The Entrepreneurial Secret Book Series

Volume III

Cedric Muhammad

CM Cap Publishing
P.O. Box 71443
Washington, D.C. 20024

CM Cap Publishing
P.O. Box 71443
Washington, D.C. 20024

For further information visit:
cmcap.com and Cedricmuhammad.com

ISBN: 978-0-578-03823-0

Cover art by Ithan Payne

First Edition 2009

Dedication

This work is dedicated to Four Females and Three Males who have suffered with me and because of my entrepreneurial path, yet continue to Believe...

To Mom, Imah, Nik, and Tonja – THANK YOU for your patient endurance, silent prayers and faith in me. Your sacrifice and love brings me to tears.

To Dad, Ant, and Charles– thank you for showing me the meaning of Proverbs 27:17. Your undying loyalty gets me through the most difficult times.

To all couples in love <u>and</u> in business together, may the story of Mr. and Mrs. Groves (in Chapter 15) inspire you.

To all first-time entrepreneurs and truly small business owners – we'll do this together...Go Get it!

Acknowledgments and Expressions Of Gratitude

Above all I thank Almighty God, Allah and His Christ for giving me Life, Light, and Power.

I am most grateful to Master Fard Muhammad and The Honorable Elijah Muhammad because Their revelation, teaching, training and purification – on the basis of the Knowledge of God, Self and Others – is the foundation for all right relationships, in life, and the science of business.

The Honorable Minister Louis Farrakhan for best representing Their Wisdom; for being a Spiritual Father to me; and for long-suffering…loving people *more* than they hate themselves.

Brother Jabril Muhammad – for <u>profound</u> spiritual insights, true friendship and a case study in the proper handling of adversity.

SAKI – for always being there and for walking me through the book writing process.

The inner circle of this book - Andy, Jeff & Regina, Tisha, Glenn, Karrima, Elaine, and Yvonne for one or all of the following: reviewing, editing, proofing, formatting, and commenting on the manuscript-in-progress. Your suggestions, corrections and advice were so helpful. The mistakes and errors that remain are mine!

The wonderful Staff at the Library of Congress who – from 2006 to 2009 – assisted with critical research, stimulating conversation, a kind word or a beautiful smile: Michelle, Bruce, Mr. Johnson, Amorie, Teree, Felicia and Antoinette… to name a few.

Frank, my dear Mentor and Friend in life – may the 'The Jonathan Files' continue…

Mook, Divine, RZA, Power and the entire Wu-Tang Clan for deep lessons in Business and Brotherhood

John – my entrepreneurial tag-team partner and corporate 'infiltration' collaborator (we lived Chapter 7)…cause we're never far from the L.A.R.

Eric – for <u>100% realness</u>, incredible ideas, and the building sessions – from the block to the boardroom.

The viewers of BlackElectorate.com [especially the 'Business and Building' Community and members of Black Electorate Economics University (BEEU)] – for supporting, critiquing, questioning, and shaping me.

Star – For a relationship of mutual respect that has evolved into a dear friendship. Your encouragement and advice has been invaluable. Thanks for embodying the greatest of all secrets – 'The total belief in one's self, with the full understanding of man's true nature.'

Sam, J'Nate, Joe, and Barnar – my wonderful and steadfast business partners.

Herm, Twila, Rahsaan, Kimberlin, Laquana, Marc, Lydia, Adrienne (ACC), Stefanie and my 'little brother' Stephen, for the closest of friendships, great advice, and listening without judging. Love you.

Cynthia – for betting on me, making history with me, and understanding entrepreneurship *is* progressive.

Reuven – more scientist than economist – for extraordinary brilliance and graciousness with time.

Stephen (SWS) – for your early 'investment' in me, and the secret science of valuation.

Wendy – for selflessly opening doors over the years and making $^!+ happen! A true power broker, you are.

Matsimela – for extending to me a platform, and for being an unparalleled Activist-Educator-Servant.

Jude Wanniski. This work was written in constant memory of his life and legacy (polyconomics.org)

The Entrepreneurial Secret Book Series

Table Of Contents

Preface – Why I Wrote This Book And A Way To Read It

"In 1900, in his book Corporations and the Public Welfare, James Dill warned that the most critical social question of the day was figuring out how to get rid of the small entrepreneur, yet at the same time retain his loyalty 'to a system based on private enterprise.' The small entrepreneur had been the heart of the American republican ideal, the soul of its democratic strength. So the many school training habits which led directly to small entrepreneurship had to be eliminated."
—**The Underground History of American Education A Schoolteacher's Intimate Investigation Into The Prison of Modern Schooling by John Taylor Gatto; published by: The Oxford Village Press, Oxford, New York, 2006.**

In many years of advising first-time entrepreneurs and small business owners and writing and commenting on economic matters, I've learned a great many things.

Perhaps the most important of which is that unless we make a great effort of our own, we are all most likely undereducated and uninformed about the business process.

There are obvious reasons for this.

First, the American public school system – from Kindergarten to 12th Grade – does not deal with the subject with any depth at all. I did not receive a course in economics until my senior year and that for only four weeks. To get any serious academic instruction in business you have to pay for it. That means college, universities and for many a huge amount of debt.

Next, the news media – which more and more revolves around political chatter, commentary, and opinion from colorful personalities – struggles to explain basic economic issues. The financial panic of 2007-2008 exposed just how little journalists knew about the banking system and the global economy, for example, and even more importantly, revealed their inability to explain it in language we all could understand. The overwhelming focus on building paper wealth, as advocated by *personal finance* columnists and 'gurus' rather than an emphasis on the basic economic principles and concepts that have guided people throughout history, contributed greatly to the crisis. Herding people into complex financial instruments and promoting investment strategies they didn't understand became more important than educating the masses about the basics of entrepreneurship and business.

However, there is a third factor contributing to our confused and ignorant condition which is my primary focus.

Here it is – the popular literature devoted to the subject of what makes for success in business has a split personality.

Let me explain.

There are primarily three categories of business literature that one can find in major bookstores and public libraries.

First, there is what I call the political economy-oriented books. These are the books that outright argue, or at least give the impression that the success or failure of a business enterprise is determined by the political process and the application (or violation) of macro or micro economic concepts and principles. Such books in this category include classic works like *The Wealth of Nations* by Adam Smith; *Wealth and Poverty* by George Gilder, *The Way The World Works* by Jude Wanniski, *Banker To The Poor* by Muhammad Yunus and *The Mystery Of Capital* by Hernando De Soto.

Next, is the material that focuses on business principle and practices. These books can read like how-to manuals and often appear as historical or reference material and detailed works on strategic concepts and techniques taught by business leaders, college professors, consultants or self-help gurus. Some that stand out in this category are; *On Competition* by Michael Porter; *E Myth Mastery* by Michael E. Gerber; *The Origin Of Brands* by Al and Laura Ries; *The 7 Habits Of Highly Effective People* by Stephen R. Covey; *Money and Power: The History Of Business* by Howard Means; *In Search Of Excellence* by Thomas J. Peters and the 2,000 page reference work, *Business: The Ultimate Resource.*

The final broad category I have identified deals with personal struggle. These books are usually either biographies or the life stories of successful entrepreneurs or deeply introspective and inspirational writings often centered on the life path of business personalities, professionals, or individuals who have overcome great odds. Among the many are: *Do What You Love, The Money Will Follow* by Marsha Sinetar; *Think and Grow Rich* by Napoleon Hill; *As A Man Thinketh* by James Allen; *The Power Of Positive Thinking* by Dr. Norman Vincent Peale; *The Purpose Driven Life* by Rick Warren; *Why Should White Guys Have All Of The Fun?*; by Reginald Lewis; *Andrew Carnegie* by David Nasaw; *Life and Def* by Russell Simmons; and *Mary Kay: You Can Have It All: Lifetime Wisdom From America's Foremost Woman Entrepreneur* by Mary Kay Ash.

Like myself, the clients that I have worked with have read or reviewed a combination of all of these kinds of books but still struggle to find a balance between them, our personal values, and exactly what (and in what order) we should apply these insights in our everyday business activity.

"Should I be pumping myself up *now*, or motivating my employees to believe that the dark days of slowing sales will pass?" or "How do I know when to spend money on marketing and whether to apply for a loan?" or "My husband thinks I am wasting my time and money on this— what can I do to convince him otherwise?" or "I believe this person can help me become successful in business but I don't know how to get their attention. How can I get a meeting with them?" or "What is the best way to write a business plan?" or "I have an idea but how do I develop and protect it?" and "I know this election is important but exactly how will the economic policies of these candidates impact my company?"

These are the kinds of questions that I have asked myself and which I have heard from friends and clients over the years. These questions are often followed by more, such as: "What book can you recommend to help me in this area?" and "Cedric, what book can I read to get a basic understanding of economics or business?"

Due to the way these subjects are ignored by elementary and high school education; inadequately handled by the news media; and split into different categories in popular books, I have never been able to recommend a single book or book series.

Is the problem the complicated and strange nature of the human being? Maybe it is. Or is it just the way human beings are being taught and informed? I think this is more of the problem. We are educated, informed and marketed to as if we were schizophrenic.

The problem is not 'us' as much as it is how educators, broadcasters, and publishers *view* us.

Consider this from economist Reuven Brenner about our divided personalities, as viewed by educators in his classic *History: The Human Gamble*:

Today human behavior is analyzed by psychologists, sociologists, economists, anthropologists, among others. Psychologists see human beings as suffering from stress, depression, obsession, oedipal complexes, and as trying to escape from freedom (according to Fromm). For economists the same human beings merely maximize their utility, have rational expectations, and are always better off when they have a greater freedom of choice. For anthropologists some human beings are bound by traditions, lack aspirations, and live near starvation. For some historians, history is made by kings, prophets, and revolutionaries, while for others the same history is made by the classes. Briefly, a look at the various disciplines in the social sciences will reveal both a rather schizophrenic human being and that very different interpretations are given to the same facts. How is this possible? After all, these fields are all supposed to deal with various aspects of behavior of the same human beings. Can it be that human beings are rational when they make their shopping lists but not when they go to a psychiatrist?

In this book I aim to give a thorough answer to modified forms of the above question posed by Mr. Brenner: Can it be that entrepreneurs are rational when they write business plans but not when a great business idea or insight first comes to them? Can it be that entrepreneurs are rational when they network with others but not when they vote for political candidates? Can it be that entrepreneurs are rational when suffer through years of not making money but not when they hire employees and pick business partners?

The answers to these questions may surprise you and that is why I titled this work *The Entrepreneurial Secret*.

Even though most of what we seek to learn about human nature and business is not truly hidden knowledge, it sure does feel that way when you try to locate it all.

With this book series I am seeking to make a contribution to ending the spilt personality that currently exists in the business publishing industry. This industry has produced what I call 'entrepreneurial schizophrenia,' where one is led to believe that the process of visualization, writing a marketing plan, negotiating a deal over dinner, and casting votes for politicians (any or all of which can be the key to success in business) are unrelated aspects of business success, to be learned by trial and error, or in 50 different book titles, magazines and newspaper articles.

Or perhaps even worse, entrepreneurial schizophrenia teaches that the elements of business *can't* be taught uniformly or presented at once.

What else explains why we can't seem to find what we are looking for in one book (I don't count the 2,000 page *Business: The Ultimate Resource* encyclopedia as a 'book.' Smile)?

This is no small matter. The divided thinking about business may be leaving us woefully unprepared to deal with the new competitive environment in which we find ourselves.

The recent economic crisis suggests that the separation of tactics, techniques, and testimony in business knowledge can be costly.

Those who have spent years focusing on inspiring themselves through the testimonial struggle of entrepreneurs, may have lacked the technical insight to understand why commercial banks were no longer lending to small business owners.

If so, they were unprepared.

Successful entrepreneurs who have mastered negotiating skills and networking techniques may have lacked the testimonial insight of personal struggle to carry them through the emotional shock of an economic recession.

If so, they were unprepared.

Qualified professionals able to manage successful businesses owned by others may have lacked the how-to tactics that could have guided them to do something for themselves, when the company they worked for went out of business.

If so, they were unprepared.

In my opinion it's past time to get prepared, and fast.

In *The Entrepreneurial Secret* I describe a new landscape and a uniform presentation of the three key areas that I believe determine the success and failure of every entrepreneur operating in the current environment: 1) an understanding of the Political Economy 2) the proper application of Business Principles and Practices 3) developing willpower and accepting suffering in the Personal Struggle that accompanies entrepreneurship.

On these three areas, I make a final suggestion on how to read this book that may surprise you.

I did not write this book expecting anyone to read it straight through like is normally the case with a novel or non-fiction work.

I wrote this book, as a series, and in a style, that I believe is best suited to accurately present it, encourage understanding and application, and facilitate further study.

Like business itself, the book will have periods where technical precision matters more; where engaging dialogue is the objective; and where providing tools for application and empowerment *after reading* are my goal.

Therefore, borrowing from my background in the music industry, I invite the reader to view this work as a compilation of songs or as the 'shuffle' feature on your mp3 player, car CD-Stereo, or turntable (yes some of us still spin vinyl records). Review the table of contents and pick and choose whatever chapter you would like to start reading. There is no wrong way to start reading this book.

Read from beginning to end, perhaps, enjoying the 'songs' or chapters, in the order in which they are placed, like a great theme album. My father raised me on great jazz music and the rhythm of Soul music and perhaps the greatest arranger-producer to confidently work in both of these musical genres – Quincy Jones. What I take from Quincy Jones (and something I have witnessed up close in working with great Hip-Hop producers or arrangers like RZA of Wu-Tang Clan) is the importance of song placement – the order in which songs appear in an album. With that art and acquired skill, in mind, I did order the chapters of this book with great care.

Any shortcomings, however, in this area are mine, and not a reflection of 'Q' or RZA.

So, if you don't wish to read cover to cover, start with the 'Business Principles and Practices' section, which features more dialogue, and tools for immediate application, *before* getting into the 'Political Economy,' section which is filled with economic insights about the current crisis; historical and cultural information about pooling capital; and my experiences in the world of electoral politics.

Another approach may be to immerse yourself with the more spiritual, emotional and scientific material presented in 'Personal Struggle,' which outlines a personal study, path, and testimony in enduring suffering, and building willpower, through the entrepreneurial journey, while managing the painful impact this journey can have on our most intimate relationships.

Why do I advocate this eclectic approach?

I am confident that eventually you will end up immersed in all three sections over time, as your interests, circumstances, and experiences in life and business make the different 'Secrets' more or less attractive to you.

The content of this book won't change, but like the seasons and the weather (all influenced by the Earth's rotation), you will.

This kind of writing and suggested approach to reading reflects not only the tempo of entrepreneurship but it also reflects my unique background.

I am not sure of this but I may be the only author on entrepreneurship who within a ten year period managed the biggest Hip-Hop group in the world, advised government leaders on international monetary policy, was published in the most influential financial newspaper in the world, and strategically guided a successful campaign for U.S. Congress.

Throughout, I had my own share of success and failure in business, much of which I include in this book.

Operating in and out of the worlds associated with these fields, has forced me to learn different languages – from the block to the boardroom, you might say.

I hope that my reference to these experiences and the manner in which I convey them are more stimulating and intriguing, than confusing.

If I'm correct in sensing the need for a new worldview that promotes the unity of the entrepreneurial personality and business experience, you will enjoy and benefit from what comes next.

If not, maybe it is I who am schizophrenic, and not those I accuse of compartmentalizing business knowledge!

I invite you to judge for yourself.

In conclusion, this book embraces the reality that business is an artistic, scientific and always human activity. In writing *The Entrepreneurial Secret* my goal was to present a practical, technical, and spiritual work that could be relevant to any person starting a business in the current environment, regardless to their stage in the entrepreneurial process.

My intention and desire is that this book will provide inspiration and insight for the recently-laid off professional. Aspects of this work are designed to be included in an economic empowerment blueprint for the homeless, previously incarcerated, and individuals struggling to move from a life of crime. And certainly chapters in this book will be most valuable to existing small business owners who need to deal with day-to-day bottom line realities.

This publication may also be suited to help better prepare students for the real world of business activity – a subject public education and higher education continues to ignore or inadequately address.

The *Entrepreneurial Secret* is also intended to challenge the thinking of intellectuals and activists who place too much emphasis on narrow or partisan aspects of the political process rather than the broader or universal economic and entrepreneurial elements of community development. In my mind it is impossible to discuss, effectively pursue, obtain, or preserve civil and human rights without carefully factoring in the spiritual, technical and practical realties of entrepreneurship, business, and economics.

In some ways, the recent financial crisis has exposed this reality.

Each of the chapters in this book, are the basis of future books, even volumes, in and of themselves. And each of them is the foundation for additional dialogue and debate, in an intellectual context, as well as additional study and application in a competitive business environment.

The online forums for those two 'follow-up' activities are my personal website Cedricmuhammad.com (http://cedricmuhammad.com/) and the website of my business consulting firm dedicated to serving first-time entrepreneurs and small business owners CM Cap.com (http://cmcap.com/).

I look forward to seeing you there.

Introduction – The Secret of State of Mind: Entrepreneur, By Necessity

"In '99 I had a vision and made a decision – being broke is against my religion."
—50 Cent, "Ryder Music" (The Massacre, 2005)

"This spirit of entrepreneurship is one born out of necessity. People cannot find jobs so they have to go out and make their own work by selling on the streets."
—"Entrepreneurial Spirit Born Out of Necessity," by Louise Redvers, July 24, 2009; Inter Press Service (IPSnews.net)

"The frost must have been severe to motivate the tortoise to climb the tree."
—Shona Proverb: Zimbabwe

"I've always been a person who needs constant change. I like when my back is against the wall and the pressure is on – when I've got to damn near fight my way out of a situation."
—Troi "Star" Torain; *Objective Hate* (2006)

"The real meaning is not the color of your skin. It's the spirit that energizes you, and moves you to action. That's the real person."
—Minister Louis Farrakhan, July 12, 2009, CNN Interview

Although I first heard of 50 Cent in the year 1999, it wasn't until this year, just months ago, in 2009 when I can honestly say I *met* him.

And I'm not talking about in a personal way.

Although I enjoyed years at the top of the music world as a result of my association with Wu-Tang Clan – a spot 50 Cent would soon enjoy for several years – our paths never crossed.

No, when I say I *met* 50 Cent, I mean I felt his spirit and came in contact with his personal drive and motivation – his entrepreneurial passion.

The moment it happened was not unlike any other day. I was doing some show prep for my radio program, "The Cedric Muhammad and Black Coffee Program" and was scouring the Internet for some good audio sound bites to weave into the hourly introductions I use during my five hour show.

On Youtube I saw a clip entitled, "50 Cent Explains The 'How To Rob' Record & Beef With Ghostface Killah."

This got my attention for two reasons. The first is Ghostface Killah is one of the members of Wu-Tang, and one of the most genuine people I met in the music business. I have a lot of respect for him. With Ghost, what you see is what you get. I always found him to be a serious-minded individual but never arrogant or over the top just for the hell of it.

The other reason this title got my attention was because it mentioned 'How To Rob.' This may be the most controversial song 50 Cent ever made and possibly the most controversial song *ever* made by any Hip-Hop artist. In it, tongue-in-cheek, 50 describes how he could rob just about all of the biggest artists in the business – a sore subject for sure.

Not because rappers have delicate egos – which all artists do – but because the song broaches a subject that many rappers would rather avoid due to its effect on their image and because of the real life danger it has represented for years.

You see, numerous rappers *have been* robbed – at gun point, at knife point – or sometimes beaten and other times made to strip down to nothing to avoid getting beaten, or worse.

You may be surprised to know which rappers have fallen victim. I'll never tell.

So, *this guy* 50 Cent decides to make an *entire* record about the touchiest and most taboo subject available. Maybe masturbation would be a close second – which 50 openly embraces in his appearance on a song called "Jerk" on the R&B group Next's album, *Welcome II Nextasy*.

And he spared no one.

The first time I heard 'How To Rob,' I thought to myself *'Who is this guy? This is not a good move.'*

Ten years later and tens of millions of album sales later, I finally got a chance to hear why 50 Cent, in his own words, made 'How To Rob.' In his own words and more importantly, through his riveting description, I got acquainted with his circumstances and his state of mind at the time:

"…'How To Rob' – I'll explain that. At the time, I'm on Columbia Records, I got a release date coming. And there's no buzz surrounding the record. When you're in my situation, *there is no plan B*. It's music, or we sell crack – 'cause that's what we did before we did music. In that environment, it may seem harsh, even when I say exactly what it is, you know? But *that's* what it is. That's what we did before we had the opportunity to do music. So it's a blessing. I am so happy to be where I am at now, that I would never – I would feel like I would be hustling backwards to go into doing something like that (sell crack) at this point. But at that particular time that was what was provided for us to provide for ourselves in that environment, so that's what we did.

When you don't have an option, *it absolutely has to work*, for you. So I'm like *I gotta' make a record that makes everybody stop right now and say 'who is this guy 50 Cent? Right now – who is this guy?'* And then the creative part is that I got $65,000 in advance from Columbia (Records). $50,000 went to Jam Master Jay to negotiate the release from JMJ records; $10,000 went to the attorney that drew the contracts up between me and

Columbia, and the release between me and Jam Master Jay. *That left me with $5,000 and I was out there for over a year before the record came out.* So I was back selling crack. How else would I provide for myself and then be on call and able to be in the studio whenever the company called me to actually be there.

And at the end of that situation it led back to 'How To Rob', and I'm like, *it doesn't matter to me if anyone is upset.* Actually it is in their best interest. I've had phone calls from people that you would think would be upset and now they're interested in doing music. It's hilarious because I'm like *hell* no. Why would I do music with you?"

That was when I first *met* 50 Cent – when I first saw him express this *spirit* in an interview recorded in 2003, made available on YouTube.

We all have experienced or witnessed what 50 explained – that realization that the help you once counted on is no longer there; the help you expected is not on its way; and the help you are relying on is not going to be available much longer.

It is in *that* state of mind that we can give up, go crazy, or, get more determined than ever and become a pure genius.

It is in *that* state of mind when there is no other option and when there is no plan B that we dig down deep emotionally, think harder and more creatively than ever before, and determine that we will accept the cards that we have been dealt but make a bold move.

History is full of such moments. The great success writer Napoleon Hill wrote about some of them in his classic *Think And Grow Rich*. He wrote of the state of mind that leads to bold action:

A long while ago, a great warrior faced a situation which made it necessary for him to make a decision which insured his success on the battlefield. He was about to send his armies against a powerful foe, whose men outnumbered his own. He loaded his soldiers into boats, sailed to the enemy's country, unloaded soldiers and equipment, then gave the order to burn the ships that had carried them. Addressing his men before the first battle, he said, "You see the boats going up in smoke. That means that we cannot leave these shores alive unless we win! We now have no choice – *we win – or we perish!*"

They won.

Are you *now* in a situation where you have no choice but to succeed?

While I don't believe that everyone will or should make the choice that 50 Cent or the unnamed great warrior did, in the music industry and in battle respectively, I do encourage you to embrace their attitude, and capture their spirit.

We've entered a time of economic turbulence which has not been seen in decades and one that may find you without the help and resources that you comfortably relied upon in years past.

The American and global economy is experiencing a double shock – mass layoffs leading to mass unemployment, and a credit freeze that makes securing access to capital and loans more difficult than ever.

Are you going to read the hand-writing on the wall and voluntarily decide that its time for a bold change – a change in attitude and a change in thinking and behavior that inspires you to make your own opportunities – realizing that you have been forced to, by these circumstances which are beyond your control?

If so, you are not alone. Many are being forced into thinking about doing something for themselves, as first time entrepreneurs.

The May 11, 2009 the *Wall Street Journal* captured this phenomenon in an article entitled 'Starting Over As An Entrepreneur,' writing:

Tough times breed a different kind of entrepreneur.

With the economy tanking, lots of people are striking out on their own. Some never thought of starting a business until they got laid off. Others kicked around the idea but never found the time or the passion to pursue it. Now, launching a start-up seems like a better bet than taking on an endless job hunt.

"I think we're going to see a lot of businesses started by people who otherwise would not have started businesses" in better times, says Bo Fishback, vice president of entrepreneurship for the Ewing Marion Kauffman Foundation, a Kansas City entrepreneurial-research organization. "Necessity-driven entrepreneurship can be a powerful motivator."

This new crowd faces lots of obstacles. Banks and investors are handing out a lot less money these days, especially to first-timers. What's more, necessity entrepreneurs have often done less of the spade work than other entrepreneurs—in part because they weren't thinking that a layoff was imminent. And the fragile economy makes just about *any* new company a chancy proposition.

A *necessity*-driven entrepreneur – that's who 50 Cent was in 1999.

A necessity-driven entrepreneur – that's who you are today.

And I'm so honored to meet you...

VOLUME III:

The Personal Struggle

Chapter 13: The Secret Of Suffering – Genius, Lessons, Character And Wealth Through Pain

We have certainly created man to face difficulties...But he attempts not the uphill road
—Holy Qur'an – Surah 90 verses 4 and 11
(Maulana Muhammad Ali translation)

"Genius is not a gift, but rather the way out one invents in desperate situations."
—Jean-Paul Sartre

"Life has a way of developing strength and wisdom in individuals through temporary defeat."
—Andrew Carnegie

"Although he was a Son, he learned obedience by what he suffered, and having been made complete, he became for all who obey him the source of eternal salvation"
—Hebrews, Chapter 5 verses 8 and 9 (Anchor Bible Translation)

"People understand the pain of sickness by experiencing it themselves."
—Lugbara Proverb: Uganda

"Now I rejoice in what was suffered for you, and I fill up in my flesh what is still lacking in regard to Christ's afflictions, for the sake of his body, which is the church."
—Colossians 1: 24 Hebrew-Greek Keyword Study Bible
(New International Version)

"Exceptional works require exceptional mental activity. This can only arise from within the mind. It can so arise in the course of resolving a conflict. Where this happens a vast flow of psychic energy previously pent up may be released and find its direction."
—George Pickering in *Creative Malady*

"Because of the awesome power that Man can come into by obeying Allah (God), he must learn valuable lessons."
—Minister Louis Farrakhan, "The Will Of God",
October 26, 1986

"Napoleon Hill had all the human weaknesses he confessed to and maybe more. But whatever else might be said of him, nobody bounced back from adversity better."
—Michael J. Ritt, Jr. and Kirk Landers in *A Lifetime Of*
Riches.

Although over 20 million people have purchased Napoleon Hill's *Think and Grow Rich* – arguably the most influential book impacting entrepreneurs, published in the last 100 years – it just may be, that the book about *his* own life and writings, *A Lifetime Of Riches,* is even more important for one to read.

That claim may be paradoxical especially when one considers the reality that of all of the persons I know who have read or heard of *Think and Grow Rich* or its release targeted for Black America, *Think and Grow Rich, A Black Choice* by Dennis Kimbro, <u>none</u>, with exception of my older blood Brother, Anthony, has ever mentioned to me the book about its author which details the *excruciating* circumstances which preceded and surrounded the writing of *Think and Grow Rich.*

In fact, I had never even *heard* of the book *A Lifetime Of Riches* until my Brother gave it to me.

In other words, while millions and millions sing the praises of that famous little book, *Think And Grow Rich*, almost all of them are possibly unaware of the life and process that went into producing it.

Perhaps that is not an accident. After all, the majority of us wouldn't go to a movie theatre to watch an unsettling tear-jerking tragedy when we could just as easily see a comedy, inspirational drama, or a thriller with a happy ending.

If properly understood, though, Napoleon Hill's life is not a tragedy, but an informative inspiration and instructive example of what an entrepreneur must go through in order to achieve success: a period, or extended periods, of suffering and adversity. The inside flap to the book, *A Lifetime Of Riches* points to much when it states:

Despite his connections with many rich and powerful people, Hill's personal life was a financial and emotional roller coaster. He watched his fortunes come and go as business enemies, world wars, a gold-digging second wife, and even the mob stole away his opportunities for wealth. Yet even when he was abandoned by his family, this incurable optimist and entrepreneur believed that every failure held a lesson for success.

How difficult was life for Napoleon Hill? Well, according to *A Lifetime of Riches*, Napoleon Hill:

- Was falsely accused of fathering a child at age 15 and deceived into marrying a woman under that pretense (The marriage was later annulled)

- Lost his job at a lumberyard when the yard went under as a result of the economic chaos produced by the Panic of 1907.

- Agreed to a book project at the age of 26 that would take twenty years to research and write without any compensation and no expenses paid except in the early stages. All in his family believed he had made a fool-hardy decision (The 20-year book project would become *Think and Grow Rich*). In giving him the vision and mission for the book, Andrew Carnegie told him, "The job will require twenty years, which during which time you must be willing to starve rather than quit."

-   Married his wife, Florence, secretly, because he had no money and did not want to face the objections of his wife's parents.

-   Had his automobile company taken over by a bank that had extended him credit for a business venture. Lost as well, at this time, was $4,000 of his wife's money which was placed in the business at the last minute

-   On November 11, 1912, Napoleon and Florence's second son, Blair, was born, not only deaf, but without ears.

-   When Blair was still an infant, and the Hills' second child, James, only a year and a half old, Napoleon left his family in Lumberport, West Virginia and headed for Chicago because he wanted to be someplace that would challenge him, and because he felt he was not doing whatever he was born to do.

-   In 1915, his three business partners in the Betsy Ross Candy Store removed him from the company, had him arrested, and then blackmailed him for his interest in the company. He was vindicated but left flat broke.

-   His wife had to borrow so much money from her family and carry so much of the financial and emotional burden of providing for the family and helping Napoleon Hill, that her parents began to think that Napoleon was conning their daughter, his wife.

-   In 1917, again, with a loan from his wife, Napoleon gave the hardest year's work he ever performed to establish his first entrepreneurial effort in teaching success principles and salesmanship through his George Washington Institute.

- In 1918, the second military draft associated with World War I practically destroyed his school, taking away most of his students in the George Washington Institute, costing him $75,000 in tuition fees.

- With the birth of their third child, and Napoleon unable to provide for his family, nor himself, Napoleon's father, James begins to think that Napoleon is taking advantage of the goodwill and generosity of his in laws – Florence's parents. The relationship between Napoleon and his father becomes more estranged as a result.

- On November 11, 1918, Napoleon Hill starts a magazine, *Hill's Golden Rule* but because he had no funds to employ outside writers he has to write and edit nearly every word of the first nine issues himself.

- In October of 1920 Napoleon loses control of *Hill's Golden Rule* to his publisher, George Williams, largely as a result of a slanderous mud slinging campaign led by a competitor and Napoleon's own secretary and associate editor. Napoleon is paralyzed for a month by grief, self doubt and self-pity.

- In April of 1921 Napoleon Hill starts his second magazine, *Napoleon Hill's Magazine*, having obtained seed capital from friends. Later that year, Florence gets sick but because communication with Napoleon is so poor and she is so used to struggling by herself with financial and family problems, she does not mention it to Napoleon. But, as *A Lifetime Of Riches* describes, "While Napoleon's domestic life began to erode, his career entered 1922 with more momentum than ever before."

-   In late 1923 after establishing a successful prisoner reform program and organization, two of Napoleon Hill's directors in this organization engaged in corruption with the resources of the business. To make matters worse, they conspired with an old and envious nemesis of Napoleon's. Together they attacked him in the media with allegations and hired 'thugs' to disrupt Napoleon Hill's public lectures, challenging his integrity before crowds and clients. The campaign cut subscribers, newsstand sales and advertising in *Napoleon Hill's Magazine*. But most devastating of all, the old nemesis was able to buy the mortgage of the printer of the magazine and when Napoleon failed to make payments, his envious enemy foreclosed and stopped publication of the magazine. To add insult to injury, he was even successful in getting Napoleon investigated for mail fraud by the U.S. Postal Service. Napoleon was exonerated but had lost everything.

-   Immediately thereafter, the building in which Napoleon stored his valuables in Chicago burned down. According to his biography, "Gone were dozens of letters and notes from Woodrow Wilson, including his approval of a Hill proposal that the president used to sell war bonds. Gone were the autographed pictures of Wilson, Bell, and others. Gone was President Taft's letter endorsing Hill for employment. Gone was a series of letters from Manuel L. Quezon, who corresponded with Hill prior to becoming president of the Philippine Commonwealth. And most devastating of all, gone were Hill's bulging files of confidential questionnaires completed by such luminaries as Luther Burbank, Thomas Edison, and hundreds more who participated in his research on the philosophy of success." Of these documents – gone for ever – Napoleon Hill expressed his sorrow, "The loss of my magazine cost all of the money I had…my confidence in men had been terribly shaken…but those losses were nothing compared to the destruction of things that could never be restored; things associated with the memories of men who had been my greatest benefactors at a time in my life when their recognition was about the only real asset I possessed."

- Borrowing $1,000 Napoleon headed to Ohio and took over the Metropolitan Business College in Ohio. As with any start-up, money was slow and scarce and had to be put back into the business. But now, his relationship with his wife and children under this added strain reached a crisis level. And emotionally in the Winter of 1925, Napoleon reached an excruciatingly painful low, knowing that his suffering wife had lost confidence in him. In a letter to her he wrote, "You have no idea what it is like when not a soul on earth encourages you, and all the negative forces pour in on you. It takes superhuman strength of will to throw them off. I would give anything if I had someone, even though they did not mean it or believe it, to tell me they KNEW I COULD SUCCEED."

- When business picked up a bit over the next few months, Florence's spirits improved a bit as did Napoleon's. In a poignant July 13, 1925 communication, Napoleon Hill wrote his wife a deeply introspective letter, acknowledging to himself what perhaps she already knew, of the paradoxical nature of his life and mission. Pointing to themes that the entrepreneur, inspired preacher and leader can relate to, Napoleon Hill wrote: "I have stood by the Law Of Success lecture and my 15 points for more than seven years. At times they only seemed to mock me, when I was talking of success to others while my own family suffered for necessities. I have not known just why I did this. At times I wondered, as you have done, if I would not have been better off to have forgotten it all and have gone back to some little job as a bookkeeper, where I could have earned at least a modest living. BUT there was something that would not let me do it... I have stood my ground, suffered, been disappointed, and given disappointment to others all because I could not do otherwise. I was simply helpless in the matter...I would have changed my course a dozen times in the past six or seven years IF I COULD HAVE DONE SO."

- In early 1926, Hill struck up a relationship with *Canton Hill Daily News* publisher Don Mellet. Mr. Mellet put together a plan to finance an 8-book success series of Napoleon Hill's. But after he exposed a bootlegging operation that targeted children, in his newspaper, and obtained a commitment from Elbert H. Gary, Chairman of U.S. Steel to pre order $150,000 worth of the new book series, Mr. Mellet was murdered at home by a gangster and renegade police officer. Napoleon Hill returned home, learned of the news, and received an anonymous call telling him he had 1 hour to get out of town. *A Lifetime of Riches* describes what happened next, "Realizing the situation was hopeless, Hill left immediately, not even pausing to pack. Once more, he had struggled and scratched to follow the course of a rainbow. Once more, he had come within an arm's length of the promised pot of gold. And once more, it had been snatched from him just as he reached to touch it. Napoleon Hill would spend the forty-third year of his life in hiding in West Virginia, destitute, unable to support his stunned family, unwilling to go out of doors without a pistol in his pocket. For the first time in his life, he experienced the pain of constant fear.

- Even after the murderers of Don Mellet, who were after Napoleon Hill, received life sentences, the writer extraordinaire could not bring himself out of hiding. He wrote, "The experience had destroyed whatever initiative I possessed," wrote Napoleon. I felt myself in the clutches of some depressing influences which seemed like a nightmare. I was alive. I could move around. But I could not think of a single move by which I might continue to seek the goal which I had so long set for myself. I was rapidly becoming indifferent; worse still, I was becoming grouchy and irritable toward those who had given me shelter in my hour of need."

- But as usual, not overcome by adversity, Hill bounced back and again received backing for his 8-book series. The first volume, *The Law Of Success*, laid out 15 principles and represented what would be much of the thesis of his masterpiece, yet to come, *Think and Grow Rich*. The book took off, lightened the financial burden of Florence and the wealth brought the family closer together. For an entire year the ride lasted. But then came the Stock Market Crash of 1929 and the beginning of the depression. By October 1930 Florence was borrowing from her family again, and Napoleon had defaulted on a property.

- And then, the final aspects of the chain reaction that would give birth to the most influential book on personal success, inspiring entrepreneurs and leaders all over the world began. In 1933 on the recommendation of Congressman Jennings Randolph, a long time supporter of Napoleon Hill's, the administration of President Franklin Delano Roosevelt hired Napoleon Hill as a speechwriter and public relations man for the National Recovery Administration. Napoleon Hill eventually requested a salary of $1 a year, and received what he asked for. But Florence and the children were not in as patriotic of a mood as he was. The sacrifice or foolishness – depending upon what perspective one takes – of Napoleon taking on such compensation and intense labor while his family languished in poverty was the final straw for Florence and in 1935 she obtained an uncontested divorce when *Napoleon's own father*, James, paid for her to make the arrangements in the state of Florida because divorce was not legal in West Virginia. James and his son Napoleon hardly communicated with one another again. During this painful time, Napoleon worked even more intensely on his success philosophy. His biography describes, "Writing lecturing and consulting to FDR kept Hill busy, but not busy enough. To cope with his post marital isolation, he found it necessary to work himself to exhaustion. Thus, to fill many long, lonely nights, he labored over several different manuscripts in preparation for the day

Americans would once again dare to dream of success and to pursue it."

- Just as his money ran out, Napoleon remarried – to a woman named Rosa Lee. The couple had so little they had to move in with Napoleon's son, Blair and his own new wife. The arrangement was a disaster – straining Napoleon's relationship with the son to whom he was closest. Their bond began to unravel under the pressure of Napoleon's criticism of his son, the close living quarters, and a loan made to Napoleon that was not repaid in a timely fashion. Blair and his wife divorced later, many believing this period doomed the marriage. The son that adored his father for helping him gain his hearing among other factors was now speaking of him like an enemy. In early 1938, Blair wrote his mother, Florence a letter wherein he calls his dad, an "unscrupulous, holier-than-thou, two-timing, double crossing good-for-nothing. Sometime I'm going to see that he pays and pays plenty for the way he treated you, treated me, treated David and Jimmy [Blair's brothers]!" Paradoxically, while Napoleon and Rosa Lee were living with Blair and his wife, the manuscript that would become *Think and Grow Rich*! was completed and re-written three times with Rosa Lee typing every page of every re-write.

Here, from *A Lifetime Of Riches* is the story of how the decision to publish the manuscript for *Think and Grow Rich* was made by publisher Mr. Andrew Pelton as well as its results:

After weeks of sleepless toil, Hill invited Andrew Pelton to the apartment and presented the manuscript to him. The publisher read the table of contents and thumbed through a few pages of text, then gave the eager Hills his verdict: It was just another self-help book, essentially the same as Hill's previous work and several other titles that he had published in recent years and which were not selling.

Despite the torture the Hills had endured to produce the manuscript, they received the publisher's sentiments with surprising aplomb. "We knew before he ever saw the manuscript that he was going to publish it," explained Hill. "We gave that matter no concern whatsoever....

"After he had talked all afternoon analyzing the book and trying to prove to us it was not very different from other books...my wife suggested that he take the manuscript home with him, read it, and then he would know what was in it that was not in my previous books or in any other book he had published."

Rosa Lee was nothing if not persuasive with men, and Pelton assented. Three days later he appeared at their apartment once more, ready to take a chance on the book on one condition – that the title be changed to something more catchy.

In the lore surrounding this particular publishing venture, one story suggested that right up to the eve of the first printing the publisher wanted to call it *Use Your Noodle to Win More Boodle*. In the end, however, the book was published under the title *Think and Grow Rich!*, and its fame and popularity would begin immediately and last enough the rest of the century.

Andrew Pelton had every right to be reluctant to invest in an inspirational self-help book that spoke of riches and success in 1937 America. Although the New Deal had succeeded in getting the economy moving forward again, the pace of improvement was agonizingly slow. Millions of Americans were still out of work and millions more were underemployed. America's Great Depression was showing only the slightest glimmerings of dissipating; it would, in fact, extend through the remainder of the decade. There was no tangible reason to believe that Nap's new title would have any more appeal to a tattered and besieged nation than *The Magic Ladder to Success* created in the early thirties.

Playing his own gut hunch, Pelton not only printed *Think and Grow Rich*, he also slapped a $2.50 retail price on it and ordered five thousand copies in the first pressrun – a fairly optimistic quantity for the day.

Incredibly, that seemingly risky print order turned out to be woefully inadequate for the demand. Three weeks after the book went into distribution, the entire print run was sold out. There followed an endless succession of printings and larger print orders as the book became a huge best-seller. If anyone in America was looking for a tangible sign that private citizens were shaking off the mental and emotional stigma of the depression, *Think and Grow Rich!* provided it in hard sales figures. Shortly after its initial appearance, one insurance company purchased five thousand copies of the book in a single order. Tens of thousands more were purchased in other bulk orders, while hundreds of thousands of single-copy sales were being rung up in direct mail and retail store offerings.

Well over a million copies of the book were sold even before the depression lifted, and it would continue to sell in large volume for decades and generations to come – all over America and throughout the world. Ten years later, *Think and Grow Rich!* ranked fourth in a leading magazine's poll on books, that most influenced the lives of the successful men of the forties. Fifty years later, the twentieth-millionth copy of the book was sold; it remained an active title in thousands of libraries and was still stocked by leading bookstores throughout the country.

Why would a book once thought to be like any other succeed on such a grand scale?

The answer probably stems from the fact that the content of Think and Grow Rich! originated from Law of Success and Hill's uniquely Carnegie-inspired, twenty-year investigation of what makes people succeed. The research itself, and the content of Law of Success, are among the most original works in modern American publishing.

Although Napoleon Hill obtained and learned much from the captains of business and industry that he studied – as well as from everyday entrepreneurs – of all of the themes that seem to dominate his legendary book, *Think and Grow Rich*, the idea that never disappears completely from view was given to him in an exchange with Andrew Carnegie, in their very first meeting:

Napoleon Hill: But what happens when a man knows what he wants, has a plan, puts it into action and meets with failure? Doesn't that destroy his confidence?

Andrew Carnegie: I hoped you would ask that, because it is important to understand what I'm about to tell you. I believe that every failure carries within it – in the circumstances of the failure itself – the seed of an equivalent advantage. If you examine the lives of truly great leaders, you will discover that their success is in exact proportion to their mastery of failures. Life has a way of developing strength and wisdom in individuals through temporary defeat.

Napoleon Hill: Most people aren't going to believe that every failure has an equivalent advantage when they are overcome with the adversity. What does one do if the experience destroys one's self-confidence?

Andrew Carnegie: The best way to guard against being overwhelmed by failure is to discipline the mind to meet failure before it arrives.

Failure, adversity, perseverance, patience, persistence, endurance and faith are all words that one will find in the life struggle of the entrepreneur. One can clearly see this at work in the life of Napoleon Hill and the subjects featured in his classic book. The ability to overcome resistance and manage pain seems to be an unavoidable aspect of those who set goals and seek them. The word and concept that best embodies all of these factors and can be applied most broadly across human disciplines is *suffering*.

In reading the life struggles of Napoleon Hill leading up and into the writing of his book about success, I was reminded of the attitude, and even some of the actual words contained in the book of Psalms. Perhaps more than any other book of the Bible, it is Psalms that people – Christian or not – have come to rely upon for guidance, comfort and even a sense of empathy and sympathy when undergoing a painful experience.

What makes the Psalms so endearing to many is not only its contents but knowledge of the fact that the man whose heart is being poured out before his God and the public, is seen as a leader – a man with stature. Not only is the David of the Bible a king, and a prophet but he is described in I Samuel 13:14 and Acts 13:22 as having a heart after God. He is said by theologians – Jewish, Christian and Muslim – to be a sign, type, or a model of the kind of person that the Messiah is, or is to be. Yet he is a picture in contrasts.

The same man that is so confident, courageous, wise, righteous and strong in the book of Kings, for example, *appears* to be so doubtful, fearful, foolish, wicked, and weak, in Psalms. But whatever he maybe, he seems to be anything but negligent in his communication with his Lord. David faithfully confides, begs, praises, and entreats the One that he sees as his Ultimate superior.

The apparent contradictions as well as the visible imperfections depict a man that almost anyone can relate to. And in spite of what is *interpreted* as a life of mistakes, errors, sins and fretfulness, David is admired by the Psalms reader for his total experience – imperfections, success, adversity, perseverance, patience, persistence, endurance and faith – his suffering.

When it comes to David and the Book Of Psalms, there is very little religious-secular competition, the admirer wants to claim David's *heart* or *his story* in one way or another – Believer or Disbeliever.

As Sir William Muir wrote nearly two hundred years ago – in *The Mohammedan Controversy*, specifically in a section called "The Psalter: Its Larger And Discretionary Use Desirable," – as part of his effort to have the Psalms used more broadly in the Church:

The Psalms have been the refuge of the soul, the voice of the Church, the song of the saint, in all generations. They are still the same, as well in privacy of the still chamber as in public ministrations of the great congregation. From the treasury of the Psalter, be his outward state or inward frame what they may, the child of God is ever borrowing words that do give shape and substance to flitting thought, life to the soul, and fire to heavenward aspiration.

Here is stored up Divine food, rich and abundant, for every time and place. Something for the morning dawn, something for the busy day, and something for the sick and solitary closet, something also for the thronging crowd. The backsliding, the penitent, the weak and afflicted, the doubting and the tempted; the soul dwelling in darkness, desolate, disowned by man, or dreading to be forsaken by the Almighty; and not less, the Saint on fire with godly zeal, hungering and thirsting after the living God, borne upwards on wings of love and joy, – each may find in the Psalms words framed, as it were, to suit his very case. And as in personal, domestic, and social life, so also, in a nation's history, whether in peace or warfare, whether the year be crowned with goodness or the staff of bread be broken, in the day of wealth and prosperity, as well as in the night of calamity and pestilence; in short, at every turn of public life the people's voice of sorrow or of joy will ascend, as it can no otherwise, ascend, in the Psalmist's very words. And, what is much to be observed, while Psalms abound with cries of anguish as well as with the "tenderest appeals to God's compassionate love that ever trembled on human lips," there is yet nothing weak or morbid, nothing extravagant or strained (as we often see in our modern Hymnody) throughout the Psalter: all is true and real, manly, simple, noble, and well-nerved."

The description Mr. Muir uses for the Psalter, also applies to the suffering associated with the successful entrepreneur, when he writes: "there is yet nothing weak or morbid, nothing extravagant or strained...all is true and real, manly, simple, noble, and well-nerved."

The horrific trials, tribulations, pain and struggles of Napoleon Hill and yes, King David, are a sign and *typical* example of the difficulty that often accompanies the successful entrepreneur.

In fact, their lives might even reveal the secret of the purpose of struggle in life itself.

Many people understand that suffering is a part of life and even progress, but few seem confident about how this phenomenon works positively on behalf of those who strive to obtain a goal. This difficulty in comprehension is partly due to semantics and the different worldviews of human beings, but even deeper than that, it seems, is the metaphysical, shapeless, and elusive nature of what suffering ultimately *is* inside of the individual and from where it originates. In this book, through this chapter, we seek to contribute to overcoming this difficulty factor. Our goal is to offer a precise definition of what suffering is that can be applied to the entrepreneurial process.

First, let's make a broader point about economic activity.

There is a critically important spiritual aspect to the relationship between economics and entrepreneurship that many may not realize. Economics is largely based upon business activity, which is largely based upon entrepreneurial activity, which is largely based upon spiritual activity within a person. Therefore it is irrational to separate economics from spirituality, and of course to do the same with *business* and spirituality; and *entrepreneurship* and spirituality.

Generally speaking, it is much easier and takes less time to show that the entrepreneurial act as we define it – *the perception of an opportunity and the creation of an organization to pursue it* – is based on a *spiritual* process, than it is to show the same regarding business and economics. This is largely because of the prevalence of certain popular beliefs regarding what is considered 'secular' and what is 'religious,' and how those beliefs impact the study of economics.

In addition, widely held views of the concept of what constitutes the 'spirit' or 'spirituality' also compound this problem, making clear demonstrations and arguments difficult, and usually dependent upon the use of clear and precise language.

So let's attempt to be clear and forthright. By human spirituality we mean *the deeper, hidden, or unseen animating reality, or intention, that exists behind, beyond, or underneath an act, appearance, or superficial reality.*

If this seems too metaphysical or mystical and not worthy of serious consideration or discussion, perhaps a couple of questions will adjust such thinking.

What is an 'intention?' And can it be seen or recognized with certainty, without a person (who holds the intention) expressing it in words?

This tension between what we can 'see' or can't 'see' through our major senses is readily apparent in entrepreneurship or creative works.

In keeping with our definition of 'spiritual' we can show that quite frequently, what gave birth to a business, product or service was not a profit-motivated, or external market-place driven activity, but rather, a powerful but deeper, hidden or unseen process or chain of events.

We touched on this in a previous chapter on the secret of capital and the business firm.

To understand this a little better we consider a section of the book, *Juice: The Creative Fuel That Drives World-Class Inventors* by Evan I. Schwartz, entitled, "Lighting The Inner Fire". In it we read:

Creating a possibility in your mind doesn't necessarily mean that the underlying problem you're trying to solve is new. What's new is your particular representation of the problem. Successful inventors often aren't the first to come up with the basic concept of their own invention. Alexander Graham Bell wasn't the first to discover the need for the telephone. Other inventors had been working on the problem for at least fifteen years before he made his first call. Thomas Edison didn't discover the need for the electric light. The need had been burning in the minds of other inventors for at least thirty years before he switched on his first bulb. Wilbur and Orville Wright didn't discover the need for the airplane. The race to build a flying machine started at least a century before Kitty Hawk. In the same vein, the future inventor of the first quantum computer, the first portable economic scanning machine, the first nanotech cell-repairing robot, or the first antigravity machine won't be the first person to have imagined those possibilities. The original dreamers were also demonstrating inventive behavior.

The most common explanation of what drives inventive activity is the age-old maxim, "Necessity is the mother of invention." But that aphorism explains almost nothing and is wrong in most instances. Because new scientific discoveries or technological possibilities often give rise to new desires, it's usually even more correct to say the opposite: "Invention is the mother of necessity." Although successful inventions seem in retrospect to fill a clear human need, what they really do is to generate the demand in the first place. Only a handful of people imagined the telephone, the electric light, and the airplane beforehand. After these things existed, however, masses of people suddenly couldn't do without them.

The task of choosing or finding the unrealized possibility isn't as straightforward as saying, What would people want? Ask yourself that question, spend some time thinking about an answer, and you'll see that there's a special habit involved. Inventors are attuned to finding the problem *inside* the problem or finding the problem *outside* the problem. They frame the challenge in such an original way that they've redefined a need and turned it into something new. That is the key: The new potential begins life in the inventor's mind.

This is where the process of invention is misunderstood. People often look at the invention and then work backward. When they see a successful new technology, they immediately relate it to the trouble it has alleviated. But you can't understand the process of invention by looking only at the inventions. You must first empathize with the inventors, the people who stirred up that trouble in the first place. The "mother of invention" adage doesn't explain why certain individuals take on a life of creative problem solving, some to the point of obsession, whereas others don't consider it. "The crucial question is why some groups respond in a particular way to the same human needs or wants that in some groups remain unfulfilled," writes technology historian Carlo Cipolla. What motivates inventors to do what they do, and why are some people, companies, and societies more inventive than others?

Psychologist Carl Jung suggests that the drive to create possibilities is actually something that comes from *within the individual* rather than from the pull of an unmet need in the marketplace of human activity. "The creative mind plays with the object it loves," Jung argues. The impulse derives from childhood experimentation and imagination. "The creation of something new," he adds, "is not accomplished by intellect but by the play instinct acting from inner necessity.'

This instinct to play describes what keeps happening with the inventors…Inventors don't have to be intellectually advanced, at least in terms of formal education. Many of them insist that they aren't especially smart. But they all display flashes of genius, and that genius is derived from their childlike proclivity to play with the things that interest them. That's the source of their urge to invent, their compulsion to create, their creative juice. In Jung's terms, inventors develop an inner necessity to imagine new possibilities and realize them. They make their own fuel and keep it burning.

Aspects of what Mr. Schwartz argues regarding 'necessity,' can be challenged or at least refined. For instance, he does not appear to appreciate that at times there is and isn't value in making a distinction between the necessity that drives entrepreneurs to supply goods and services (with no initial concern for the marketplace) and the necessity that drives consumers to purchase these goods and services (which often motivates the creative act of the entrepreneur).

Either way, what propels the entrepreneur comes from within – whether by creative habit or through the perception of an opportunity.

His primary focus on habitually creative persons causes him to obscure, deny or ignore that there is obviously a direct correlation between the two 'necessities.'

People create because they enjoy it and people create because they wish to make money.

We see no need in making one motivation any less important than the other. We also see no need – in the context of explaining necessity – to make one appear more internal and the other to appear more external in nature.

Mr. Schwartz appears confused or conflicted about why necessity matters in the first place.

He feels a need to simultaneously deny and acknowledge the words of Carl Jung which he quotes, "The creation of something new is not accomplished by intellect but by the play instinct acting from inner necessity." Here he acknowledges a form of necessity. Yet earlier Mr. Schwarz largely denies the role of necessity in creativity, "The most common explanation of what drives inventive activity is the age-old maxim, 'Necessity is the mother of invention.' But that aphorism explains almost nothing and is wrong in most instances."

If it is wrong than what is 'inner necessity?'

Yet, much of Mr. Schwartz's central point is in harmony with what we mean by *spiritual*. The creative or innovative act is always something that takes place inside of the person and is part of a process that "comes from *within the individual*…" as he states.

The creative act "comes from *within the individual* rather than from the pull of an unmet need in the marketplace of human activity," quite frequently but why that should be a sticking point is not clear. Our concept of the entrepreneur (the primary agent of creative acts) recognizes that the "pull of an unmet need in the marketplace of human activity" is not unrelated to the process that is taking place inside of a human being. It is actually part of it. It is very likely that the "pull of an unmet need in the marketplace of human activity" is one of the factors affecting the 'inner necessity' within the person to create a product, service and business and offer it in the marketplace.

Therefore there is no contradiction in what Jung describes as the 'inner necessity' of the individual, and the unmet need or necessity in the marketplace. The definition of an entrepreneur that we promote (a person who perceives an opportunity and creates an organization to pursue it) reconciles both 'necessities.'

Therefore, necessity (the inner drive to create or the perception of a need in the marketplace) absolutely is the mother of invention!

And here is the point of departure we have with mainstream economic theory and the vast majority of what academia has to say about the nature of entrepreneurial activity. This is also an area that popular business literature fails to address.

Economic theory is influenced by the dichotomy – the religious vs. secular and spiritual vs. material divide – and artificial division of reality that plagues the social sciences altogether. As a result, of the two factors Evan Schwartz describes, the economics profession places far more emphasis on the "the marketplace of human activity" (treating it as an external activity with no spiritual component) than it does on "the drive to create possibilities…that comes from *within the individual.*" It rarely if ever identifies where these two areas connect.

And this is why the metrics of the establishment economics profession are inadequate and unable to measure, quantify and qualify the nature of the economic process. As a result, if we only consider standard economic statistics and analysis we don't know *why* people create or innovate; or just *how creative* people truly are, nor do we know how *well* they are doing, outside of their income level (derived from the 'marketplace').

This shortcoming or oversight prevents accuracy in economic development models and measurements of economic growth, opening the door to mistakes, errors and even corruption.

To back this assertion we consult three sources, first the book, *Confessions Of An Economic Hitman* by John Perkins; *From Subsistence to Exchange and other Essays* by Peter Bauer; and *History The Human Gamble* by Reuven Brenner.

Mr. Perkins writes of his role as an 'economic hit man,' specially trained, while employed by private corporations to persuade governments to assume debt and multilateral agencies like the World Bank to fund projects in nations, which Perkins claims, the United States wanted leverage over. He explains his work for Chas. T. Main, Inc. (MAIN), and the training received for it (from a woman named Claudine), and finally how commonly used economic statistics like Gross National Product (GNP) were part of the deception (bold emphasis is mine):

Claudine told me that there were two primary objectives of my work. First, I was to justify huge international loans that would funnel money back to MAIN and other U.S. companies (such as Bechtel, Halliburton, Stone & Webster, and Brown & Root) through massive engineering and construction projects. Second, I would work to bankrupt the countries that received those loans (after they had paid MAIN and the other U.S. contractors, of course) so that they would be forever beholden to their creditors, and so they would present easy targets when we needed favors, including military bases, UN votes, or access to oil and other natural resources.

My job, she said, was to forecast the effects of investing billions of dollars in a country. Specifically I would produce studies that projected economic growth twenty to twenty-five years into the future and that evaluated the impacts of a variety of projects. For example, if a decision was made to lend a country $1 billion to persuade its leaders not to align with the Soviet Union, I would compare the benefits of investing that money in power plants with the benefits of investing in a new national railroad network or a telecommunications system. Or I might be told that the country was being offered the opportunity to receive a modern electric utility system, and it would be up to me to demonstrate that such a system would result in sufficient economic growth to justify the loan. The critical factor, in every case, was gross national product. The project that resulted in the highest average annual growth of GNP won. If only one project was under consideration, I would need to demonstrate that developing it would bring superior benefits to GNP.

The unspoken aspect of every one of these projects was that they were intended to create large profits for the contractors, and to make a handful of wealthy and influential families in the receiving countries very happy, while assuring the long-term financial dependence and therefore the political loyalty of governments around the world. The larger the loan, the better. The fact that the debt burden placed on a country would deprive its poorest citizens of health, education, and other social services for decades to come was not taken into consideration.

Claudine and I openly discussed the deceptive nature of GNP. For instance, the growth of GNP may result even when it profits only one person, such as an individual who owns a utility company, and even if the majority of the population is burdened with debt. The rich get richer and the poor grow poorer. **Yet, from a statistical standpoint, this is recorded as economic progress**.

This final point of Mr. Perkins – regarding how development statistics do not accurately reflect economic activity – connects to one made in an earlier chapter in this book on capital and the business firm. There, we referred to the work of Peter Bauer who wrote, of the entrepreneurial and economic activity of small farmers in poor countries (bold emphasis is ours):

"Farmers in poor countries producing for wider exchange have to make investments of various kinds. These investments include the clearing and improvement of land and the acquisition of livestock and equipment. Such investments constitute capital formation. A part of this capital formation is financed from personal savings and borrowing from traders and others. But much of it is nonmonetized. For example, the clearing or improvement of land is the result of additional effort on the part of the farmer and his family. Very little monetary expenditure is involved. **These forms of investment, when made by small farmers, are generally omitted from official statistics and are still largely ignored in both the academic and the official development literature**."

Now, let's add an additional element from Reuven Brenner who writes (italics mine):

Economic development as conventionally understood and measured might not tell us much about either wealth per capita or general welfare. One of the major points of this book is that much of what we consider to be signs of progress or development – the rise of markets, and of social institutions, literacy, legislation, and so forth are, in a historical perspective, an illusion. These new institutions substitute for the trust, customs, and beliefs that are shared when human populations are much smaller and are maintained at stable levels, while *innovations and discoveries, or the gambling on novel ideas in general, are due to people's suffering.* It should then be that development, as measured by a rising gross national product, cannot be equated with either progress, an evolutionary process, or increased welfare, as is done now by most Western minds.

These insights suggest that a significant amount of what leads to or constitutes economic activity like non-monetary investments made by poor people (often without access to bank loans, no collateral and little or no cash revenue), and innovations and gambling on new ideas by individuals is not being measured by economists who insist on focusing only on a monetary marketplace (which seems to have a need to ignore non-monetary forms of capital and harder to see or more spiritual aspects of human motivation, like suffering).

These two factors are ignored though for two different reasons.

In the case of non-monetary investments, as noted earlier in this book, the problem stems from the unwillingness of economists to broaden their definition of 'capital,' beyond simply 'money and machines,' and from their inability to understand that a business firm is an entity that pools forms of capital for reasons other than monetary profit.

The second factor – the motivation for innovations and gambling on new ideas, or risk-taking – is ignored because of disrespect for the spiritual aspects of human existence, and a reliance on a research process, and statistical and development models which rarely incorporates it.

We have already examined the first factor – of the non-monetary capital investments and pooling of resources entrepreneurs and the poor make every day.

Now, it is toward this process of innovation, creativity and risk-taking and their relationship to suffering to which we will now turn.

Is suffering the spiritual process by which unseen realities are perceived; the circumstantial fuel that reveals and manifests intention to, and within a person; and the means by which people make critical life-changing decisions and determine to persevere through obstacles and difficulty factors?

Could it be that pain and loss hold a key to pleasure and gain through entrepreneurship?

Could it be that the foundation of economic development and growth – entrepreneurship – is built upon the insight, knowledge, force and power that come to us through suffering?

These possibilities seem to be consistent with the view expressed in both the Bible, Holy Qur'an and various disciplines regarding the natural and spiritual progression of man.

Before we can definitively see how clearly suffering impacts entrepreneurship for better or worse it would be helpful to see the efforts to understand and explain this phenomenon from a variety of perspectives. Then, we can see more clearly how this force for change affects entrepreneurs and how it can be mobilized on behalf of any of us.

We now look at "suffering" from the perspective of theology, sociology, psychology, psychiatry, and economics, before, finally, business and entrepreneurship.

Theology

In Christian theology there may be no subject bigger than that of the Suffering Servant, those verses contained in the book of Isaiah 53 which paint a picture of the experience of the Messiah, the Messianic nation or both (depending upon which interpretation one accepts). According to scholars and preachers, although the majority of the passages in scripture pertaining to the Suffering Servant are contained in between the 40th and 55th chapters of the book of Isaiah – 42:1-9; 49:1-6; 50:4-9; 52:13-53:12 in particular – the crux of these passages appear in Isaiah 52:13-53:9 which reads:

See, my servant shall prosper; he shall be exalted and lifted up, and shall be very high.

Just as there were many who were astonished at him – so marred was his appearance, beyond human semblance, and his form beyond that of mortals – so he shall startle many nations; kings shall shut their mouths because of him; for that which had not been told them they shall see, and that which they had not heard they shall contemplate.

Who has believed what we have heard? And to whom has the arm of the LORD been revealed?

For he grew up before him like a young plant, and like a root out of dry ground; he had no form or majesty that we should look at him, nothing in his appearance that we should desire him.

He was despised and rejected by others; a man of suffering and acquainted with infirmity; and as one from whom others hide their faces he was despised, and we held him of no account.

Surely he has borne our infirmities and carried our diseases; yet we accounted him stricken, struck down by God, and afflicted. But he was wounded for our transgressions, crushed for our iniquities; upon him was the punishment that made us whole, and by his bruises we are healed.

All we like sheep have gone astray; we have all turned to our own way, and the LORD has laid on him the iniquity of us all.

He was oppressed, and he was afflicted, yet he did not open his mouth; like a lamb that is led to the slaughter, and like a sheep that before its shearers is silent, so he did not open his mouth.

By a perversion of justice he was taken away. Who could have imagined his future? For he was cut off from the land of the living, stricken for the transgression of my people.

They made his grave with the wicked and his tomb with the rich, although he had done no violence, and there was no deceit in his mouth.

While some Christian and Jewish scholars have been preoccupied with the identity of the servant(s) pictured in these verses, it seems that it is equally important to note the paradoxical nature of what is depicted.

Here, the servant is despised, rejected, marred, afflicted and 'by a perversion of justice, taken away....cut off from the land of the living, stricken for the transgression of my people." Yet, we are told earlier, the servant "shall prosper; he shall be exalted and lifted up, and shall be very high." Some theologians make it very clear that the exalted status of this servant is made possible *because* of what the servant suffers.

This theme is not exclusive to Isaiah in the Bible.

This picture and a relationship between the suffering of God's servant and the servant's eventual glorification and exaltation as part of a Divine plan is similarly displayed in the New Testament:

In *What The Bible Says About Suffering* by Willie W. White we read:

One of the greatest evidence of God's love for His children is that He permits them to suffer – and gives them the grace to see it through. "But no one has ever suffered as I have suffered." Don't you believe it! Jesus did- and He was made perfect through sufferings.

For it became him, for whom are all things, and through whom are all things, in bringing many sons unto glory, to make the author of their salvation perfect through sufferings (Heb. 2:10)

Can this be possible: Jesus Christ, the Son of God, the Saviour of men, the One Who made all things and for Whom all things were made, the Author of our salvation, "made perfect through sufferings?" Was He not divine? Was He not always perfect? Wherein was His imperfection, His weakness, His sin? Who was able to respond when He issued the challenge, "Which one of you convicteth me of sin?" (John 8:46). Does the author of the Hebrew letter contradict himself when he declares that Jesus was "without sin" (Heb. 4:15), and that He was "holy, guileless, undefiled, separated from sinners, and made higher than the heavens" (Heb. 7:26)? What can it mean: "Perfect through sufferings?"

In commenting on this dilemma, the splendid Greek scholar, A.T. Robertson, observes, "If one recoils from the idea of God making Christ perfect, he should bear in mind that it is the humanity of Jesus that is under discussion." Note carefully the picture of the Son which is drawn in the preceding verses. He is superior to the angels and more to be heeded, yet for those brief years in which He was subjected to human limitations He was made "a little lower than the angels" (v.9) . Our Lord was qualified to be the Saviour of men only by suffering as a man.

Those who knew the language in which the author wrote did not share the problems of understanding the word "perfect." It is the Greek word Teleiosai (first aorist active infinite of teleioo). The outstanding Greek authority Thayer defines the word as "wanting nothing necessary to completeness...to bring the end (goal) proposed." The word might well be translated "finished," "completed," or "done." It contains the thought of fulfilling the purpose for which a thing is made, completed for a task. His sufferings completed the process of His training. "By means of sufferings" God perfected His Son in His human life for His task as Redeemer and Savior. Without suffering there can be no completion of the plan of God.

The writer enlarges upon this wonderful theme in Hebrews 5, where, in verses 8 and 9, he declares, "Though He was a Son, yet learned obedience by the things which he suffered; and having been made perfect, he became unto all them that obey him the author of eternal salvation." Our salvation is perfected through His perfection!

..."Perfect" – what a wonderful and meaningful word! And how its meaning is enhanced when we discover that this was next to the last word to fall from the lips of our Lord as He offered Himself for our sins on the cross of Calvary: "It is finished" (John 19:30).

...It was Peter who took the lead on Pentecost, as the church was established. It was Peter who was first to carry the gospel of redeeming grace to the gentiles. It was Peter who became a pillar of the church in Jerusalem. After Peter met the risen Christ and experienced the purging of forgiveness he never wavered. He knew what it was to suffer with Christ and not be ashamed. As he wrote to the saints who were being scattered through persecution, he reminded them, "Christ also suffered for you, leaving you an example, that ye should follow his steps (I Peter 2:2). If Christ suffered for us, and if we are to follow His steps, we are obligated to face up to the question, "What did Christ suffer, and as I follow Him what suffering may I expect?"

In describing the forms of suffering one who follows Christ can expect, Mr. White lists: 1) The suffering of physical pain 2) The suffering of sin 3) The suffering of poverty 4) The suffering of misunderstanding and loneliness 5) The suffering of the loss of loved ones.

Then in a section called, "The Fellowship of His Suffering" Mr. White adds:

The paramount goal of the apostle was that he might know Christ, and the power of His resurrection, and the fellowship of His suffering (Phil. 3:10). Earlier in this letter to his beloved church Paul has declared that "to you it *hath been granted* in the behalf of Christ, not only to believe on him, but also to suffer on his behalf" (Phil. 1:29. Italics are the author's). How strange! Who among us *desires* to suffer? But here the inspired apostle declares that "it has been granted" us to suffer. Those early disciples had captured this truth, and it enabled them to depart from the religious council where they had been beaten for their testimony, "rejoicing that they were counted worthy to suffer dishonor for the Name" (Acts 5:41).

Although some have expressed otherwise, the suffering of the Messiah and those who follow the Christ figure of the Bible does not take place in a vacuum. The purpose and objective for those so enduring this phenomenon, made clear in numerous places in the scriptures, is the eventual 'victory' over those that oppose the movement of which they are a part of, *and* the obtaining of a closer communion – even a spiritual and physical presence – with God and one another, in a spiritual or physical location.

All of this – just described – of course, has been interpreted differently by numerous scriptural scientists and theologians. But the main point is that there was a motive, objective, and even agreement between the follower and God and the Christ, according to the scriptures. Actions and thoughts are rewarded, forgiven and punished as part of a process that includes judgment, forgiveness, repentance, atonement and mercy – providing a real context for suffering and even an explanation of why it is readily accepted by the Believer.

In the mind of the disciples, the suffering is justified or worth it all – in relation to something(s) or Someone (s) other than themselves, and an eventual state of development within their own being which they hope to obtain, reach, and experience.

In Christian theology, a question has perplexed and concerned scholars and preachers for ages – why do Believers suffer? If the Believers are the most righteous people on earth, why, then do they endure so much pain, experience so much injustice and have to patiently hope and have faith in a future that is brighter than the present or past?

Perhaps, more than any other book in the Bible, the book of Job, has been the reference point for the deepest consideration of these paradoxical questions.

The book of Job is the story of a man by that name who is both faithful to God and wealthy, but who has his good fortune replaced by loss due to an arrangement by God and Satan, at Satan's request.

Satan, apparently seeking to prove that Job was only faithful to God because he was the recipient of Divine blessings, challenges God to remove his providence from his servant, Job. According to Job 1: 9-10 we read, "Does Job fear God for nothing?" Satan replied. "Have you not put a hedge around him and his household and everything he has? You have blessed the work of his hands, so that his flocks and herds are spread throughout the land."

Satan is suggesting that God's blessings and protection of Job are the reason for his loyalty for God.

So, God agrees to give Satan the power to test Job.

Everything that Job owned was placed under Satan's authority. And what was the result? In one day, disaster strikes. Job's servants are attacked and killed and have their donkeys and oxen stolen from them. Lightning strikes and kills all of his sheep and shepherds. Raiders kill more servants and take the camels. A storm blows down Job's eldest son's house and kills all of his children. And what is Job's response? "I was born with nothing, and I will die with nothing. The LORD gave and now He has taken away. May his name be praised!" (Job 1: 21)

As if that were not enough, Satan requests and receives the power to hurt Job physically.

His hope is that this kind of suffering will cause Job to curse God directly to his face. So God permits this, but will not allow Satan's effort to go to the extreme of killing Job. Job's body is racked by pain with boils and sores covering him from head to toe.

The suffering of Job affects his relationships. Beginning with his wife, they all react in different ways. His wife asks Job "Why don't you curse God and die?" (Job 2: 9)

Three of Job's friends, Eliphaz, Bildad and Zophar, come to console him. They are so shaken and overcome by what their friend is experiencing that they are with him for seven days, but say nothing. Job's anguish deepens and he begins to complain about his state of affairs openly wishing he had never been born.

He wants to die in order to end to his pain.

One of the most powerful aspects of suffering that is visible in this story (and many others), is the effect that the suffering of an individual has on those closest to them; and how that effect impacts the sufferer.

Of the evolving perceptions among Job's friends regarding the adversity he is facing and their judgment of why it is occurring, followed by the God's view, we consider the following summary drawn from three sources: Good News Bible, Canadian Bible Society, 1992; Halley's Bible

Handbook, Zondervan, 2000; and William Neil's One Volume Bible Commentary, Hodder & Stoughton, 1962:

The bulk of the text of Job is the content of three cycles of dialogue by the friends and Job's responses to them.

In the first cycle (Job 4-14) Eliphaz speaks first. Reflecting the standard Hebrew line of theology, he urges Job to repent of his sins since he is obviously being punished. The other two friends deliver the same line of thought. Job defends himself with each one and maintains his trust and faith in God. He is bitterly disappointed in their accusations and attitude towards him.

Cycle number two (Job 15-21) is like the first only more heated. The friends have only one answer to Job's situation: Job is wicked and won't admit it. There is no other explanation for the torment that God is allowing him to endure. They don't believe Job's claims of innocence and are blunt, sarcastic and accusatory. Job wants to know why the wicked prosper. He feels that everyone is against him.

The third cycle of dialogue begins in chapter 22 and Eliphaz lays into Job harder than ever. He accuses Job not only of guilt but also of being God's enemy. It's a final plea for Job to confess and end the misery. Bildad resigns himself to state that no one can claim to be without fault and leaves it at that. They are at a stalemate. What is the answer to the suffering of the righteous? Can anyone be declared righteous?

Job makes a final plea to all three and claims to be innocent of all charges against him. The friends are silenced; they give up. A bystander who has been listening to the whole exchange introduces himself. His name is Elihu and his speech takes up six chapters. He is angry with the friends for their accusations. He is mad at Job because Job was hinting that maybe God is not just. He accuses Job of trying to undermine the sovereignty of God.

Finally God speaks in chapters 38 – 41. The Lord basically asks Job, Who do you think you are? It is a lesson on the sovereignty of God. We cannot question or understand God's motives and Job is reprimanded for doubting God's justice. The Lord then takes Eliphaz, Bildad and Zophar to task for their accusations. God asks them to make sacrifices for their sin and asks Job to pray for them. In the end Job is rewarded for his refusal to curse God. He becomes twice as prosperous as he was before.

Why do the righteous suffer? Why do bad things happen to good people? The lesson in Job is that we can't know the answer. The only attitude to have is one of faith and trust in an almighty, sovereign, loving God who knows all and sees the beginning and end of everything.

For a thorough analysis on the story of Job and what it suggests about the purpose and consequences of suffering, from the perspective of theology, we turn to respected Christian theologian Dr. Thomas 1. Constable. From his "Notes on Job" 2006 Edition we read:

I believe the primary application of the Book of Job is that we do not need to know why God does what He does if we know Him. Job is a book that deals with persevering faith
(cf. 2 Cor. 5:7).[224]

> "To sufferers in all ages the book of Job declares that less important than fathoming the intellectual problem of the mystery of suffering is the appropriation of its spiritual enrichment through the fellowship of God."

In this book the writer clarified the basis of human relationship with God. It is not retribution. Retribution is the theory that before death God always pays someone in kind according to what that person gives Him, blessing for righteousness or suffering for unrighteousness. We should not return to God what God sends us either, worship for blessing or cursing for pain. Rather the basis of our relationship is grace. God owes people nothing. Because people are sinful creatures God can justly curse us. However because God is a loving Father He chooses to bless us in many cases. People's response to God's grace should be trust and obedience.

Why do the godly suffer?

Person(s)	Answer	Evaluation
Job's wife	God is unfair.	Never
Job's three friends	God is disciplining (punishing) them because of sin.	Sometimes
Job	God wants to destroy them because of sin.	Sometimes
Elihu	God wants to direct (educate) them because of ignorance.	Sometimes
God	God wants to develop them and to demonstrate His glory.	Always

The different characters in the book based their understanding and their convictions on different sources of knowledge.

Person(s)	Epistemological base
Job's wife	Empiricism
Job's three friends	Rationalism
Job	Rationalism
Elihu	Human inspiration
God	Revelation

Job's three friends each had a different basis of authority.

Person	Authoritative base
Eliphaz	Experience
Bildad	Tradition
Zophar	Intuition

Some of the practical lessons the Book of Job teaches include the following. God is in control even when He appears not to be. The good will of God includes suffering, in spite of what faith healers say. Bad things happen to good people because God allows Satan to test them, not because God seduces them to do evil (cf. James 1:13). God is just in spite of appearances. Whatever God does is right because He does it. We can and should worship God even when we are suffering. We can trust God even when we have no explanation for what is happening to us. It is futile and foolish to criticize God or to challenge Him. We create problems for ourselves when we put God in a box. When we feel anxious we should seek to get to know God better by consulting His special revelation, the Bible.

"The book of Job makes an outstanding contribution to the theology of God and man. God is seen as sovereign, omniscient, omnipotent, and caring. By contrast, man is seen as finite, ignorant, and sinful. And yet, even in the face of suffering, man can worship God, confident that His ways are perfect and that pride has no place before Him."

Among other streams of thought, it appears that one of the reasons for suffering identified by Christian theologians is that God uses it to develop human beings.

<<<>>>

In the Holy Qur'an, the concept of suffering is most frequently embodied by the use of words, translated from the Arabic language into English, as adversity, difficulty, steadfastness and patience.

In the Holy Qur'an the nature of suffering is laid bare and intimately connected to other concepts such as struggle, striving, trials and tests. The purpose of suffering, afflictions, adversity, difficulty, struggle, striving, trials and tests is three-fold: 1) to develop qualities and character in the human being enabling his or her progress in life 2) to reveal man's qualities and character before Allah (God) and 3) to bring man closer to Allah (God).

A sampling of a variety of verses and footnotes makes this clear.

Surah 2 verse 177 (Yusuf Ali translation):

It is not righteousness that ye turn your faces towards East or West; but it is righteousness – to believe in Allah and the Last Day and the Angels, and the Book, and the Messengers; to spend of your substance, out of the love for Him, for your kin, for orphans, for the needy, for the wayfarer, for those who ask, and for the ransom of slaves; to be steadfast in prayer, and practice regular charity, to fulfill the contracts, which ye have made; and to be firm and patient, in pain (or suffering) and adversity, and throughout all periods of panic. Such are the people of truth, the God-fearing.

Surah 2 verse 214 (Yusuf Ali translation):

Or do ye think that ye shall enter the Garden (of Bliss) without such (trials) as came to those who passed away before you? They encountered suffering and adversity, and were so shaken in spirit that even the Messenger and those of faith who were with him cried: "when (will come) the help of Allah" Ah! Verily, the help of Allah is (always) near!

Surah 6 verses 42 to 43 (Yusuf Ali translation):

Before We sent (Messengers) to many nations, and We afflicted the nations with suffering and adversity, that they might learn humility. When the suffering reached them from Us, why then did they not learn humility? On the contrary their hearts became hardened, and Satan made their (sinful) acts seem alluring to them.

Surah 3 verse 134 (Yusuf Ali translation):

Those who spend (freely), whether in prosperity, or in adversity; who restrain anger, and pardon (all) men – for Allah loves those who do good –

Surah 7 verse 168 (Yusuf Ali transalation):

We broke them up into sections on this earth. There are among them some that are the righteous, and some that are the opposite. We have tried them with both prosperity and adversity: in order that they might turn (to Us).

Surah 10 verse 21 (Yusuf Ali translation):

When we make mankind taste of some mercy after adversity hath touched them, behold! They take to plotting against Our Signs! Say: "Swifter to plan is Allah!" Verily, Our messengers record All the plots that ye make!

Surah 11 verses 9, 10 and 11 (Yusuf Ali translation):

If We give man a taste of mercy from Ourselves, and then withdraw it from him, behold! He is in despair and (falls into) blasphemy. But if We give him a taste of (Our) favours after adversity hath touched him, he is sure to say, "All evil has departed from me;" Behold! He falls into exultation and pride. Not so do those who show patience and constancy, and work righteousness; for them is forgiveness (of sins) and a great reward.

Surah 41 verses 49 and 50 (Yusuf Ali translation):

Man does not weary of asking for good (things), but if ill touches him, he gives up all hope (and) is lost in despair. When We give him a taste of some mercy from Ourselves after some adversity has touched him, he is sure to say, "This is due to my (merit): I think not that the Hour (of Judgment) will (ever) be established; but if I am brought back to my Lord, I have (much) good (stored) in His sight!" But We will show the Unbelievers the truth of all that they did, and We shall give them the taste of a severe penalty.

Surah 2 verse 148 (Yusef Ali translation):

To each is a goal to which Allah turns him; then strive together (as in a race) towards all that is good. Wheresoever ye are, Allah will bring you together. For Allah hath power over all things.

Surah 53: verses 36 to 42 (Yusef Ali translation)

Nay, is he not acquainted with what is in the books of Moses and of Abraham who fulfilled his engagements – namely that no bearer of burdens can bear the burden of another; that man can have nothing but what he strives for; that (the fruit of) his striving will soon come in sight; then will he be rewarded with a reward complete; that to thy Lord is the final Goal.

Surah 90 verses 4 and 11 (Maulana Muhammad Ali translation):

We have certainly created man to face difficulties...But he attempts not the uphill road;

Surah 90 verses 4 and 11 (Yusef Al translation):

Verily we have created man into toil and struggle...But he hath made no haste on the path that is steep.

If all of these verses, and numerous others, were connected, compared and contrasted (which is beyond the scope of this book) a set of common themes regarding the relationship between suffering, afflictions, adversity, difficulty, struggle, striving, trials and tests would emerge.

One theme would be that difficulty, pain, adversity and suffering are an essential aspect of life and that they are produced or utilized by Allah (God) as a means of developing, qualifying and disqualifying man for rewards and progress, and ultimately divine access to the Supreme Being. By suffering, man is persuaded or forced to think more deeply and recognize the reality of a Supreme Being. This is the dominant theme.

That this phenomenon is a major aspect of the purpose of life is made clear in Surah 90 and verse 4, *"We have certainly created man to face difficulties."* This verse makes clear or at least strongly implies that one of the reasons or inherited realities of the human being is to actually deal with problems, adversity and opposition. In the footnote to this verse, in commentary, Yusuf Ali quotes and cites several verses from the Bible and Holy Qur'an, writing, " 'Man is born unto troubles as the sparks fly upward' (Job v. 7); 'For all his days are sorrows and his travail grief' (Ecclesiastes, ii. 23). Man's life is full of sorrow and vexation; but our text has a different shade of meaning: man is born to strive and struggle; and if he suffers from hardships, he must exercise patience, for Allah will make his way smooth for him (65:7; 94:5-6)...."

In his commentary, Yusuf Ali cites two other chapters (and verses) in the Holy Qur'an: Surah 65 verse 7 and Surah 94 verses 5 and 6. They read as follows:

Surah 65 verse 7 (Yusuf Ali translation):

Let the man of means spend according to his means: and the man whose resources are restricted, let him spend according to what Allah has given him. Allah puts no burden on any person beyond what He has given him. After a difficulty, Allah will soon grant relief.

Surah 94 verses 5 and 6 (Yusuf Ali translation):

So, verily, with every difficulty, there is relief. Verily, with every difficulty there is relief.

In the footnote in relation to verse five and verse 6, Yusuf Ali writes, "This verse is repeated for extra emphasis. Whatever difficulties or troubles are encountered by men, Allah always provides a solution, a way out, a relief, a way to lead to ease and happiness, if we only follow His Path and show our Faith by patience and well-doing. The solution or relief does not merely come *after* the Difficulty: it is provided *with* it."

Now let's go back to, and look again, at Surah 90 verse 4.

On this verse, in a footnote, Maulana Muhammad Ali writes of the Arabic word, which he translates as difficulty, and the meaning and implications of this verse, "*Kabad* means *distress* or *difficulty*. We are here told that the advancement of man, *even physically*, lies along a path of hard struggle. Every conquest that man has made has been the result of suffering on his part. The same is the case in the sphere of the spiritual advancement of man. Abraham suffered great hardships in the cause of Truth; and so must the Prophet now, in order to bring about a spiritual awakening in the world. It is only a long and hard struggle on the part of certain benefactors of humanity that makes man's advancement possible, physically as well as spiritually."

A clear summation of much of what the Holy Qur'an presents on the phenomenon of suffering, its purpose, and the attitude of the human deemed best in handling it is distilled in an excerpt from Maulana Muhammad Ali's book, The *Religion of Islam:*

The Holy Book throws further light on this subject where it makes mention of the Divine intention to bring the faithful to perfection through adversities. Thus, speaking of the believers in particular, it says: "And We shall certainly try you with something of fear and hunger and loss of property and lives and fruits; and give good news to the patient, who, when a misfortune befalls them, say: 'Surely we are Allah's and to Him we shall return'. Those are they on whom are blessings and mercy from their Lord and those are the followers of the right course" (2:155 – 157). The principle is laid down here that the faithful are brought to perfection through adversities and trials, because we are told that Allah intends to try the believers by means of various kinds of affliction, and through patience in suffering, they make themselves deserving of Divine blessings and mercy. Therefore when the faithful are made to say, "Nothing will afflict us save what Allah has ordained for us" (9:51), it is in reference to the Divine will, as expressed above, and they are made to suffer afflictions for their own perfection. God's writing down afflictions for them, means, therefore, only that the Divine law is that they will be brought to perfection through afflictions...

Both the verses quoted above and other similar verses, which speak of the writing down of afflictions for the believers, only teach that greatest lesson of life, resignation in adversities. Muslims are taught to remain absolutely contented when they have to meet adversity or death in fulfillment of their duties. If a Muslim meets adversity or even death, he must believe that it is by God's order, that being the real meaning of *kitabat* [author's note: *kitabat* means "written down"] in such cases. That faith upholds a Muslim in adversity because he knows that, out of adversity which is by the order of the good God, will undoubtedly come good. There is a message in these verses that Muslims must face all adversities manfully and never despair of the mercy of God.

Now let's move into a look at this concept from other disciplines.

<<<<>>>>

Sociology, Psychology, Psychiatry

In the discipline of sociology the concept and phenomenon of suffering is addressed with some trouble, with scientists and professionals in these fields openly admitting that explaining the process and what causes it has involved, well, some suffering of its own.

In *Suffering: A Sociological Introduction* by Iain Wilkinson we read:

Throughout this discussion I have drawn attention to the ways in which the effort to conceptualize the existential components of human suffering draws researchers to debate the adequacy of the language of the social sciences to address the reality of this phenomenon. Without exception, researchers labour under the conviction that something vital is always being left out of their accounts of what suffering *does* to people. They are repeatedly brought to the conclusion that they are both conceptually and methodologically ill-equipped to make human suffering their object of investigation.

...Accordingly, this research tends to be embroiled in fundamental questions of origins, significance and purpose, in an effort to clarify the constitution of suffering in human experience and identify the optimum ways in which its antagonism might be opposed. While looking to promote this endeavor, I have nevertheless worked to highlight the possibility that, not only might a burden of analytical frustration always remain to obstruct these aims and objectives, but also that this is perhaps inevitable and even necessary if we are to arrive at a fuller understanding of what suffering *does* to people.

Interestingly, Mr. Wilkinson more confidently suggests that the search for a definition of suffering is what has enabled him to arrive at a clear definition:

 I have argued that it is when placed under the frustration of being driven to ask such fundamental questions of origins, significance and purpose that, paradoxically, we may be in position to share in a vital component of what suffering 'is' in human experience: namely, a cultural struggle to reconstitute a positive sense of meaning and purpose for self and society against the brute force of events in which these are violated and destroyed.

Some sociologists state that suffering is impossible to quantify and explain due to three reasons.

First, suffering is a subjective reality, although common. It does not allow us to enter into the realm of another person's personal experience with it, they contend. They also hold that the intense nature of the pain of the person who is suffering keeps them from sharing it with others, as they are unable to represent what they are experiencing.

Secondly, suffering appears in such a wide variety of forms that it is hard to say exactly what 'it' is. Suffering is said to be comprised of humiliation, distress, boredom, depression, anxiety, guilt and taking place in experiences of bereavement and loss, social isolation and personal estrangement. It can take place in cultural, political, economic, physical, psychological and social life. It can occur through the denial of civil liberties, social injustice, and the deprivation of material things.

Mr. Wilkinson writes, "In the final analysis, there may be no symbolic forms of culture that are adequate to represent *all* the ways in which suffering may afflict our humanity. Perhaps we ask too much of our capacity for language when we seek to represent a phenomenon which appears to be so dynamically adapted to the purpose of negating every aspect of our being."

That final point, that suffering, is "a phenomenon which appears to be so dynamically adapted to the purpose of negating every aspect of our being", relates to the third belief in much of sociology, that because suffering represents a lack or a denial of something or someone, it is counter to our nature or reality and somehow indescribable.

In a 2001 article, "Can We Research Suffering?" published in *Qualitative Health Research*, A.W. Frank writes:

Suffering involves experiencing yourself on the other side of life as it should be, and no thing, no material resource, can bridge that separation. Suffering is what lies beyond such help. Suffering is the unspeakable, as opposed to what can be spoken; it is what remains concealed, impossible to reveal; it remains in darkness, eluding illumination; and it is dread, beyond what is tangible even if hurtful. Suffering is loss, present or anticipated, and loss is another instance of no thing, an absence of what was missed and now is no longer recoverable and the absence of what we feel will never be. At the core of suffering is the sense that something is irreparably wrong with our lives, and wrong is the negation of what could not have been right. Anyone who suffers knows the reality of suffering, but this reality is what you cannot 'come to grips with'.

One area of these disciplines that has shown more promise than others in terms of actually quantifying what suffering is, might be the study of the impact that society and social interaction has on the physical and psychological health of the individual.

This has a bearing on our search for a meaningful definition of the relationship between suffering and entrepreneurship, as entrepreneurship is first a mental activity, beginning with an awareness of self and influenced by one's view of themselves in relation to their physical environment and others – in a household or community. That there might exist a relationship between society and a person's psychological health, suggests that any external factor or force that affects the physiology and anatomy of a person also might impact the perception and thinking of an individual and their view of 'loss' and 'opportunity.' This would allow us to better understand entrepreneurs, the circumstances in which they appear and operate, and perhaps identify the types of individuals who have excelled the most in that field.

Another work that looks at suffering from the perspective of sociology and psychology is *Social Causes Of Illness* by Richard Totman. In his book he devotes an entire chapter to the relationship between suffering and disease. It is called, "Life Events and Illness." In this chapter he explores what events in the lives of everyday people can affect their health.

His findings point in the direction of the human perception of a loss – actual or expected – bringing on an illness. His research shows that the loss can be more than just a person in one's life, writing, "...the essential factor may not be the loss of another person in itself but rather the loss of a familiar, well-established pattern of life, a pattern which perhaps was only made possible through another person's company....all change involves losing something, and changes demanding the revision of long-held attitudes, beliefs, values and life-styles are those most resisted and those which people find hardest to cope with."

Here is a sampling, of excerpts from a few categories in which Mr. Totman's research showed the impact a 'loss' could have on health:

Social Mobility

Several researchers have been interested to know whether an especially high incidence of disease is to be found among people who change social class during their lifetime. Such transition is referred to by sociologists as 'social mobility', most frequently meaning movement from a lower to a higher social class (upward mobility). There are a variety of reasons why a high rate of disease might be expected in association with a significant change in social status. Someone who finds himself in a new social milieu has to conform to expectations with which he is unfamiliar. Demands on him to revise his old customs may be severe, inducing conflict and strain in the new situation.

Two comprehensive reviews of findings in relation to heart disease reveal a solid body of findings supporting a link between social mobility and disease.

The 'comprehensive reviews' that Richard Totman is referring to are 1) *Social stress and cardiovascular disease. Milbank Memorial Fund Quarterly, 45* and 2) Psychological and social precursors of coronary disease. *New England Journal of Medicine*, 284 pgs.244-255, 307-317

Status Incongruity

Quite apart from any change in his own personal status, an individual may move in different social circles, and these may make incongruous, or even incompatible, demands on him. This eventually has become known as 'status incongruity'. The pattern of findings relating to incidence of disease to status incongruity is very similar to that on social mobility....Where status incongruity is defined and measured in terms of a discrepancy in status between a person's parents, what findings there are support a link between status incongruity and disease more consistently than if some other definition is used, such as a difference between an individual and his spouse. An unusually high incidence of status incongruity has been discovered among parents of women with rheumatoid arthritis. Also, it has been noticed that heart disease is especially prevalent among people whose parents belong to different religious denominations.

Geographical Mobility

Evidence relating the extent to which people change their place of residence (other than by immigration) to incidence of disease shows somewhat better agreement than do studies of social mobility and studies of status incongruity, possibly because moving home is a less ambiguous business, and thus easier to identify and record.

Holmes found that tuberculosis rates were higher than normal among ethnic groups who were in the minority in their neighbourhood, and also among people who lived alone and made many occupational and residential moves. He describes them as 'strangers trying to find a role in the contemporary American scene.'

A study of executives by Christenson and Hinkle revealed that the highest proportion of illnesses of all sorts occurred among those working and living in a social environment perceived as new and unfamiliar

Rapidly changing social environment

If a society is forced to change its established way of life at such a rate that long held traditions suddenly become redundant and inappropriate to the new social demands, we might expect a similar effect on its members to that on an individual when he moves to an alien cultural setting. A number of anthropological and sociological observations on the effects of intensive urbanization on primitive rural cultures and sub-culture provide information on the occurrence of disease in such a situation.

Scotch studied Zulus living in urban and rural settings in South Africa. The rural native reserve was ethnologically classified as more culturally stable than the urban setting. Those Zulus in the urban environment were found to have significantly higher average blood pressure levels than the rural Zulus. Dietary factors were not believed to explain the difference. A similar pattern was noted…in relation to Guatemalan Indians.

There are some who suggest that there is plenty of reason to believe that a state of ease, comfort, and stability might be good for one's health. But what is the relationship between these states, character development and entrepreneurship – especially considering that pain and risk-taking are natural conditions of the latter two?

Could it be that creativity, character development, and risk-taking thrive in a condition that borders on or could even be considered *unhealthy*?

In his book, *Creative Malady*, George Pickering gives a snapshot of the type of person likely to be in relatively good health. "The research gives us one fairly clear directive: Most resistant to illness is the socially involved individual: the person who is well adjusted to a stable role within a supportive community."

This certainly does not sound like a person who has experienced the just described social mobility, status incongruity, geographical mobility, or rapidly changing social environment.

And is this "socially involved individual: the person who is well adjusted to a stable role within a supportive community," the same person that we have seen on the pages of scripture, in a state of anxiety, grief, psychological pain, with every fiber of their being seemingly tested by the difficulty they are commanded to face by their Lord?

Where is this form of stability, described by Mr. Pickering, in the life of a Believer who is going through suffering, under the hand of the Lord Jesus Christ, Jehovah, G-d, or Allah?

And would the majority of us qualify as "the socially involved individual: the person who is well adjusted to a stable role within a supportive community?"

Furthermore, what is it about theology that apparently does not allow it to place 'stability' in the development of the human being on par with adversity and suffering and the changing condition it imposes on the Believer?

Could it be that psychology and psychiatry and sociology recommend what theology and entrepreneurship don't?

Could it be that what is best for health is worse for economic development and wealth creation?

Or is there something else at work, not yet expressed in what we have reviewed from the disciplines of Sociology, Psychology and Psychiatry?

The work of Mr. Pickering may hold keys to a missing link between instability – even what is considered to be 'mental illness' – and the process of creativity that makes for successful entrepreneurship.

In his work Mr. Pickering divides illness into three categories, "organic illness, by which is meant disease of one of the organs of the body; psychosis by which is meant disorder of the mind severe enough to produce insanity in its legal sense; and psycho neurosis, by which is meant a lesser degree of mental disorder."

Of these, he says, of their relationship to creativity, "Organic or physical disease is not, to my knowledge, in general an aid to creativity. Vigour is essential to creativity…. The psychoses are, as we have seen… associated with mental deterioration at least in their advanced stages. At that stage those afflicted are not creative even though they may have been earlier."

But in the area of psychoneurosis, Mr. Pickering seems to speak with a forked tongue, acknowledging that a further difficulty is that achievement may at once be *the result of, and the cure* for a neurosis.

First he writes:

There is, as far as I know, no convincing evidence of exceptional creativity among psychoneurotics in general. At the present time, the psychoneuroses are some of the commonest diseases affecting society. Exceptional creativity, on the other hand, is very rare. Nor is there any evidence that there is a correlation between intelligence and psychoneurosis, though the question has not been submitted, as far as I know, to rigorous scientific scrutiny. However, the impressions of most psychiatrists would be that psychoneurosis occurs with all levels of intelligence and that in a given population of psychoneurotics, there is no preponderance of the highly intelligent.

Approaching the problem from the other direction, is there any evidence that men and women who have achieved distinction through their own creations are unusually prone to psychoneuroses? Ernest Jones seemingly thought so when he remarked: 'Neurotics are the torchbearers of civilization.'

In looking at this problem more closely, we may begin with the scientists. I happen to be acquainted with many of the most distinguished of living scientists. I have known personally, or known a good deal about, the Presidents of the Royal Society during the last forty years. None of them had, as far as I know, a psychoneurosis.

So, according to the above, it appears that Mr. Pickering finds nothing obvious about a connection between psychoneurosis and exceptional creativity, brilliance or genius.

But elsewhere he writes of his expectations in his research, admitting a curious insight in conclusion, which I have placed in boldface:

I hoped it might, as a by-product, throw some light on the creative personality. I think it does. It emphasises the singlemindedness of many men of genius, their obsession with the object of their passion to the exclusion of the ordinary conventions of daily life. Geniuses are very peculiar. And the dividing line between the odd and the mentally ill is tenuous.

My study emphasizes particularly the importance of passion, which is to be distinguished from ambition or the desire for fame, Passion is the chief characteristic that I can find which relates the psychoneuroses of the characters here described and the creative work which brought them fame. **Psychoneurosis arises when there is a conflict between a wish and its fulfillment. The more passionate the desire the more likely is its frustration to lead to psychoneurosis. This in turn may make possible the fulfillment of the wish, or act as a spur to the mental catharsis which produces a great creative work. This seems to be the basis of the relationship between psychoneurosis and creativity.**

In brief, a psychoneurosis represents passion thwarted, a great creative work, passion fulfilled.

With his statements, *"Psychoneurosis arises when there is a conflict between a wish and its fulfillment …a psychoneurosis represents passion thwarted, a great creative work, passion fulfilled,"* Mr. Pickering has presented a theme and even thesis worth exploring.

Again, exploring deeper, this idea that there is a relationship between social or external pressure, a mental disorder and creativity we look at his words, elsewhere in his book:

Many creative artists, painters and musicians have gone through a period of great turmoil and torment of mind before producing a masterpiece. The Agony in the Garden of Gethsemane was a necessary prelude to Christ's sacrifice on Calvary. Such disturbances of the mind may be regarded as part of the act of creation, in that this turmoil provides the drive or the directive, or both, for what happens subsequently.

And of the human subjects of his research – individuals famous for their creativity – he continues to write. In boldface I have placed those points he makes which support the thesis, *"Psychoneurosis arises when there is a conflict between a wish and its fulfillment ...a psychoneurosis represents passion thwarted, a great creative work, passion fulfilled."* He writes:

These sketches serve as an introduction to the more substantial characters shortly to be described. All of them display the same type of relationship. **Each subject was afflicted with a psychoneurosis, the attempted self-cure of which produced the ideas and the energy to establish those ideas that made him or her famous. This process was given the name mental catharsis by Joseph Breuer**, to explain what a young woman with a hysterical paralysis had discovered in herself. When she talked freely about her affliction and how it began, she was temporarily cured. In using this term, Breuer tried to bridge concepts of mental disease into line with concepts then common about the nature and cure of physical disease....**What Breuer meant by his term mental catharsis was a process by which the mind was purged of what was disturbing it. Nowadays we believe that psychoneurosis is, in general, the result of a conflict between a wish and its fulfillment. The more intense the desire, and the more completely it is frustrated, the more severe the psychoneurosis. If by some process the force opposing the desire can be removed or materially reduced, then the psychoneurosis may be cured.**

Adding more support for his unintended thesis that an unfulfilled desire can represent a mental disorder – a psychoneurosis – and that a personal and internal creative act resolves this state of mental instability, Mr. Pickering writes:

There seems to be an important difference in the process as it is generated within the patient's own mind, and as it is induced from without. **In every case known to me where a great creative work has resulted, the solution to the conflict has originated in the subject's own mind.** The method of bringing peace of mind from without through the confessional has long been used by the Roman Catholic Church. A similar method, using a different technique, underlies contemporary psycho-therapy. Neither of these induced methods of clearing the mind results in an act of creation. This is not surprising. As an eager, curious child or adolescent knows, there is all the difference in the world between discovering something for oneself and being shown it. In one the mind is active, in the other, passive. **Exceptional works require exceptional mental activity. This can only arise from within the mind. It can so arise in the course of resolving a conflict. Where this happens a vast flow**

of psychic energy previously pent up may be released and find its direction.

That suffering begets creativity is generally accepted. That the human being is quite often in a state of discomfort, dissatisfaction and tension while in the midst of a creative act is also widely believed. That the accomplishment, fulfillment or *actualization* of a creative desire and goal can be good for one's self-confidence and esteem, and therefore their psychological health, is a benefit to which many bear witness.

This actualization of a goal results in a form of actualization of one's self. Yet and still, in spite of these propositions many leading thinkers still wrestle with the paradox that they find in the relationship between creativity; self-actualization; the process of betting on new ideas as the result of 'loss' or the desire for 'gain' on one hand; and the 'health' of the creative person on the other.

One example is a writing, "Self-Actualization" by Mark A. Runco of California State University, Fullerton, which appears in the *Encyclopedia of Creativity Volume I*. He articulates the challenge:

Both creativity and self-actualization are indicative of psychological health. As is the case with most signs of health, however, it is not easy to determine which comes first. It is possible that self-actualization allows the individual to be creative, or that the creative tendency supports self-actualization. It is also possible that both are results of a third variable. This third variable might be the capacity for effective coping, adaptability, or intrapersonal intelligence. Recall here…that self-actualization and creativity both reflect an underlying motivational force.

We agree so far with Mr. Runco, but as we shall see later in this chapter, we can be more specific in that our model clearly stating that that 'underlying motivational force' of the entrepreneur is very frequently the suffering of 'loss' or the unrealized desire for 'gain.'

Mark A. Runco continues:

There is evidence that creativity and self-actualization are related. This relationship follows from the theories of Carl Rogers and Abraham Maslow, and was apparent in both clinical observations and some correlational studies. As is the case with all correlations studies, however, there is some uncertainty about the direction of effect. Creativity may lead to self-actualization, or self-actualization may support creativity. They both reflect a third variable, such as coping or adaptability. And neither guarantees the other.

Runco would do better if he more directly attempted to connect this 'third variable' which he calls 'coping or adaptability' with the thinking process and decision-making that goes on in the mind of a person *before* they engage in a creative act or reach the state of self actualization.

He might discover that suffering is both the 'coping or adaptability' process and the 'underlying motivational force' that leads to creativity which leads to a form of self-actualization (once the completed act is achieved or completed.)

He concludes:

There are many cases of unhealthy creative persons. This is not much of a surprise, if we keep in mind that there are different ways to be creative. Some individuals are creative in their work, and some in their leisure. Some are creative when they solve problems; others are creative only when they are not threatened by problems. Although some creative persons may be self-actualized, and that self-actualization may in fact be necessary for their creativity, other individuals may be creative without self-actualizing. Both creativity and self-actualization are multifaceted constructs, and this gives them any number of possible intersections.

What Runco writes is plausible, but there is more correlation and causation between these factors than he indicates. The 'unhealthy creative person' may be going through the 'psychoneurosis' and 'mental catharsis' associated with creativity. That state may have been reached due to the stress that one is under from experiencing a 'loss' or the dissatisfaction of an unrealized 'gain.'

The 'coping or adaptability' process that he describes can be the suffering leading to decision making to become creative in order to make up for the loss or to realize this gain, not yet attained. Runco's statement that "there are different ways to be creative," is of course true but not necessarily a problem in addressing the problem of correlation. His pointing out that, "Some individuals are creative in their work, and some in their leisure. Some are creative when they solve problems; others are creative only when they are not threatened by problems," is more of an emphasis on setting and circumstance during creativity, rather than specifically addressing what precipitated or affected the state of mind the person was in when they *decided* to engage in a creative act.

Without focusing on, or seeking to identify the moment of decision and what caused it, the psychologist, in particular, will always grope around in the dark, searching for correlation.

<u>Economy</u>

In looking at the subject of suffering from the perspective of economics we turn to a review of the thinking of one of the most influential men to ever impact the field, Karl Marx. He, uniquely, among the most influential economic historians and commentators of the last 200 years, addresses the relationship between human suffering and economics. His thinking, not only address the subject directly, but in many respects, it opens the door for further exploration in the area of how economic suffering impacts the decision making of a society in a political context. His point of view dovetails with much of what we have already considered.

From *Suffering: A Sociological Introduction* by Iain Wilkinson we read:

Perhaps as a consequence of academic infatuation with issues of substantive theory, there has been a tendency to give only minimal attention to the passages in his writing where Karl Marx seeks to elucidate his arguments with reference to the empirical evidence of suffering. Marx was greatly affected by Friedrich Engel's account of *The Condition of the Working –Class in England* and this directly influenced his own attempts to detail the social degradation, physical torment and misery of industrial labour in *Capital, volume 1*. Engels provides one of the first, and certainly most passionate, attempts to describe the rank squalor of the living conditions of workers in slum districts of new industrial towns. Moreover, particular attention is given to the bodily afflictions suffered by men, women, and children who have no choice but to work in conditions of brutal hardships. Large sections of his study are given over to harrowing descriptions of the physical deformities, atrophying weariness, chronic diseases and painful early deaths of mine workers, machine operatives and agricultural labourers as they struggle to exist in the direst circumstances. Likewise, in the chapters on 'The Working Day', 'Machinery' and 'The General Law Of Capitalist Accumulation' of the first volume of *Capital,* Marx dwells on such details so as to emphasize the 'physical deterioration', 'intellectual degeneration' and 'moral degradation' that takes places as a consequence of capitalist exploitation of the labouring classes.

More than any other theorists in the 'classical' tradition, Marx and Engels worked to document the brute facts of human suffering in conditions of extreme poverty and cruel toil. In *Capital, volume 1,* Marx is not only concerned to expose and explain the law of capitalist economic organization, but also, in the most vivid terms, to detail its tragic human consequences. Indeed, perhaps we have not gone far enough to recognize the extent to which Marx presents suffering not only as the result of the logic of capitalist accumulation, but also as necessary for making people into docile bodies for exploitation. His extensive cataloguing of experiences of suffering are intended to provide analytical insight into methods of capitalist production, as well as to cast their oppressive tendencies in moral perspective. As Marx explains:

Within the capitalist system all methods for raising the social productivity of labour are put into effect at the cost of the individual worker; that all means for the development of production undergo a dialectical inversion so that they become means of domination and exploitation of the producers; they distort the worker into a fragment of a man, they degrade him to the level of an appendage of a machine, they distort the actual content of his labour by turning it into a torment; they alienate from him the intellectual potentialities of the labour process in the same proportion as science is incorporated in it as an independent power; they deform the conditions under which he works, subject him during the labour process to a despotism the more hateful for its meanness; they transform his life-time into working-time, and drag his wife and child beneath the wheels of the juggernaut of capital…the law which always holds the relative surplus of population or industrial reserve army in equilibrium with the extent and energy of accumulation rivets the worker to capital more firmly than the wedges of Hephaestus held Prometheus to the rock. It makes an accumulation of misery a necessary condition, corresponding to the accumulation of wealth. Accumulation of wealth at one pole is, therefore, at the same time accumulation of misery, the torment of labour, slavery, ignorance, brutalization and moral degradations at the opposite pole, i.e. on the side of the class that produces its own product as capital. (Marx [1867] 1976: 799)

According to the view expressed by Mr. Wilkinson "Marx makes clear that the tendency of the working class to revolt will grow in proportion to 'the mass of misery, oppression, slavery, degradation and exploitation' experienced within capitalist relations of production." Mr. Wilkinson's only complaint is that Mr. Marx does not explain exactly *how* suffering contributes to such strength of solidarity and purpose. He also charges that "it is possible to highlight an ambiguity that is largely neglected within the domain of Marxist scholarship."

How is it that through their 'physical deterioration', 'intellectual degeneration' and 'moral degradation' the working class might become a united force in pursuit of communism? How can experiences that are so painfully negative and essentially dehumanizing be made into a positive force for the construction of social conditions for realizing our 'essential powers'? What are we to make of the apparent paradox that, while on the one hand Marx would alert us to the oppressive force of suffering upon the physical and social body, on the other he would have us understand this as a necessary constituent of the historical process whereby people are physically and socially empowered to fulfill their human potential?

It is only in the *Economic and Philosophic Manuscripts of 1844* that Marx begins to sketch some possible answers to these questions. But by no means are we presented with an unequivocal point of view on how people are liable to experience and relate to their suffering. Indeed, in these essays he provides some arguments to highlight the potential for suffering to heighten the condition of alienation and obstruct the realization of class consciousness, as well as reasons for us to identify this as a potential spur for the struggle for human freedom. For example, on the negative side, in the introduction to the critique of Hegel's *Philosophy of Right*, human suffering features not so much as a force of radical social change, but rather as a contributing factor to the maintenance of the *status quo*; for it is this which guarantees the psychological appeal of religion, and leads people to ignore 'the truth of the here and now' in favour of the 'illusory happiness' of life in the hereafter. However, in a more positive vein, in a section of manuscript where he attempts to outline the 'essence' of human nature, he maintains that 'suffering, humanly considered, is a kind of self-enjoyment of man.' Indeed, in the essay where he offers a 'Critique of the Hegelian Dialectic and Philosophy as a Whole', he appears to hold to the view that suffering is always necessary for us to engage in 'passionate' pursuit of the 'objective' truth of our human condition. Accordingly, in this context Marx may be interpreted as holding two contradictory points of view on the relationship of humanity to suffering; while on one hand there is the suggestion that suffering works to obstruct the realization of human potential, on the other it is conceived to be an integral part of the process whereby we might attain full 'enjoyment' of self and others.

In my reading of Karl Marx I find no such contradiction. And Mr. Wilkinson is wrong about when and where Karl Marx "begins to sketch some possible answers" to the questions he poses: "How is it that through their 'physical deterioration', 'intellectual degeneration' and 'moral degradation' the working class might become a united force in pursuit of communism? How can experiences that are so painfully negative and essentially dehumanizing be made into a positive force for the construction of social conditions for realizing our 'essential powers'? What are we to make of the apparent paradox that, while on the one hand Marx would alert us to the oppressive force of suffering upon the physical and social body, on the other he would have us understand this as a necessary constituent of the historical process whereby people are physically and socially empowered to fulfill their human potential."

Although he actually cites pg. 929 of *Capital* Volume I by Karl Marx he does not seem to understand how that portion of *Capital* answers these questions. Here is that section of Karl Marx classic work – the entire Chapter 32, "The Historical Tendency Of Capitalist Accumulation" (bold emphasis is mine):

What does the primitive accumulation of capital, i.e. its historical genesis, resolve itself into? In so far as it is not the direct transformation of slaves and serfs into wage-labourers, and therefore a mere change of form, it only means the expropriation of the immediate producers, i.e. the dissolution of private property based on the labour of its owner. Private property, as the antithesis to social, collective property, exists only where the means of labour and the external conditions of labour belong to private individuals. But according to whether these private individuals are workers or non-workers, private property has a different character. The innumerable different shades of private property which appear at first sight are only reflections of the intermediate situations which lie between the two extremes.

The private property of the worker in his means of production is the foundation of small-scale industry, and small-scale industry is a necessary condition for the development of social production and of the free individuality of the worker himself. Of course, this mode of production also exists under slavery, serfdom and other situations of dependence. But it flourishes, unleashes the whole of its energy, attains its adequate classical form, only where the worker is the free proprietor of the condition of his labour, and sets them in motion himself: where the peasant owns the land he cultivates, or the artisan owns the tool with which he is an accomplished performer.

This mode of production presupposes the fragmentation of holdings, and the dispersal of the other means of production. As it excludes the concentration of these means of production, so it also excludes co-operation , division of labour within each separate process of production, the social control and regulation of the forces of nature, and the free development of the productive forces of society. It is compatible only with a system of production and a society moving within narrow limits which are of natural origin. To perpetuate it would be, as Pecquuer rightly says, ' to decree universal mediocrity.' **At a certain stage of development, it brings into the world the material means of its own destruction. From that moment, new forces and passions spring up in the bosom of society, forces and passions which feel themselves to be fettered by that society. It has to be annihilated; it is annihilated. Its annihilation, the transformation of the individualized and scattered means of production into socially concentrated means of production, the transformation, therefore, of the dwarf-like property of the many into the giant property of the few, and the expropriation of the great mass of people from the soil, from the means of subsistence and from the instrument of labour, this terrible and arduously accomplished expropriation of the mass of the people forms the pre-history of capital.** It comprises a whole series of forcible methods, and we have only passed in review those that have been epoch-making as methods of the primitive accumulation of capital. The expropriation of the direct producers was accomplished by means of the most merciless barbarism, and under the stimulus of the most infamous, the most sordid, the most petty and the most odious of passions. Private property which is personally earned, i.e. which is based, as it were, on the fusing together of the isolated, independent working individual with the conditions of labour, is supplanted by capitalist private property, which rests on the exploitation of alien, but formally free labour.

Here, it is clear that Marx is explaining the process of transformation quite plainly. He describes how, "At a certain stage of development, it brings into the world the material means of its own destruction. From that moment, new forces and passions spring up in the bosom of society, forces and passions which feel themselves to be fettered by that society. It has to be annihilated; it is annihilated."

The society, according to Marx is annihilated by the "new forces and passions" that spring up in the society. The forces and passions are fettered or oppressed, and confined by that society. I would venture to say that it would not be a stretch to say that these forces and passions might reflect a form of suffering in those individuals or entities that are 'fettered.' In any event this represents phase 1 of the process.

Marx continues:

As soon as this metamorphosis has sufficiently decomposed the old society throughout its depth and breadth, as soon as the workers have been turned into proletarians, and their means of labour into capital, as soon as the capitalist mode of production stands on its own feet, the further socialization of labour and the further transformation of the soil and other means of production into socially exploited and therefore communal means of production takes on a new form. **What is now to be expropriated is not the self-employed worker, but the capitalist who exploits a large number of workers.**

This expropriation is accomplished through the action of the immanent laws of capitalist production itself, through the centralization of capitals. One capitalist always strikes down many others. Hand in hand with this centralization, or this expropriation of many capitalists by a few, other developments take place on an ever-increasing scale, such as the growth of the co-operative form of the labour process, the conscious technical application of science, the planned exploitation of the soil, the transformation of the means of labour into forms in which they can only be used in common, the economizing of all means of production by their use as the means of production of combined, socialized labour, the entanglement of all peoples in the net of the world market, and, with this, the growth of the international character of the capitalist regime. **Along with the constant decrease in the number of capitalist magnates, who usurp and monopolize all the advantages of this process of transformation, the mass of misery, oppression, slavery, degradation, and exploitation grows; but with this there also grows the revolt of the working class, a class constantly increasing in numbers, and trained, united and organized by the very mechanism of the capitalist process of production.** The monopoly of capital becomes a **fetter** upon the mode of production which has flourished alongside and under it. The centralization of the means of production and the socialization of labour reach a point at which they become incompatible with their capitalist integument. This integument is burst asunder. The knell of capitalist private property sounds. The expropriators are expropriated.

It appears that what is clearly a phase 2 of the revolutionary process, is not understood by Mr. Wilkinson. In the first phase, Marx clearly describes: "At a certain stage of development, it brings into the world the material means of its own destruction. From that moment, new forces and passions spring up in the bosom of society, forces and passions which feel themselves to be fettered by that society." In what I call phase 2, Marx again uses the word fetter. The fetter in phase 2 is the "monopoly of capital." So just as we saw forces and passions that were bound by the fetters of society in phase 1, we should expect to see the same in reaction to "the mass of misery, oppression, slavery, degradation, and exploitation" – the suffering – that Karl Marx describes as growing under "the monopoly of capital."

Mr. Wilkinson's claim that Marx does not answer the three questions that follow is not credible: "[1] How is it that through their 'physical deterioration', 'intellectual degeneration' and 'moral degradation' the working class might become a united force in pursuit of communism? [2] How can experiences that are so painfully negative and essentially dehumanizing be made into a positive force for the construction of social conditions for realizing our 'essential powers'? [3] What are we to make of the apparent paradox that, while on the one hand Marx would alert us to the oppressive force of suffering upon the physical and social body, on the other he would have us understand this as a necessary constituent of the historical process whereby people are physically and socially empowered to fulfill their human potential."

Karl Marx makes it abundantly clear that the suffering of the working class gives birth to forces and passions that break the fetters that bind and oppress it. In closing this chapter, "The Historical Tendency Of Capitalist Accumulation", Marx makes the process of revolution clear and how it is effected by the human misery of the working class. Mr. Wilkinson seems to not understand that *Marx is implying if not outright saying that the forces and passions of people, when suppressed, break loose in search of freedom and a better condition.* This cycle will continue as long as there are "fetters" that are suppressing the human spirit. Obviously Marx does not believe that misery is the natural condition of man, even though he might believe it is the natural condition of capitalism.

Marx concludes this important chapter with a summary:

The capitalist mode of appropriation, which springs from the capitalist mode of production, produces capitalist private property. This is the first negation of individual private property, as founded on the labour of its proprietor. But capitalist production begets, with the inexorability of a natural process, its own negation. This is the negation of the negation. It does not re-establish private property, but it does indeed establish individual property on the basis of the achievements of the capitalist era: namely co-operation and the possession in common of the land and the means of production produced by labour itself.

The transformation of scattered private property resting on the personal labour of the individuals themselves into capitalist private property is naturally an incomparably more protracted, violent and difficult process than the transformation of capitalist private property, which in fact rests on the carrying on of production by society, into social property. In the former case, it was a matter of the expropriation of the mass of the people by a few usurpers; but in this case, we have the expropriation of a few usurpers by the mass of the people.

In other words, phase one is the "expropriation of the mass of the people by a few usurpers" and phase two is: 'the expropriation of a few usurpers by the mass of the people." Both phases characterized by what can be defined as suffering.

His words, "What is now to be expropriated is not the self-employed worker, but the capitalist who exploits a large number of workers," should be considered carefully in any economic study of the relationship between economics, entrepreneurship and suffering.

Business

One of the most powerful accounts of adversity in the world of business is told by Anthony Robbins, of the establishment of the Honda Corporation by Soichiro Honda.

Mr. Robbins writes, in *Awaken The Giant Within*:

In 1938, while he was still in school, Mr. Honda took everything he owned and invested it in a little workshop where he began to develop his concept of a piston ring. He wanted to sell his work to Toyota Corporation so he labored day and night, up to his elbows in grease, sleeping in the machine shop, always believing he could produce the result. He even pawned his wife's jewelry to stay in business. But when he finally completed the piston rings and presented them to Toyota, he was told they didn't meet Toyota's standards. He was sent back to school for two years where he heard the derisive laughter of his instructors and fellow students as they talked about how absurd his designs were.

But rather than focusing on the pain of the experience, he decided to continue to focus on the goal. Finally, after two more years, Toyota gave Mr. Honda the contract he dreamed of. His passion and belief paid off because he had known what he wanted, taken action, noticed what was working and kept changing his approach until he got what he wanted. Then a new problem arose.

The Japanese government was gearing up for war, and they refused to give him the concrete that was necessary to build his factory. Did it mean to him that his dream died? No. Did he focus on how unfair this was? Absolutely no. Again, he decided to utilize the experience, and developed another strategy. He and his team invented a process for creating their own concrete and then built their factory. During the war, it was bombed twice, destroying major portions of the manufacturing facility. Honda's response? He immediately rallied his team, and they picked up the extra gasoline cans that the U.S. fighters had discarded. He called them "gifts from President Truman" because they provided him with the raw materials he needed for his manufacturing process – materials that were unavailable at the time in Japan. Finally, after surviving all of this, an earthquake leveled his factory. Honda decided to sell his piston operation to Toyota.

Here is a man who clearly made strong decisions to succeed. He had a passion for and belief in what he was doing. He had a great strategy. He took massive action. He kept changing his approach, but *still* he'd not produced the results that he was committed to. Yet he decided to persevere.

After the war, a tremendous gasoline shortage hit Japan, and Mr. Honda couldn't even drive his car to get food for his family. Finally, in desperation, he attached a small motor to his bicycle. The next thing he knew, his neighbors were asking if he could make one of his "motorized bikes" for them. One after another, they jumped on the bandwagon until he *ran out* of motors. He decided to build a plant that would manufacture motors for his new invention, but unfortunately he didn't have the capital.

As before, he made the decision to find a way no matter what! His solution was to appeal to the 18,000 bicycle shop owners in Japan by writing them each a personal letter. He told them they could play a role in revitalizing Japan through the mobility that his invention could provide, and convinced 5,000 of them to advance the capital he needed: Still, his motorbike sold to only the most hard-core bicycle fans because it was too big and bulky. So he made one final adjustment, and created a much lighter, scaled-down version of his motorbike. He christened it "The Super Cub," and it became an "overnight" success, earning him the Emperor's award. Later he began to export his motorbikes to the baby boomers of Europe and the United States, following up in the seventies with the cars that have become so popular.

Today, the Honda Corporation employs over 100,000 people in both the United States and Japan and is considered one of the biggest car-making empires in Japan, outselling all but Toyota in the United States. It succeeds because one man understood the power of a truly committed decision that is acted upon, no matter what the conditions, on a continuous basis.

There is much to be considered in what makes some businesspersons more resilient, persistent, able to manage pain and overcome adversity, than others.

A book looking into this phenomenon was *The Adversity Challenge: how successful leaders bounce back from setbacks,* by Charles R. Stoner and John F. Gilligan. In the book the authors profile 35 successful business leaders and their attitude, beliefs and experiences in relation to overcoming adversity.

In their book, they illuminate an interesting aspect of this, which they call "The Paradox of Success:"

We experience the same dynamics. We are all engaged in a quest to fulfill our dreams, to capture a vision of what we want for ourselves professionally and personally. Yet, there is no guarantee in life that what we pursue will be achieved. Success is not a given.

There is a deep dimension, a revealing connection between success and adversity. It is truly paradoxical. The very nature of success implies failure, and any claim to success without a risk of failure is nothing less than self-deception and personal fraud.

There is no such thing as success if there is nothing to overcome. In fact, the essence of success, that sense of personal significance, is strangely defined through the experience of adversity. We refer to it as the ***Paradox of Success:*** *The meaning and value of success are heightened as adversity experiences increase and intensify.*

They also describe the different levels of adversity:

Just as success has both personal and public components, adversity is always a struggle at two levels: personal (internal) and public (external). Effective resolution of any crisis or adverse event requires that both levels be managed simultaneously. For example, leaders are public figures. Despite their personal struggles, the business must move ahead. The real world has its own demands which cannot be ignored. However, the internal or personal level is the center from which all adversity is conquered. This is where issues are emotionally felt and mentally sifted and sorted.

The heart of adversity is always a personal battle. While adversity may have a public face, it must be confronted and addressed at the personal level. For successful leaders, adversity is not so much a function of what has happened, but how adversity's events affect and move them at a personal level.

Its categories:

Experience teaches us that no one's life and leadership journey is free from disappointments, frustrations, obstacles, and crises. They come in a variety of forms: death, illness, financial loss, divorce, angry employees, interpersonal conflicts, ethical challenges, and jealousies. All are events that can block the leader's path to success. No one is spared. Like death and taxes, adversity is constant.

Not only is adversity a given, but in today's turbulent and chaotic business environment, adversities seem to appear with more frequency and intensity than ever. As one executive noted, "They just seem to crop up more. And the lows seem lower."

Sifting through our interviews, we sought logical and meaningful ways to categorize leaders; adversities – their misfortunes, trials and tribulations. We drew interpretations from our analysis and from careful consideration of the previous work in the adversity field. Typically, adversities fall into one of three categories – business, career, or personal. Each category may have many bases.

The authors write that they discovered three categories of business adversities: 1) Mistakes and Missteps, 2) Volatility of Business Environment, 3) Interpersonal or People Issues.

But perhaps the most interesting part of their research revolved around the actual process of how business leaders handle adversity when it occurs, and the process that is involved. In a chapter called, "The Great Disruption" they write:

Some disruptions occur without notice while others are anticipated. Like the CEO quoted above, surprise is the typical reaction for those sudden and unforeseen big events. But since we are talking about adverse events that threaten personal and organizational equilibrium, shock is the more descriptive word. Shock disorients, confuses, and puzzles. One loses clarity of thought and direction for a period of time. And at the biological level, a state of arousal occurs. The entire immune system can be affected.

The above, again, bears witness to the real physiological and psychological changes that occur when one suffers. Remember psychoneurosis, and the mental catharsis. The authors continue:

The majority of us will never be fired, declare bankruptcy, be held hostage, suffer from life-threatening cancer, or face other threatening disasters. Yet all human beings have similar reactions to shocking events, even though they may not show it in their behavior. Disruptions and subsequent reactions are experienced in degrees. They may be short or long-lived, but from the extreme cases we learn how the process of disruption is best handled.

…Shock, that initial disrupting event, has a tendency to sever or loosen us from our anchors of stability, either personal or professional. A period of confusion ensues. "I can't figure out why it happened" is a typical response to this stage of disruption. We seem to think that if we know why it happened, we can reverse events or find a clear path of action. But shocking events can't be reversed, and there is no clear path of action. We have conceptualized the initial phase of the rebound as disillusionment.

What should be noted here is how shock causes instability, which is one of the elements previously described by George Pickering, when he wrote, "The research gives us one fairly clear directive: Most resistant to illness is the socially involved individual: the person who is well adjusted to a stable role within a supportive community."

But remember we previously learned that shocks are also stimulating, when Charles F. Stoner and John F. Gilligan wrote (boldface emphasis is mine), "Shock disorients, confuses, and puzzles. One loses clarity of thought and direction for a period of time. And at the biological level, **a state of arousal occurs**."

Shocks appear to force us to be more fully aware of ourselves, and to think more carefully about our environment and into the meaning and significance of persons, events, institutions, and circumstances.

The authors of *The Adversity Challenge* write on about the stages one goes through after experiencing a shock:

Denial and fear surround the phase of disillusionment. Denial takes many forms from "this can't be true" to "it's not all that bad." Denial is one mechanism that is used to manage our confusion about what should be done. Others manage confusion by repetitively reviewing and analyzing what happened.

Fear is manifested through disappointment, embarrassment, hopelessness, loss of energy, and feelings of depression that can envelop a person. Everyone experiences some degree of fear and denial. If not managed well, they can become overwhelming and immobilizing. Some careers end up on these rocks.

The second phase of the rebound is reflection. This phase of recovery often includes anger. The mix of feelings experienced in the first phase usually consolidates into anger. If properly expressed, this is a healthy step. The person is in touch with energy – the kind of psychic energy that will be needed to overcome adversity. But anger must be transformed into creative action.

…This process takes time and even then the emotional reactions to a great disruption usually linger. It can last from hours to months, depending upon the depth of the disruption. Crises where business, career or personal survival is threatened, will likely take longer than more common inconveniences or missteps.
…The leader must pass through a set psychological process to constructively adjust to the disruption. If one step is bypassed the disruption will come back and haunt.

The great disruption creates shock and confusion. This is followed by a phase of fear and denial. This is a period when the pain from the blow is being absorbed psychologically and physically. It is the recognition that this really hurt in so many ways. It is the moment when every sense of competence and worth is threatened. Depression and a sense of loss dominate.

A period of anger follows. Anger is a form of energy. Like all energy it can be used for constructive as well as destructive purposes. Anger counters the initial depressive effects of the disruption's assault on self. The challenge is to harness this energy for constructive, even creative purposes.

Finally, the leader emerges into the reframing and redirecting stage of the rebound. This is the period when the event is no longer seen as devastating or as a set-back, but as a challenge or an opportunity to improve.

What *The Adversity Challenge* describes is a detailed process compiled from their study of 35 business leaders faced with difficulties that they had to overcome. The critical part of the process is the decision and ability to reframe and redirect the meaning and emotions produced by a disruptive experience.

Once the suffering is reinterpreted as the basis of action, it can become a source of motivation, even if that suffering is not the fault of the victim. As Dr. Martin Luther King said in his famous "I Have A Dream Speech", "unearned suffering is redemptive."

Entrepreneurship

As was highlighted by the account of how Honda was established, the story of the entrepreneur is that of the legendary Phoenix bird – which rises from the ashes. It seems as if every entrepreneur that we hear of renown, once their story is fully told, experienced labor-like pains in the 'birthing' of their business and the struggle to nurture and cultivate it to success.

But as common as this story is, the study of entrepreneurial economics is woefully underdeveloped and lacking in the study of this phenomenon, as was touched upon earlier in this book.

And that is what makes the work and unique attention that economist Reuven Brenner has paid to the subject valuable.

In three of his major works, in particular, *History – The Human Gamble*, *Rivalry: In Business, Science, Among Nations*, and *Betting On Ideas*, Mr. Brenner explains how suffering relates to innovation, risk-taking, creativity and decision-making by entrepreneurs.

He clearly identifies the experience of human suffering as a factor principally motivating the emergence of the entrepreneur, which he clearly defines, in his works.

Citing the insights and views of many, across various fields and disciplines, here is an excerpt from *Betting On Ideas*:

Many writers from ancient to modern times have implicitly associated "thinking" and "creativity" with suffering, loss of status, and some disorder. Moreover, some of them have advocated order, recognizing that the price paid for it is diminished creativity. Some of these writers were mentioned in my first book; this brief section complements that picture by quoting others.

Aristotle in the Politics objects to the proposal to Hippodamus for awards for new ideas. In a settled regime he considers them suspect. For a "citizen will receive less benefit from a change in the law than damage from being accustomed to disobey authority…the law itself has no power to secure obedience save the power of custom, and that takes a long time to become effective" (pp.82-83). Oscar Wilde echoed this view when he said that in "The Soul Of Man Under Socialism" that "it is through disobedience that progress has been made."

Adam Smith in a lesser-known essay, "The History of Astronomy," wrote explicitly that men "have seldom had the curiosity to inquire by what process of intermediate events [a] change is brought about because the passage of thought from the one object to the other is by custom become quite smooth and easy" (pp.44-45), and that it is well known that custom deadens the vivacity of pain and pleasure, abates the grief we should feel for the one, and weakens the joy we should derive from the other. The pain is supported without agony, and the pleasure enjoyed without rapture; because custom and the frequent repetition of any object comes at last to form and bend the mind or organ to that habitual mood and disposition which fits them to receive its impression, without undergoing any violent change" (p. 37).

Similar statements have been made by poets and writers and not just philosophers. Wordsworth wrote that "Wisdom is oftimes nearer when we stoop; than when we soar"; Jean-Paul Sartre stated that "genius is not a gift, but rather the way out one invents in desperate situations"; and Proust, in Remembrance of Things Past, wrote that "Everything great in the world comes from neurotics. They have composed our masterpieces. We enjoy lovely music, beautiful paintings, a thousand delicacies, but we have no idea of their cost, to those who invented them, in sleepless nights, spasmodic laughter, rashes, asthmas, epilepsies…" and in the chapter "The Past Recaptured" he notes that "Happiness is beneficial for the body, but it is grief that develops the powers of the mind." One can also find this opinion expressed in Samuel Johnson's statement that "the mind is seldom guided to very rigorous operations but by pain or the dread of pain,"…John Dewey argued long ago in Human Nature and Conduct that thinking was an adaptive behavior triggered by unfulfilled expectations, while William Faulkner said more than once that he created characters in violent circumstances in an effort to get at the truth of the human heart. One can also find this viewpoint, expressed differently by Isaiah Berlin (p.981). In the essays on Moses Hess, Marx, and Disraeli, he suggests that only when one belongs to a community can one manage a full life undistorted by neurotic self-questioning about one's true identity and be free from feelings of inferiority, real or imaginary. Those who do not belong, however, "hit upon various more or less conscious solutions to their problems of self identity." These lead, eventually, to original insights – "a neurotic distortion of the facts," as Berlin puts it. In fact Berlin thinks that many of Marx's and Disraeli's ideas evolved in the first place not as tools of analysis, but as comforting myths to rally oppressed spirits, perhaps those of the authors themselves.

In the more technical language of the management literature some similar views have been expressed by Herbert Simon (1959) (although he admits in his 1957 work that his intention was to build a new vocabulary rather than a theory):

(a) Where performance falls short of the level of aspiration, search behavior (particularly search for new alternatives of action) is induced.

(b) At the same time, the level of aspiration begins to adjust itself downward until goals reach levels that are practically attainable.
(c) If the two mechanism just listed operate too slowly to adapt aspirations to performance, emotional behavior – apathy or aggression, for example – will replace rational adaptive behavior. [p.87]

Simon's first proposition exactly reflects one facet of my model. His second proposition, while plausible, will not always hold true. Some people (call them "entrepreneurs") may turn out to be determinate enough and may gamble on new ideas until they achieve their expectations. But Simon is right, in part, in his third proposition when he states that when aspirations are not achieved one may gamble on criminal acts and that the lack of achievement takes its emotional toll. However, he is misleading in calling the alternative "rational" adaptive behavior. If somebody becomes suddenly poorer, why is it "rational" to adapt to the new situation by just staying poorer, rather than starting to gamble on new ideas and trying to restore one's position in the distribution of wealth? It should be emphasized that if one defines "search behavior" (described in Simon's first proposition) as "rational," one must also define the aggressive one as such, since both types stem from the *same* trait, a trait precisely defined in the model. But there seems to be little doubt that Simon's view of human nature bears some strong resemblance to mine (although his vocabulary is different). In his book with James G. March he writes:

…we may conclude that high satisfaction, per se, is not a particularly good predictor of high production nor does it facilitate production in a causal sense. Motivation to produce stems from a present or anticipated state of discontent and a perception of a direct connection between individual production and a new state of satisfaction.

The definition of the entrepreneurial act within the model gives precision to these words.

In Mr. Brenner's model, more thinking is likely to occur when people suffer a loss in their standing in society's wealth distribution. He likens the wealth distribution in that of most societies, writing, "…the distribution of wealth is pyramidal – that is, there is a small 'upper-class,' a larger 'upper middle class,' a still larger 'lower middle class,' and so forth." In his model, the entrepreneurial act – thinking, or betting on new ideas – occurs "when an individual's position in the distribution of wealth has suddenly been (or is expected to be) significantly worsened." In other words, when a person has suffered a loss of some kind that negatively affects their wealth in relation to others in the society.

Still, with more detail, Reuven Brenner explains:

"Thinking," defined as "bets on ideas," is the subject that I tried to shed light on in my previous book, and the one that I also try to shed light on here, though I am examining new directions. Summarized briefly the views suggest that bets on new ideas are triggered when customary ways of behavior fail to produce expected results and lead to the perception of a loss in one's relative standing in society. One can attribute this adaptive behavior to "envy," "ambition," or "fear of being hindered by others". This perception and these sentiments lead to the following types of behavior:

- people may start to participate in games of chance that they have previously shunned;
- they may commit a crime, or an act not in accordance with existing customs;
- they may gamble on new (i.e., noncustomary) ideas in business, science, technology, the arts, and politics. The appeal of gambling on political ideas – going to war in particular – is greater when a whole group's standing in a society or the society of nations has suddenly been significantly worsened....

And the contrary: when aspirations are more than fulfilled, and people suddenly outdo their fellows, they

- will tend to take out insurance that they previously shunned;
- may avoid committing a crime that they contemplated before:
- may avoid betting on new ideas.

Suffering is directly correlated to entrepreneurship. On this, Reuven Brenner writes, in *Rivalry*:

In previous studies a wide range of evidence on entrepreneurship has been examined: from data on minorities who have been discriminated against, to data on the emergence of the entrepreneurial trait within some well-defined historical circumstances (the industrial Revolution), to a detailed examination of the relationship between patents (taken as a crude proxy of "novel ideas") and changes in people's position in the distribution of wealth. The picture that emerged from all the verifications are similar: Within groups that suddenly fall behind, or following periods of deepening depressions, the entrepreneurial trait surfaced (although not always directed toward business, but sometimes toward criminal activities too – as indeed one should expect.)

Brenner cites an excerpt from an interesting November 1975 study by Albert Shapero, "The Displaced Uncomfortable Entrepreneur," published in *Psychology Today*. Suggesting conditions in which entrepreneurship thrives it reads:

The simplest route is falling on hard times. Most entrepreneurs are…displaced persons who have been dislodged from some nice, familiar niche, and tilted off course. Sometimes they are [displaced persons] in the most literal sense; political refugees often produce a surge of company formations in their adopted country. The French refugees who left North Africa for France, the East Germans who escaped to West Germany and the Cubans who fled to Miami are all known for their entrepreneurial energy.

If that is correct, it is possible that it will be that among those who are enduring or suffering the most, where we might find entrepreneurship in its finest quality and greatest quantity.

It also further suggests that the stability sought after and described previously by social scientists and psychologists as the basis for good health is not the starting point or initial quality of life for the most likely and successful greatest entrepreneurs.

Stress is good, it seems, for business.

It would be appropriate to end this chapter by illuminating how suffering helps us to become more conscious of our own 'self.' In that sense perhaps it is easier to see a benefit in recognizing loss and realizing that the pain in and of itself is a sign of 'life' rather than of death.

To drive that point home dramatically and perhaps metaphorically we turn to the perspective of medicine and specifically that of a doctor working with leprosy victims – *individuals whose lives are sadly marked by experiencing life without sensing pain*. From *Pain The Gift Nobody Wants* by Paul Brand and Phillip Yancey we read of the three-stage process of pain and the incredible ability to re-conceptualize and overcome pain (in order to obtain a goal):

A simple, everyday mishap – a little girl's fall while running – illustrates the interplay among these three stages of pain. When her knee first scrapes against the sidewalk, she rolls sideways to avoid further contact. This emergency maneuver, ordered by the spinal cord, takes place at the reflex level (stage one). Half a second passes before the girl becomes conscious of stinging sensations from her scraped knee. How she then responds will depend on the severity of the scrape, her own personality makeup, and what else is going on around her.

If the girl is running in a race with friends, chances are the noise and overall excitement of play will produce competing messages (stage two) that block the further progress of the pain. She may get up and finish the race without even glancing at her knee. When the race is over, though, excitement dies down, pain messages will likely stream through the spinal gate to the thinking part of the brain (stage three). The girl looks at the knee, sees blood, and now the conscious brain takes over. Fear enhances the pain. Mother becomes important, and that is where the child turns. A wise mother first hugs her daughter, replacing the fear with reassurance. Then she fusses over the sore, washes away the blood, covers the wound with a decorative adhesive bandage, and sends the child back to play. The girl forgets about the pain. Later, in the night, when nothing is distracting the mind, the pain may return and her parents will be called back on duty.

All this time the actual pain signals have not changed much. Loyal neurons in the knee have been sending in damage reports all afternoon and evening. The girl's perception of the pain varies mostly by the extent to which the pain was blocked at stage two, by competing input, and, at stage three, by the parents' resourcefulness in calming anxiety.

In adults, who have a larger pool of experience and emotions to draw from, the mind plays a more paramount role. As a doctor I have gained an ever-increasing appreciation for the mind's ability to alter the perception of pain in one direction or the other. We can become adept at converting pain into the more serious state that we call *suffering*. Or, to the contrary, we can learn to harness the vast resources of the conscious mind to help cope with the pain.

The Orphan Sense

In medical school I mainly encountered pain at stage one. Patients came to me with specific complaints about signals in the periphery ("My finger hurts." "My stomach aches." "My ears are ringing.") No patient ever said to me something along this line: "Among the many transmissions entering my spinal cord, signals of pain from my finger have been judged of significant value to be forwarded on to the brain." Or "I am feeling pain in my stomach; could you please administer a morphine-like drug to my brain so that it will ignore the pain signals emanating from my stomach?"

Although I had to rely on the patient's report of stage one to help me diagnose the cause of pain, I soon realized the importance of responding to stage three from the start. Now I would probably rank the stages of pain in the reverse order, giving prominence to the third stage first. What takes place in a person's mind is the most important aspect of pain – and the most difficult to treat or even comprehend. If we can learn to handle pain at this third stage, we will most likely succeed in keeping pain in its proper place, as servant and not master.

I once knew a ballerina who felt severe pain in her foot every time she performed one particular maneuver on the point of her toe. Tchaikovsky's *Swan Lake* called for this maneuver thirty-two times in the course of the ballet, and for that reason she dreaded *Swan Lake*. Whenever the music came over the radio she would leap to her feet and switch it off. "I can actually feel the pain in my foot when I hear those chords!" she said. What took place in her mind affected what she perceived in her foot.

I first became aware of the power of the mind when I treated the soldier named Jake, the war hero with shattered legs who shrank I fear from a hypodermic needle full of penicillin. Later I learned that Jake's attitude at the front, strange as it seemed at the time, was a classic response to combat injury. Dr. Henry K. Beecher of the Harvard Medical School coined the term "Anzio effect" to describe what he observed among 215 casualties from the Anzio beachhead in World War II. Only one in four soldiers with serious injuries (fractures, amputations, penetrated chests or cerebrums) asked for morphine, though it was freely available. They simply did not need help with the pain, and indeed many of them denied feeling pain at all.

Beecher, an anesthesiologist, contrasted the soldiers' reactions to what he had seen in private practice, where 80 percent of patients recovering from surgical wounds begged for morphine or other narcotics. He concluded, "There is no simple direct relationship between the wound *per se* and the pain experienced. The pain is in very large part determined by other factors, and of great importance here is the significance of the wound…In the wounded soldier the response to injury was relief, thankfulness at his escape alive from the battlefield, even euphoria; to the civilian, his major surgery was a depressing, calamitous event."

My study of the brain…helped me understand why the mind plays such an important role in pain. The structure of the brain requires it. Only one-tenth of one percent of the fibers entering the cerebral cortex convey new sensory information, including pain messages; all the other nerve cells communicate one with another, reflecting, sifting through memory and emotion. Am I afraid? Is the pain producing something of value? Do I really want to recover? Am I getting sympathy?

Moreover, the conscious brain composes its responses to this swirl of data inside the skull, secluded from the stimulus that caused pain in the first place. Most sensations have a referent "out there," and we enjoy inviting others to share what excites our senses: "look at that mountain!" "Listen closely, here comes the good part." "Feel this fur – it's so soft." But along comes the overpowering sensation of pain and each of us is orphaned. Pain has no "outside" experience. Two people can look at the same tree; no one has ever shared a stomachache. This is what makes the treatment of pain so difficult. None of us, doctor, parent, or friend, can truly enter into another person's pain. It is the loneliest, most private sensation.

How do you feel? How bad does it hurt? We can ask these questions, and form an idea about someone else's pain but never with certainty. Patrick Wall, a pioneer in pain theory, states the dilemma: "Pain is my pain as it grows as an imperative obsession, a compulsion, a dominating reality. Your pain is a different matter…Even if I have experienced a similar situation I only know my pain and guess at yours. If you hit your finger with a hammer I squirm as I remember how my thumb felt when I hit my own thumb. I can only assume how you feel." Wall says he has learned to respect a patient's own description, no matter how hazy, for despite what any high-tech diagnostic instruments may indicate, in the final analysis the patient's verbal report is the only possible account of the pain.

And yet, although pain is an orphan sense that no one else can truly share, it seems to be indispensable in helping form one's personal identity. I hurt, therefore I am. The brain relies on a "felt image" of body parts to construct its inner map of the body; when nerve damage disrupts the flow of data to the brain that puts the basic sense of self at risk. Speaking metaphorically, we use the word *dead* to describe a temporary sense of painlessness, as when a dentist deadens a tooth or when we leave a leg crossed so long that it goes numb. Leprosy patients seem to regard their hands and feet as truly dead. The limb is there – they can see it – but with no sensory feedback to nourish the felt image in their brains, they lose the innate awareness that the numbed hand or foot belongs to the rest of the body.

I have seen this principle at work rather grotesquely in laboratory animals. For a while I used white rats to help determine the best design of shoes for the insensitive feet of leprosy patients. I would deaden a pain center in one hind leg and then imitate the stress of different types of shoes on the rat foot. I had to keep these research animals well fed, for if they got hungry they would simply start to eat the deadened leg, a rat no longer recognizing it as part of self. Similarly, a wolf, its leg gone numb from the pressure of a trap and the cold, will calmly gnaw through fur and bone and limp away.

A Dominant Role

An amoeba, brainless, senses, danger directly and galumphs away from harsh chemicals and bright lights. "Higher" animals perceive pain indirectly – the central nervous system reports to a brain isolated from the stimulus – and this in turn gives them much freedom to modify the experience. Almost a century ago the Russian scientist Ivan Pavlov trained a dog to overcome basic pain instincts by rewarding it with food just after applying electrical shocks to a particular paw. After a few weeks, instead of whining and struggling to get away from the shocks, the dog responded by wagging its tail excitedly, salivating, and turning toward the food dish. Somehow, the dog's brain had learned to reinterpret the negative, 'It hurts!" aspect of pain. (Yet when Pavlov applied a similar shock to a different paw, the dog reacted violently.)

More recently, Ronald Melzack took Pavlov's experiments a step further. He raised Scottish terrier pups in individual, padded cages so that they would encounter none of the normal knocks and scrapes of growing up. To his astonishment, dogs raised in this deprived environment failed to learn basic responses to pain. Exposed to a flaming match, they repeatedly poked their noses into the flame and sniffed at it. Even when flesh burned, they showed no sign of distress. They also failed to react when he pricked their paws with a pin. In contrast their littermates, raised normally, yelped and fled after just one confrontation with the match or pin. Melzack was forced to conclude that much of what we call pain, including the "emotional" response, is learned, not instinctive.

In human beings mental powers reign supreme, and that is what gives us the ability to alter pain so dramatically. A cat that steps on a thorn instinctively begins limping, which will give the injured foot rest and protection. A man who steps on a rusty nail will also limp. But greater brain power allows him to reflect consciously, even obsessively, on the experience. In addition to limping, he may search for other coping aids: pain relievers, crutches, a wheelchair. If concern over the injury swells into fear, the pain will intensify so that it really does "hurt" the man more than it would presumably hurt a cat. He may worry about tetanus. If, like my patient Jake, this man has an exaggerated fear of needles, he may talk himself out of a tetanus shot and risk far greater pain. On the other hand, if he is paid ten thousand dollars a game to kick field goals in the National Football League, most likely the limper will bandage the foot, ignore the pain, and head for the practice field.

From whatever field we may view suffering it is evident that the "human ability to alter pain..." is quite impressive.

All of these views of suffering, examined in this chapter, from a variety of disciplines are telling us much about the nature of suffering and its influence on the human being. And all of these view inform the model and success strategy for entrepreneurs with the least amount of monetary resources available to them, presented in this book.

From theology, we learn that suffering is ordained, comes with the territory for those seeking to develop their character and connect their spirit with a Higher Purpose or Supreme Being. From this perspective we learn that the human being must struggle and overcome difficulty in order to make progress. This is the path to God. It is abundantly clear in theology that the most powerful human beings are those that suffer greatly and learn from it.

If there were two verses from the Bible and Qur'an that summarize the theological perspective presented here, it would be, "*We have created man to face difficulties...Although he was a son, he learned obedience from what he suffered...*" a combination of Surah 90: 4 (Maulana Muhammad Ali translation) and Hebrews 5: 8 (New International Version translation). Our model, informed by these verses suggests that 'through suffering we perceive opportunity,' or 'through suffering we learn creativity (or '...become creative')'.

From the worlds of sociology, psychology and psychiatry we learn that suffering is a biological reality and that what happens in our daily lives and interaction with others affects us greatly. When we experience a 'loss' – whether of familiar surroundings, a loved one, money, or status – we suffer mentally, and that experience affects our thinking deeply, about ourselves, our quality of life and our relation to others.

We also learn that it appears that what might be interpreted as an unhealthy condition, may actually be the natural experience of the human being involved in the process of creativity. Psychoneurosis, clinically considered a mental disorder is no such thing to the inventor or artist. It is, at times, only an aspect of the 'birthing' process of the creative genius. This does not mean that we get sick in order to create. *But what it does mean is that the stress that can make us sick, also makes us creative.* And it means that while we are creative, we may appear to be ill.

Furthermore, the "mental catharsis" that we encountered in our view of suffering in the fields of psychology and psychiatry suggests that the state of anxiety, grief and even depression that we might be in, can only be relieved by the creative act. There is no drug that we can take that can remove the cause of our condition, it seems – only accomplishment will bring relief.

When we set a goal that is not reached or have an unfulfilled desire, we have set up a gap from where we are to where we want to be that can only be bridged by achievement and the completed act of creativity. Dissatisfaction brings about a creative change.

Emphasizing this point, the *Encyclopedia of Creativity Volume I, Mark* – A. Runco and Steven R. Pritzker, Editors In Chief states:

Rooted in yearning to make things better than they are, creativity should be distinguished from the mere manipulation of familiar objects for the sake of novelty. The need to make a more efficient tool, a better weapon, or an improved mode of transportation or communication is, in popular parlance, "the mother of invention." Innovation, according to Jean Piaget, is a necessary component of the process of transformation, itself a form of interpreting the objective world "to make sense of it," and improve on it.

Creativity emerges from a longing for unrealized perfection in its absolute sense. It carries with it a dissatisfaction with things as they are, and a zeal to reform them – to "ennoble" or even to emancipate them from the fetters of conditions that now prevail, or to bring the actual world into conformity with the ideal world.

From *Creative Malady* we were reminded by George Pickering of the delicate and complicated state of affairs that accompanies our efforts to make something new, while keeping sane, "Passion is the chief characteristic that I can find which relates the psychoneuroses of the characters here described and the creative work which brought them fame. Psychoneurosis arises when there is a conflict between a wish and its fulfillment. The more passionate the desire the more likely is its frustration to lead to psychoneurosis. This in turn may make possible the fulfillment of the wish, or act as a spur to the mental catharsis which produces a great creative work. This seems to be the basis of the relationship between psychoneurosis and creativity".

Abraham Maslow addressed this aspect of 'the fulfillment of the wish' and catharsis in his 1954 book, *Motivation and Personality*, connecting these to a concept called 'release behavior' he writes:

There is a special type of behavior which, though essentially expressive, has nevertheless some usefulness to the organism. Sometimes even a wished-for usefulness, e.g. what [David M.] Levy has called release behavior...

Probably all such release behaviors can be generally defined as keeping the organism more comfortable, i.e., keeping tension level down, by (1) allowing an incompleted act to be completed; (2) draining off accumulations of hostility, anxiety, excitement, joy, ecstasy, love, or other tension-producing emotions by allowing consummatory motor expression, or (3) permitting simple activity for its own sake of the type indulged in by any healthy organism.

It is very likely that catharsis, as originally defined by Breuer and Freud, is in essence a more complex variant of release behavior. This, too, is the free (and, in a special sense, satisfying) expression of an impeded, uncompleted act that, like all impeded acts, seems to press for expression.

Embodied in what we have looked at in terms of mental catharsis and release behavior, is a key to understanding why persistence and will power are assets to the entrepreneur (when not driving them crazy.)

Alluding to this quality, in a way that corresponds to our view of the entrepreneurial act as that which starts as an internally recognized perception of opportunity and which grows into an externally visible organization that pursues it (a business), Maslow writes that "...simple perseverations, catharsis, or release...do no more than complete the uncompleted and resolve the unresolved."

In other words, perseverance, mental catharsis and release behavior are aimed at the fulfillment of that which is not complete, but which is recognized as possible and desirable as an objective. Maslow wrote that the person was insecure until they accomplished what they desired:

Apparently the insecure human organism cannot accept defeat gracefully. It must keep on trying again and again, useless though this may be. Here we may recall the experiments of Ovsiankina and Zeigarnik on the perseveration of uncompleted tasks, that is to say, unsolved problems. Recent work has shown that this tendency appears only where threat to the personality core is involved, i.e., where failure means loss of safety, self-esteem, prestige, or the like.

From economics, we learned from Karl Marx that it is when the passion of the masses is fettered and individuals suffer that cyclical societal change occurs.

In the area of entrepreneurship we gained the insight that the suffering of a relative loss can be the principal event that causes one to 'think' or 'bet on a new idea.' When people believe that they are dropping in the relative distribution of wealth in society, they are more likely to consider doing something they have not before. Their willingness to take risks increases. They think more. They develop more businesses.

This view informs us by making it clear that the process of suffering, on a daily, hourly, minute-by-minute basis is motivating changes yet to be seen. In other words we have new ideas, organizations, political decisions, inventions and ideologies being formulated and introduced as a result of shifts of wealth inside of families, firms, communities, and nations.

This view of the individual and society makes us sensitive to every part of the planet Earth, and the potential of every individual to be the vessel through which we experience revolution, profits, an improved quality of life, and adjustments in our relationships to others. Any one 'loss' suffered by a person, under the right circumstances, can lead to that which causes pain and pleasure for countless others.

So what's the secret of suffering you ask?

If you understand and accept a purpose of pain and 'loss' in your life (and its benefits in the form of knowledge and motivation) it is not hard to see that many forms of loss and shock –including the current financial crisis – has created the environment, not just for tragedy, but for your triumph as an entrepreneur!

The next step is to unite your being around your identity as an entrepreneur and develop the will-power necessary to persevere through what you must suffer.

The Secret of Suffering

- *Entrepreneurship is the perception of an opportunity and the creation of an organization to pursue it - is based on a spiritual process.*
- *The spiritual essence the deeper, hidden, or unseen animating reality or intention that exists behind, beyond, or underneath an act, appearance, or superficial reality.*
- *Although over 20 million people have purchased Napoleon Hill's Think and Grow Rich - arguably the most influential book impacting entrepreneurs, published in the last 100 years - it just may be, that the book about his own life and writings, A Lifetime Of Riches, is even more important for one to read.*
- *Failure, adversity, perseverance, patience, persistence, endurance and faith are all words that one will find in the life struggle of the entrepreneur. The word and concept that best embodies all of these factors and can be applied most broadly across human disciplines is* **suffering.**
- *Theology, sociology, psychology, psychiatry economy,, and business all bear witness to the association between loss, pain, adversity, and the decision to take risk for future gain or achievement – which is the essence of entrepreneurship.*
- *In the area of entrepreneurship we gain the insight that the suffering of a relative loss can be the principal event that causes one to 'think' or 'bet on a new idea.' When people believe that they are dropping in the relative distribution of wealth in society, they are more likely to consider doing something they have not before. Their willingness to take risks increases. They think more. They develop more businesses.*
- *If you understand and accept a purpose of pain and 'loss' in your life (and its benefits in the form of knowledge and motivation) it is not hard to see that many forms of loss and shock –including the current financial crisis - has created the environment, not just for tragedy, but for your triumph as an entrepreneur!*

Chapter 14: The Secret Of Will Power – Unite Your *Self,* Before Others

"Michael, I recall you sitting on a chair, in your bedroom, staring at the television, watching the 1980 Grammy awards show, crying to me because you had won only one Grammy award and you said, 'Watch, LaToya, my next record, I am going to sell more records and win more Grammys than anyone in the history of music... I will be the biggest and the greatest entertainer of all time.' You began to write that dream all throughout your bedroom, on the walls, on the mirrors, in your books and anywhere else you could find space.... You've lived your dream, you've proven to us all that if we believe, you will achieve; you believed, and oh my, did you achieve!"

—words from LaToya Jackson contained in the program for Michael Jackson's memorial service, July 7, 2009

"God is a man and we just cannot make him other than man, lest we make Him an inferior one; for man's intelligence has no equal in other than man. His wisdom is infinite; capable of accomplishing anything that His brain can conceive. A spirit is subjected to us and not we to the spirit."

... *"What helps to bring about new creation? When you make a new way of thinking in a person, he is bound to do something new; for he cannot do something other than new since he has a new mind, new ideas. A new mind and new ideas produce a new thing."*

"Get business minded; get a creative mind."

—The Honorable Elijah Muhammad, from *Message To The Blackman* and *Our Saviour Has Arrived*

A magnetized piece of iron will lift about twelve times its own weight. But if you demagnetize this same piece of iron, it will not lift even a feather. In the same way, there are two types of people. Those who are magnetized are full of confidence and faith. They know they are born to succeed and to win. Others, so many others, are demagnetized. They are full of fears and doubts.
—Joseph Murphy, from *The Power Of Your Subconscious Mind*

I have no accidental works to share with you. My success is not the result of luck or reckless, drug-induced behavior. I have earned it through sheer will and determination. My fortune is owed to no one but myself. Yes, I was given the breath of life from a creative force, but I really don't think it is concerned with any of our silly, minute goals or accomplishments.
—Troi "Star" Torain, *Objective Hate: The Prequel* (2006)

Before one heals others, heal oneself.
—Wolof Proverb: The Gambia, Senegal

There I was, just 21 years of age, and in spectacular and public fashion my first major entrepreneurial venture had failed.

Due to opposition from a school university and my own mistakes and errors, a rap concert that I had put together had to be cancelled at the last minute. I mean, *the very last* minute.

The artists wanted to get paid. The people wanted their money back, and so did a few investors.

It wasn't pretty.

But for some reason, *I just felt numb.*

I had just gotten off of the stage and performed what some of my closest friends had told me was the bravest thing I ever did or they ever saw – some very close to me later told me they cried over it.

Another person, a spiritual teacher of mine at the time, said, "No matter what anybody ever says about you, Cedric, you got heart, man."

I just did what I felt I had to do.

I got on a stage in front of hundreds of very disappointed and angry people – including friends – and told them what had happened. There would be no show and at that time there was no money to refund.

The whole scene is still a little bit foggy but I do remember some people throwing things at me.

I can still recall a quarter whizzing by my head. I can see it *right now*, as clear as day.

Things must have gotten very bad in an obvious way because at one point, prior to breaking the bad news, I stepped outside of the building looking for fresh air. I actually ended up picking up the unmistakable scent of marijuana. One of the artists and his entourage (in the location where the weed was coming from, no doubt) who was contracted to perform (and still willing to do so) offered me a gun to protect myself ('*...yo, you need some steel?*') is how the offer was presented).

I declined the kind offer, didn't seek or ask for protection – as it didn't matter to me whether anybody hurt me or not. I was prepared to face the consequences.

That, for me, *was the easy part.*

What was not so easy would come next.

It was dealing with the aftermath of facing hurt friends, admirers turned haters (there was a very cute young lady on campus who suddenly took an interest in me just weeks before the show – afterward, she disappeared), and the anguish of what could have been.

In keeping with the material just presented in the last chapter on suffering, I was experiencing loss, shock, and deep pain.

For over a month I rarely ventured out of my dormitory room – only to eat, when I had an appetite.

I went into a depression, traveling only in my own mind.

The shock and disbelief was unbelievable, almost indescribable. I never thought this could happen.

I still couldn't find the strength to listen to Hip-Hop music or urban radio, but at some point I did begin to read, not at my previous level, but enough to pick up my favorite column published in the *Final Call* – written by Jabril Muhammad, called 'Farrakhan The Traveler.' I was in luck, so to speak, blessed in other words, to be fortunate enough to encounter the column – always illuminating – but in the midst of a poignant series on pain and how it empowers.

The series changed my attitude and helped me to reinterpret or form a new conception of what had just happened to me in business and in my social life, and even, what I had done to others.

Somehow someway, the strangest thing happened over a relatively short period of time.

It was incredible.

I was able to transform a deeply demoralizing experience into one that I knew was going to be the basis of an even greater success – a concept most plainly described by Napoleon Hill, in his book *Think and Grow Rich* as: *"every defeat, every disappointment, and every adversity carries with it the seed of an equivalent or greater benefit."*

I was able to find purpose, meaning, and power in my suffering and my personal and professional 'failure' which fueled me toward the day that I sought the most, when it would not hurt so bad and when I would achieve an equivalent or greater benefit.

Little did I know – or maybe deep down I did – that exactly three years later I would be serving on the management team of the most popular Hip-Hop group in the world!

I was consciously entering into my first profound encounter with the secret, even mysterious power of the human will and about to embark on a journey to understand the power of my*self*, studying self, from every discipline with something to offer.

Every entrepreneur already has or will do the same – in some form or fashion – on their way to success.

There are a great many mysteries in life today. But whether they are religious, scientific, or in natural phenomena, the root of what makes them 'mysterious' is the same. There is something that we do not understand, haven't been taught, and cannot explain about the subject in question.

If it is the origin of life itself, it is, perhaps because there is not a witness giving a detailed account of the process.

If it is the intelligence that evolves a sperm and egg from a clot, to an embryo, to a fetus, to a baby within nine months, it is because none of us remembers that experience.

If it is finding a cure for cancer, it is, perhaps, the inability to grasp all of the relationships that are associated with the human cell.

If it is the power of electricity, it is, perhaps, our inability to perceive its cause as compared to its effect.

For lack of a better word, there appears to be something we 'can't see' about these phenomenon or problems that makes them a mystery, unexplainable or solvable at our current level of understanding, education, or development.

But not being able to 'see' something in the physical sense of that word, has never prevented human beings from accepting or *relying* upon realities they can't explain or observe in totality.

One can see this very clearly in the world of science and the attitude of the scientist.

As Jabril Muhammad wrote very clearly years ago in *This Is The One,* there appears to be something surprisingly spiritual in the worldview and work of the scientist, whose outlook is usually seen as 'rational' or 'empirical.'

Mr. Muhammad articulates what he does after having critiqued those that have a proud or dismissive view towards believers in religion:

…people will usually tell you that "science" deals only with perceptible and verifiable realities. Therefore, the findings of "science" are superior to the results of "religion," which they say concerns that which cannot be demonstrated. Is this so? Is it not true that the scientists of this world depend on the unseen universal reign of law that is inherent in everything everywhere? Is not their ability to reason rooted in the belief, if not the conviction, of the rationality of existence, which is grounded in that which they cannot see with the physical eye? What prevents us from believing that there may be dimensions of existence transcending the level we are now aware of?

…We are all acquainted with the fact that the universe is graded. That is, we observe and experience, matter (stone, sand), life (insects, plants), animal life (dogs, camels) and humans. We also know that the human mind has grades. There is nothing irrational in believing that there are realms, or mental levels, beyond the experience most of us live on.

The most intelligent men, fully aware of the achievements and contributions of "science," were and are, believers in the Divine Supreme Being with all that such belief implies.

What Jabril Muhammad is addressing is manifold. He is putting forth part of an argument that reality occurs on levels that not everyone perceives. He is also questioning the legitimacy of the notion that science is more demonstrable, verifiable or real than religion. He does so by placing attention on the numerous laws in the physical or supposedly 'hard' sciences that require faith and confidence in the existence of phenomenon and law, the cause and origin of which scientists admit ignorance of or cannot explain.

All of this is important to the entrepreneur – whether atheist, agnostic, religious, or naturalist – as it is their values, beliefs, and worldview regarding life itself that can determine their view of themselves, what is possible, and the best way to achieve what is possible, in the face of difficulties.

In those times of shock, loss, and pain, we all manifest who and what we are, and what we truly think is right, wrong, possible, and desirable.

The ability to bring forth what exists in the mind but which we or others don't currently see in front of us in the physical form, is an attribute of great entrepreneurs and achievers in all walks of life.

In the Holy Qur'an, in Surah 2 verses 1 to 3 (Maulana Muhammad Ali translation) it reads: "I, Allah, am the Best Knower. This Book, there is no doubt in it, is a guide to those who keep their duty, who believe in the Unseen…"

In a footnote, Maulana Muhammad Ali elaborates on the Arabic meaning of the word translated as "Unseen," saying "Al-ghaib is *that which is unseen or unperceivable by the ordinary senses.*"

What are the ordinary senses?

In short they are generally recognized as taste (gustatory), touch (kinesthetic), hearing (auditory), sight (visual) and smell (olfactory).

What are the major ways in which we learn?

In short they are generally recognized as reading, conversation, observation and experience.

But where do such factors as intuition or even revelation fit in these major categories? Are they senses or forms of learning of a more intangible nature? How do they relate to such concepts as faith?

In an answer to question 6b in Minister Louis Farrakhan's Study Guide 8: "Building The Will – Part IV", we read:

Unseen does not mean Unreal. A terrible impediment to us in this world is that most of us only believe in what we can physically see, which is, of course extremely limited in scope. This is primarily due to the fact that we only know ourselves as material beings; we do not know the spiritual self.

…The Will is the Power behind your being, but the Will is Unseen. To deny the existence of what we cannot see is to deprive ourselves of access to the true Power behind the Universe. The physical things we see are mere variations in forms of manifestation of that Power. The "things" come and go, but the power that produces them is eternal.

A baby draws milk from his mother's breast. He can see the breast, but he cannot see the milk. The first time he pulls on the breast, he is acting not out of knowledge of what is contained therein, but out of faith that something is there. Again, as indicated in previous study guides, the scripture is true: "Faith is the <u>substance</u> of things hoped for; the <u>evidence</u> of things unseen."

On this subject I am reminded of the words of the Honorable Elijah Muhammad in a talk he gave, July 2, 1972, during the 'Theology of Time' teaching series. In explaining the unseen power that exists in the universe, moving matter, he said, of the phenomenon that exists in space:

Now, if we see one emerged out of all this darkness, what force of power in the darkness brought it out? One could not have come out of darkness unless force was in the darkness to bring it out.

In the universe now there is a force in the universe that moves seemingly unmovable stars. After so long, and so long, the star, which we saw here – at this point – has moved over here, to another point. And if that star moved over here to another point, within ten, twenty, thirty, forty, or fifty or a hundred years or a thousand years – force made it to move. It could not move alone.

So this teaches us, Brother – you go back and get your scientists and I will contend with him and he will contend with me, that the force of the actual space, seemingly looking as though it doesn't, is moving, to bring us objects that is hidden in it, to our view.

We don't wind up the universe like that and tell it to bring Jupiter over to us. No, Jupiter is moving by force. It is already out.

Again, we don't say to a star that is a hundred trillion years, probably, back out there to 'come out and show us yourself.' There are already forces…out there to bring it to our view.

Think deeply over that word 'forces.' Can the 'force' that drives you as a person be seen?

Maybe the apparent gulf between science and religion and life itself, when it comes to mysteries, is not as large as we have been led to believe. Certainly the concept of suffering, as we have seen from last chapter, suggests that this could be so.

Perhaps it is in the entrepreneurial experience where the human being is forced to merge rational thought, creative and critical thinking, with belief, faith and vision, where we may find answers to some of life's remaining questions.

What greater mystery is there than that of the power of our own selves and where it comes from? Most specifically our mental powers and the physiology of our brains? According to the *Webster's New Collegiate Dictionary*, the brain is: "the portion of the vertebrate central nervous system that constitutes the organ of thought and neural coordination, includes all the higher nervous centers receiving stimuli from the sense organs and interpreting and correlating them to formulate the motor impulses, is made up of neurons and supporting nutritive structures, is enclosed within the skull, and is continuous with the spinal cord through the foramen magnum."

The most mysterious aspect of the brain is this portion of the definition above, "...constitutes the organ of thought and neural coordination, includes all the higher nervous centers receiving stimuli from the sense organs and interpreting and correlating them to formulate the motor impulses," and how this function relates to what is called the mind and will of the human being.

The mystery of the relationship between the brain, mind and will has perplexed scientists, theologians, doctors and psychologists for as long as they have studied the brain, it seems. For more anecdotal and empirical evidence regarding the mystery of the power of the brain and its effect on and relationship to the human body, one should read *Love, Medicine, and Miracles: Lessons Learned About Self-Healing From A Surgeon's Experience With Exceptional Patients* by Bernie S. Siegel and *Anatomy Of An Illness As Perceived By The Patient: Reflections On Healing And Regeneration* by Norman Cousins.

Something that is important to realize in this study of the relationship between brain, mind and will is that the brain and mind are not the same thing as most people commonly indicate by how they use those words interchangeably. The 'mind' is defined as "the element or complex of elements in an individual that feels, perceives, thinks, wills, and esp. reasons." These capabilities go well beyond the brain and involve other parts of your anatomy and physiology.

One can see this in the study of neurotransmitters which are the chemicals that transmit impulses along your nerves. Think of them as the messengers in the communication system between your brain and the rest of your body. Your thoughts reach every part of your body through the work of the neurotransmitters. It has been recently discovered that the same neurotransmitters that are in the brain can also be produced in other parts of your body. That means messages are not just sent from the brain to the body, they can be initiated in the body and transmitted by organs. The neurotransmitter represents the nexus point of mind – bridging the brain and body.

If the importance of the 'mind' is hard to see through a basic study or review of anatomy and physiology, it becomes clear when one considers them from the lens of marketing and advertising and psychological warfare.

If you want a field in which to consider how the mind – "the element or complex of elements in an individual that feels, perceives, thinks, wills, and esp. reasons" – works and why it is so important, there may be no better place to start than in the world of commercial advertising on television. One of the best and clearest explanations I have seen accomplishing this objective is provided in *Awaken The Giant* by Anthony Robbins. In a section titled, "If You Don't Have A Plan For Your Life, Someone Else Does," Mr. Robbins wrote two decades ago:

The mission of Madison Avenue is to influence what we link pain and pleasure to. Advertisers clearly understand that what drives us is not so much our intellect as the sensations that we link to their products. As a result, they've become experts in learning how to use exciting or soothing music, rapid or elegant imagery, bright or subdued color, and a variety of other elements to put us in certain emotional states; then, when our emotions are at their peak, when the sensations are their most intense, they flash an image of their product continuously until we link it to these desired feelings.

Pepsi employed this strategy brilliantly in carving out a bigger share of the lucrative soft-drink market from their major competitor, Coca-Cola. Pepsi observed the phenomenal success of Michael Jackson, a young man who spent his entire life learning how to heighten people's emotions by the way he used his voice, his body, his face, and his gestures. Michael sang and danced in a way that stimulated huge numbers of people to feel incredibly good – so much so that they'd often purchase one of his albums to re-create the feelings. Pepsi asked, 'How can we transfer those sensations to *our* product? Their reasoning was that if people associated the same pleasurable feelings to Pepsi as they did to Michael Jackson, they'd buy Pepsi just as they bought his albums. The process of anchoring new feelings to a product or idea is the integral transference necessary to basic condition...consider this: any time we're in an intense emotional state, when we're feeling strong sensations of pain or pleasure, anything unique that occurs consistently will become neurologically linked. Therefore, in the future, whenever that unique thing happens again, the emotional state will return.

You've probably heard of Ivan Pavlov, a Russian scientist who, in the late nineteenth century, conducted conditioned-response experiments. His most famous experiment was one in which he rang a bell as he offered food to a dog, thereby stimulating the dog to salivate and pairing the dog's sensations with the sound of the bell. After repeating the conditioning enough times, Pavlov found that merely ringing the bell would cause the dog to salivate – even when food was no longer being given.

What does Pavlov have to do with Pepsi? First, Pepsi used Michael Jackson to get us in a peak emotional state. Then, at that precise moment, they flashed the product. Continuous repetitions of this created an emotional linkage for millions of Jackson's fans. The truth is that Michael Jackson doesn't even drink Pepsi! And he wouldn't even hold an empty Pepsi can in his hand on camera! You might wonder, "Isn't this company crazy? They hired a guy for $15 million to represent them who doesn't even hold their product, and tells everybody that he won't! What kind of spokesperson is this? What a crazy idea!" Actually, it was a brilliant idea. Sales went through the roof – so high that L.A. Gear then hired Michael for $20 million to represent their product. And today, because he's able to change the way people feel (he's what I call a "state inducer") he and Sony/CBS just signed a 10-year recording contract that's reputed to be worth more than $1 billion. His ability to change people's emotional states makes him *invaluable.*

What we've got to realize is that this is all based on linking pleasurable sensations to specific behaviors. It's the idea that if we use the product, we'll live our fantasies. Advertisers have taught all of us that if you drive a BMW, then you're an extraordinary person with exceptional taste. If you drive Hyundai, you're intelligent and frugal. If you drive a Pontiac, you'll have excitement. If you drive a Toyota, what a feeling you'll get! You're taught that if you wear Obsession cologne, you'll soon be entwined in the throes of androgynous orgy. If you drink Pepsi, you'll be able to jam with M.C. Hammer as the epitome of hip. If you want to be a "good" mom, then you feed your children Hostess fruit pies, cupcakes and Twinkies.

Advertisers have noted that if enough pleasure can be generated, consumers are often willing to overlook the fear of pain. It is an advertising adage that "sex sells," and there's no question that the pleasurable associations created in print and on TV by using sex do the job. Take a look at the trend in selling blue jeans. What are blue jeans anyway? They used to be work pants: functional, ugly. How are they sold today? They've become an international icon of everything that's sexy, fashionable, and youthful. Have you ever watched a Levi's 501 jeans commercial? Can you explain one to me? They make no sense, do they? They're totally confusing. But at the end, you have the distinct impression that sex took place nearby. Does this type of strategy really sell blue jeans? You bet! Levi is the number-one blue-jeans manufacturer in America today.

...Of course, the use of advertising as a form of conditioning is not limited to physical products. Fortunately or unfortunately, we consistently see television and radio used as tools for changing what we associate to candidates in the political process. No one knows this better than the master political analyst and opinion-shaper Roger Ailes, who was responsible for key elements of Ronald Reagan's successful 1984 campaign against Walter Mondale, and who in 1988 masterminded George Bush's successful campaign against Michael Dukakis. Ailes designed a strategy to convey three specifically negative messages about Dukakis – that he was soft on defense, the environment, and crime – and caused people to link painful sensations to him. One ad portrayed Dukakis as a "kid playing war" in a tank; another seemed to blame him for pollution in the Boston Harbor. The most notorious one showed criminals being released from Massachusetts jails through a revolving door, and played on the widespread negative publicity generated around the country by the "Willie Horton incident." Convicted murderer Willie Horton, released from jail as part of a controversial furlough program in Dukakis's home state, failed to return and ten months later was arrested for terrorizing a young couple, raping the woman and assaulting the man.

Many people took issue with the negative focus of these ads. Personally, I found them highly manipulative. But it's hard to argue with their level of success, based on the fact that people do more to avoid pain than to gain pleasure. Many people didn't like the way the campaign was fought – and George Bush was one of those people – but it was hard to argue with the reality that pain was a very powerful motivator in shaping people's behavior. As Ailes says, "The negative ads cut through quicker. People tend to pay more attention to [these types of ads]. People may or may not slow down to look at a beautiful pastoral scene along the highway. But everyone looks at an auto accident." There is no questioning the effectiveness of Ailes's strategy. Bush won a clear majority of the popular vote and soundly trounced Dukakis in one of the biggest landslides in electoral college history.

The force shaping world opinion and consumer buying habits is also the same force that shapes *all* of our actions. It's up to you and me to take control of this force and decide on our own actions consciously, because if we don't direct our own thoughts, we'll fall under the influence of those who would condition us to behave in the way they desire. Sometimes those actions are what we would have selected anyway; sometimes not. Advertisers understand how to change what we link pain and pleasure to by changing the sensations we associate to their products. If we want to take control of our lives, we must learn to "advertise" in our own minds...

Just think over all of the above. But there are two excerpts in particular to consider carefully.

First, "Advertisers clearly understand that what drives us is not so much our intellect as the sensations that we link to their products. As a result, they've become experts in learning how to use exciting or soothing music, rapid or elegant imagery, bright or subdued color, and a variety of other elements to put us in certain emotional states; then, when our emotions are at their peak, when the sensations are their most intense, they flash an image of their product continuously until we link it to these desired feelings."

Secondly – "If we want to take control of our lives, we must learn to "advertise" in our own minds..."

If advertisers are '*experts in learning how to use exciting or soothing music, rapid or elegant imagery, bright or subdued color, and a variety of other elements to put us in certain emotional states...*' and '*when our emotions are at their peak, when the sensations are their most intense, they flash an image of their product continuously until we link it to these desired feelings,*' couldn't entrepreneurs be mindful of how these elements can serve or work against them in pursuit of what they desire – a successful business?

What if entrepreneurs through the use of music, photography, statements, and audio recordings imagined, rehearsed or 'advertised' their own success to themselves and experienced it in advance to some degree through their senses?

Now, on to psychological warfare.

In April of 1976, the United States Army put out a little-known two-volume study of the relationship between military and political operations and influencing human psychology.

It was entitled, *The Art and Science of Psychological Operations: Case Studies Of Military Application.* From Volume One of this work we can gain valuable insight into the working of the human mind and how important influencing it is.

Here we provide some introductory material from this reference (boldface emphasis is ours):

ORIGIN OF PSYOP TERMINOLOGY BY William E. Daughtery
An account of the origin of the terms PSYWAR and PSYOP

It has been amply demonstrated that American employment of propaganda, psychological warfare (PSYWAR), psychological operations (PSYOP), or whatever one chooses to call activity that these terms are intended to describe is neither revolutionary nor un-American. In this essay the origins of the terms "PSYWAR" and "PSYOP" will be described.

PSYWAR and PSYOP

The terms "psychological operations' and "psychological warfare" are often used interchangeably to identify an activity or function as old as human conflict or intercultural group relations. Both terms, however, are known to be of relatively recent origin. Psychological warfare was first used in 1920 and psychological operations in 1945.

The British military analyst and historian, J.F.C. Fuller, is believed to have been the one who coined the term "psychological warfare," when in 1920, in a scholarly analysis of lessons learned during World War I, especially as these related to the employment of such new weapons as armor, he allowed his mind to wander imaginatively about the character of the future battlefield. In his treatise on tanks he prophesied what traditional means of warfare, as then known and understood, might in time be.

Replaced by a purely psychological warfare, wherein weapons are not used or battlefields sought...but [rather]...**the corruption of the human reason, the dimming of the human intellect, and the disintegration of the moral and spiritual life of one nation by the influence of the will of another** is accomplished.

Although Fuller's employment of the term is believed to have been the earliest recorded use of the phrase, there is not thought to be any direct connection between his use and the widespread adoption of it by Americans on the eve of World War II. The British did not...describe what both they and the Americans hesitated to describe as propaganda operations. Instead of employing the term "PSYWAR," the British adopted the term "political warfare" to describe those activities that Americans came to identify in time as psychological warfare or PSYWAR. Since World War II the British have followed American practice and now use the term "PSYWAR" to describe the activities they previously identified as political warfare. The earliest recorded use of the term "psychological warfare" in an American publication occurred in January 1940 when an article entitled "Psychological Warfare and How to Wage It" appeared in a popular American journal.

The earliest recorded use of the term "psychological operations" occurred early in 1945 when Captain (later Rear Admiral) Ellis M. Zacharias, U.S. Navy, employed the term in an operation plan designed to hasten the surrender of Japan. Without any description or explanation, the term was used in the context "All psychological operations will be coordinated both as to times and trends in order to avoid reduction of effectiveness of this main operation." The next use of the term was in 1951, when the Truman Administration renamed an interagency strategy committee giving it the title Psychological Operations Coordinating Committee. Neither in 1945 nor in 1951 did the use of the term "psychological operations" create so much as a ripple of interest.

Although the Department of the Army made the change in 1951, it was not until the 1960s that psychological operations came to supplant psychological warfare as the all-inclusive term in common use. Any explanation of this development must take into account the fact **Americans have become increasingly concerned about the continued use of a term that includes the word "warfare" to describe an activity that is directed to friends and neutrals as much or more than to hostile or potentially hostile people.** Examples are the Lebanon of 1958 and the Dominican Republic intervention of 1965.

In the late 1960s, with the widespread use of psychological operations in Indochina, emphasis was placed upon the need to reintegrate PSYOP with other training and operations and upon the reinforcement which other missions could lend to psychological operations. The psychological objective military assistance and civic action, for example, was more fully stressed.

WHAT IS COMMUNICATION? By Yasumasa Tanaka

From mentalists to behaviorists, over the last quarter century, an intensive effort has been made to construct a general model of human behavior. Models which can explain human behavior have recently been constructed by a number of behaviorists. Among these is a variety of "cybernetic models" that variably take into account the communication and control aspects of human behavior. In the simplest terms, these models presuppose a series of psychological processes in which one individual's or organization's behavior, in the form of explicit "output" information produced by him or it, is dependent upon the "input" information that an individual or organization may receive from other people or organizations and from the environment. In order to examine their validity and discover their relevance to our problems, let us look briefly at a few of them.

As an initial point of reference, it is useful to keep H.D. Lasswell's classic formula in mind. The scientific study of communication, he says, involves discovering "Who Says What, In What Channel, To Whom, With What Effect."

There is another type of model, the "cybernetic" one, first introduced by C.E. Shannon for telephone communication and subsequently adjusted for human communication situations by C.E. Osgood.

On the basis of the "theory" of these models, we now can make a more formal statement about the nature of human communication behavior. We can assume the existence of various processes of *decoding* and *encoding* between input and output events. Decoding here refers to the way in which the individual human (or organization) receives input information from his environment – namely, the internal reaction caused by the input of the subject. Encoding designates those processes whereby the individual human (or organization) chooses some response, in the form of output, to the environment surrounding and affecting him. That which psychologists call the "mediation process" is thus considered as the bridge between decoding and encoding. In the simplest terms, it is the process which mediates between sensory nervous processes of *decoding* on the "input" side and the motor nervous processes *encoding* on the "output" side. Even in comparatively simple acts, such as making a speech, an individual's communicating behavior is complex, susceptible to many factors, as suggested above, and it is a continuously renewing process whereby he is always adapting to his environment.

At this point the term feedback is also relevant. It has been stated thus:

The action is initiated by an "incongruity" between the state of the organism and the state that is being tested for, and the action persists until the incongruity... is removed [Excerpts from "Psychological Factors in International Persuasion." The Annals of the American Academy of Political and Social Science, Vol. 398 (November 1971), pp. 50-54.]

According to this view, the fundamental building block of the social system is the feedback "loop."

Dealing with the complex organization and mechanisms of government, **Karl Deutsch defines feedback as a "communication network that produces action in response to an input of information, and includes the results of its own action in the new information by which it modifies its subsequent behavior.** In other words, by this feedback mechanism, individual humans (and organizations) can correct errors and adjust their behavior to the continuously renewing environment.

Furthermore, in view of the present state of communication technology, interpersonal interaction is not necessarily limited to a face-to-face situation. The whole or part of an encoded message may be quoted in a newspaper, or broadcast by radio and television, or even relayed via a communication satellite to local stations in foreign countries, for literally universal "mass consumption." Then, as the feedback loops became more complex, the source will need some extended "scanning" devices or "monitors," to gather feedback information. He will continuously need to keep an eye on local and national newspapers, radio, or television newscasts, and even on the mass media in foreign countries!

PERSUASION AND THE EFFECTS OF COMMUNICATIONS

Persuasion may be defined as the art of "winning men's minds by words." The basic premise here is that persuasion is an act of communication. We must note, however, that it is a special kind of communication, and it is not involved in all communication situations in which behavior is influenced by a set of input stimuli. In order to be persuasive in nature, the communication situation must involve a conscious attempt by the communicator to influence the thought and behavior of the receiver through the transmission of some message. Persuasive communication, therefore, implies a judgment of the situation in terms of the intentions of the communication and the resultant thought or behavior change of the receiver. **Persuasive communications can thus be judged with respect to their success in producing desired thought or behavior, or their failure to do so. Examples of success or failure of persuasive communications can be easily seen in election campaigns, advertising, or international diplomacy.**

Research on persuasive communication embraces the study of persuasiveness, on the one hand, and persuadibility on the other. It also involves the study of attitudes – how they are formed and how they can be changed.

What election campaigns, advertising, and international diplomacy and psychological operations reveal, is that *all* human beings are *always* under the influence of persuasive communication directed at their senses and learning experience.

Your brain and senses are the target of everyone who wants to influence you.

But how conscious are entrepreneurs of these techniques and methods, and how many use these methods and insights to persuade and influence themselves towards a goal?

Those who understand this process and apply its principles to themselves stand the best chance of control over their own heart, mind and soul – their *self*.

And an entrepreneur in possession of them*selves*, is more creative, more disciplined, and more determined to accomplish their goal.

The more power you have over your will, the greater your power over your own thoughts and actions in pursuit of any opportunity you perceive and build a business organization around.

<<<<>>>>

Now that we have looked at the relationship between brain and mind, we can consider the relationship between the mind and will. In order to do that we must start by thinking *about* thoughts and feelings and the relationship between thoughts, feelings *and* the will.

It may be useful to consider these three factors – thoughts, feelings and will – like a tripod in one sense, and like three ingredients in a recipe. In the sense of a tripod, they represent three aspects of the foundation upon which the human being experiences and lives. In the sense of ingredients they represent an inter-related whole, incapable of being separated, as they are mixed together in unity.

Although there is much literature (much of which is confused and uncertain) that abounds on these three areas, one is well served by consulting two fields – psychology (with an assist from philosophy) and theology (with an assist from religion).

In psychology, thoughts, feelings and will are looked at, frequently and traditionally from the perspectives of three main areas: cognition, emotion, and conation.

According to *A Dictionary of Psychology* by Andrew Colman, cognition is defined as "the mental activities involved in acquiring and processing information"; emotion is defined as "any short-term evaluative, affective, intentional, psychological state, including happiness, sadness, disgust, and other inner feelings…"; and conation is defined as "the psychological processes involved in purposeful action."

Hopefully by the language used to define these terms it becomes clear that they can be studied separately but have a union that makes them related and even one.

From the perspective of theology, thoughts, feelings, and will are looked at from the perspective of three areas as well: the mind, heart and soul.

Excerpts and portions of definitions for these three areas, correspond and compliment some of what psychology puts forth.

Mind, according to *The Expository Dictionary Of Bible Words* by Lawrence Richards can be defined, from an examination of Greek words used in the New Testament. He identifies three words that relate to the mind or psychological functions: *Phronesis* which he defines as "one's way of thinking"; *Nous* which he defines as "one's capacity to perceive" and *dianoia*, "the faculty or organ of perception."

In summary Richards writes, "The NT [New Testament] explores human cognitive capacity."

The heart, according to the *Evangelical Dictionary of Biblical Theology* edited by Walter A. Elwell is the center of emotional functions. He writes:

The Lord, who knows our hearts (Luke 16:15), experiences its full range of emotions; for example, its joy (Deut. 28:47; 1 Sam. 2:1; Prov. 15:15) and its sorrow (1 Sam. 1:8); its raging (2 Kings 6:11) and its peace (Col. 5:15); its feeling troubled (John 14:1) and its rejoicing (1 Sam. 2:1; Ps. 104:15); its love (Rom. 5:5; 1 peter 1:22) and its selfish ambition (James 3:14); its modes of doubts (Mark 11:23) and of fear (Gen. 42:28) and its mode of trusting (Prov. 3:5); when it rises up in repulsive pride (Deut. 8:14) or, as in the case of Jesus, is lowly and humble (Matt. 11:29); and when one loses heart (Heb. 12:3) or takes heart (John 16:33).

The emotional state of the heart affects the rest of a person: "A happy heart makes the face cheerful. But heartache crushes the spirit" (Prov. 15:13); "a cheerful heart is good medicine, but a crushed spirit dries up the bones" (17:22)

The heart also wishes, desires…

Soul, according to the *Catholic Biblical Encyclopedia* (1956) compiled by John E. Steinmueller and Kathryn Sullivan is, "A spirit having understanding and free will…It is the rational seat of man's intentions, will, or conscience."

This certainly seems to connect with the definition from psychology for conation as "…purposeful action."

The purpose of pointing out the distinction between how these attributes and processes are described in psychology and theology is not to put one field at opposition to the other.

Rather is the deliberate opposite – to show unity across worldviews that people commonly put at variance to one another and show the relationship between human attributes and processes and entrepreneurial activity.

The heart, mind, and soul – or feelings and emotions; ideas and thinking; and purposeful determination – are all essential factors or the means by which the entrepreneur perceives an opportunity and then creates an organization to pursue it.

Our thinking is that the more deeply one looks into the fields of psychology and theology the more likely they will see no rigid barrier dividing certain insights in both worlds.

This view is shared or alluded to by others.

Gregory Berkely, according to *The Oxford Companion To The Mind* edited by Richard L. Gregory, wrote, "the soul is the will properly speaking."

In *The International Standard Bible Encyclopedia* edited by G. W. Bromley we read of the heart having a function more closely related to conation than to emotion (affection). Under a section called, "Volition and Purpose" we read:

The heart's role as the center of emotions is important, but its role as the center of will and purpose, intentionality and decision making, is even more significant.

Will and purpose originate in the heart (Dt. 8:2; 1 S. 2:35; 2 S. 7:3, 21; 1 K. 8:17; 1 Ch. 17:2; 28:2) and thus also intentionality (Jer. 23:20…; RSV "intents of the mind" –. which is often a matter of "setting the heart" (1 Ch. 22:19; Ezr. 7:10). Resolve comes from the heart (Acts 11:23…NEB "resolute hearts"; RSV "resolved")…

The heart's desire (2 S. 3:21; Ps. 10:3; 21:2; 37:4) often refers to determination, i.e, that on which one's heart is set (Dt. 24:15; Prov. 19:18; Eph. 6:5; Col. 3:22)…

An idiomatic way of expressing willful purpose or intent is that of "incline the heart"…(Josh. 24:23; Jgs. 9:3; 1 K. 8:58; Ps. 117:36)…

The inner impulse (Ps. 108:1) for decision or choice comes from the heart (Ex. 35:21, 29; 2 K. 12:4)…Reluctance or indecision can be seen in the expression "slow of heart to believe" (Lk. 24:25). Persistence in a decided course of action even against sound advice is stubbornness or obduracy of heart (Dt. 29:19; Isa. 46:12)…When people agree, they have 'one heart" (…1 Ch. 12:38; 2 Ch. 30:12; Jer. 32:39…"one way. A person "after one's own heart" (1 S. 13:14; Jer. 3:15; Acts 13:22; cf. Jgs. 16:15) thinks or wills the same things one does. The idiom for discord or duplicity is having a "double heart" (Heb; 1 Ch. 12:33; Ps. 12:2)

And in the book *The Power of Your Subconscious Mind*, Joseph Murphy writes, "your subjective mind perceives by intuition. It is the seat of your emotions and the storehouse of memory," and "…as a man thinketh in his heart [subconscious mind] so is he."

From another perspective we can see the equation of the will with the soul of the human being.

First, in Minister Louis Farrakhan's Study Guides, *Self Improvement: The Basis For Community Development*, psychology and theology meet when the will of the human being is referred to as the essence of the human being, the power he or she receives from the Supreme Being.

He writes, "Brothers and Sisters, each time we turn away from the struggle to overcome difficulty, there is deterioration of character and there is destruction of the Will – and the Will that is within you is God's gift. It is His Essence that He gives to man and anything that deteriorates your Will destroys your ability to cope with the problems of life. Struggle is ordained by God. God is not a vicious God. He is a Loving, a Beneficent, and Merciful God, but He ordains struggle. Because without struggle, you cannot bring out of yourself that which God has deposited within you. It is something that has to be brought out and it is a struggle overcoming difficulties that manifest your own gifts and your own sublime qualities."

With that in mind, from the Holy Qur'an the essence of the human being is called "nafs." From a footnote to Surah 4 verse 1, in the Maulana Muhammad Ali translation we read, "The word *nafs* is used in the language of the Arabs in two ways, one of which is your saying *kharajat nafsu-hu* where by *nafs* is implied *the soul*, and according to the other use the significance of *nafs* is *the whole thing, and its essence*."

In addition, the Minister also explains the interconnected nature of the three pillars of psychology – conation, cognition and emotion – from a spiritual perspective in his October 26, 1986 speech, "The Will Of God – Part I" stating:

Will is Power, but Power must be guided. Guided by what? The power of Will must be guided by knowledge. But there is an emotional force that gives direction to Will. And the emotional force – which is the creative force upon which the entire Universe is constructed – is Love. And it is out of this awesome power of Love that the Will springs up; it springs up out of this emotion and it is directed and guided by that emotion. When you couple Will and Knowledge and Love, then you have a balanced individual, whose Will is being used in a creative, constructive way; not in the way of destruction.

The depiction of the relationship between "Will and Knowledge and Love" can easily be studied from our identification of the three major categories of psychology, that align perfectly with the trio identified by Minister Farrakhan as essential to achieving balance in the individual. Those three areas of psychology which equate to Will, Knowledge and Love are Conation, Cognition and Volition.

Some psychologists define Conation as a combination of Volition and Emotion.

In advising clients, I spend a considerable amount of time on the relationship between the spiritual and emotional aspects of the human brain and mind, and entrepreneurship and business activity. For some this seems strange. But when properly reminded of just what is involved in a creative or innovative act, or in organizing people around it; it does not take long before a person sees the deep connection between the unseen reality of inner human nature and personality, and the manifestation of behaviors, events, and institutions outside of us.

I promote the general definition of an entrepreneur as one who conceives or perceives an opportunity and creates or coordinates an organization to pursue it.

The largely internal or unseen acts of perception and conception are critical factors in our ability to obtain what we strive for in entrepreneurship and business, much less life itself.

For this reason, of the major elements of the model at the center of this book – power, standardization, capital, suffering and willpower—if I had to choose I would say that the relationship between willpower and suffering matters the most. Again, these two emotional and spiritual factors occur most intensely on the inside of the individual, and represent the unseen force that underlies motivation and drives human actions.

In all of the great stories and biographies of the most successful businesspersons that I have read or studied, not a single one of them achieved and sustained success without developing and supporting the power of their will through suffering and adversity.

Every single one of these great ones practiced one, two, or all three of the following methods: prayer, affirmation, or visualization. They did so whether or not they claimed a religious or spiritual faith, or belief system.

Reflect over the following regarding visualization from "How To Find a More Satisfying Career" by Victor M. Parachin:

Legendary hotelier Conrad Hilton knew how to use this technique. The Great Depression was exceptionally hard for Mr. Hilton. After the stock market crash of 1929, people didn't travel as much, and when they did they didn't stay in the hotels Mr. Hilton had acquired during the roaring 1920s. Business at his hotels was so poor that by 1931 his creditors were threatening to foreclose. He was so financially destitute that even his laundry was in hock and he had to borrow money from a bellboy to eat. That year, Mr. Hilton came upon a photograph of the Waldorf Hotel. It had six kitchens, 200 cooks, 500 waiters, 2,000 rooms and a private hospital and railroad in the basement. He clipped the photograph out of the magazine and scribbled across it, "The Greatest of Them All."

"The year 1931 was a presumptuous, outrageous time to dream," Mr. Hilton would later write. Nevertheless, he put the photo of the Waldorf in his wallet, and when he had a desk again, slipped the picture under the glass top. The magazine photo was always in front of him. As he worked his way back up and acquired new, larger desks, he would slip the cherished photo under the glass. In October 1949, 18 years later, Mr. Hilton bought the Waldorf.

Since so much of what we are discussing in terms of the brain, mind, will and suffering relates to feelings and emotions, we should now take a little time to view feelings and emotions more closely.

Aristotle and other prominent philosophers and scientists throughout Western civilization considered emotions to be 'co-comittant' with thinking, meaning they were intertwined and closely related. But around two centuries ago, psychologists and others began to separate emotions from their study of thought and mind, placing it in a category of its own.

Separating or systematizing part of a whole for the purpose of study is fine.

But when that separation becomes a whole until itself, problems can develop. And that has been the case with the study of science and even emotion, from well before the time of Aristotle.

Today, the study of emotions is a mess, to put it mildly, with neuroscientists, psychologists, psychiatrists among others, disputing what emotions are and how they work, in relation to human behavior and the mind.

The surprising popularity of the book, *Emotional Intelligence* by Daniel

Goldman in 1995, revealed the gap that existed between the general public's intense interest in the subject and what formal education and science had been able to provide to satisfy that interest. The book's popularity also showcased the ability of human beings to understand the process of how their minds and bodies work if the language used to communicate to them is precise and simple enough.

That is also the approach and objective of this chapter.

But regardless to how plain something is put, we all – as students of self – must work a bit harder than we have in order to understand the nature in which we were created and have evolved. After all the Knowledge of Self is that essential knowledge that is basic to everything else we may learn or do, including entrepreneurship.

There are three factors that determine our emotions and our emotional states.

They are: our anatomy and physiology; our individual experience, programming and conditioning; and our cultural experience, programming and conditioning. We look now at all three.

1) Anatomy and Physiology. In order to understand the relationship between our senses and our emotions we have to understand a part of the brain known as the limbic system. The limbic system is an important control center of the brain. It is a collection of organs near the middle of the brain. Different authorities include different organs of their body in their description, but the main components listed tend to be 1) The hippocampus which is involved with most incoming sensory information, and memory. It passes information to other parts of the limbic system and brain. 2) The hypothalamus which is the emotional and functional barometer/control unit of the brain controlling things like body temperature, hormones, metabolism. The hypothalamus therefore influences our emotions chemically as well as maintaining function and 3) The amygdala which is thought to be involved more directly in controlling the experience and expression of emotion.

From a publication put out by The Society For Neuroscience, *Brain Facts: A Primer On The Brain And Nervous System* the following definitions for these three appear:

Hippocampus: A seahorse-shaped structure located within the brain and considered an important part of the limbic system. One of the most studied areas of the brain, it functions in learning, memory, and emotion.

Hypothalamus: A complex brain structure composed of many nuclei with various functions, including regulating the activities of internal organs, monitoring information from the autonomic nervous system, controlling the pituitary gland, and regulating sleep and appetite.

Amygdala: A structure in the forebrain that is an important component of the limbic system and plays a central role in emotional learning, particularly within the context of fear.

The limbic system, according to this same primer, is "A group of brain structures – including the amygdala, hippocampus, septum, basal ganglia, and others – that help regulate the expression of emotion and emotional memory."

The forebrain is defined as "The largest part of the brain, which includes the cerebral cortex and basal ganglia. The forebrain is credited with the highest intellectual functions."

Giving a broader context, in the book, *The Brain and Psychology* edited by M.C. Wittrock, we read, in a section, "The Hypothalamus and the Limbic System":

Just anterior to the brainstem is a region called the hypothalamus, combining many nuclei and pathways related to metabolic, hormonal, and motivational aspects of behavior. Stimulation of this brain area can result in intense pleasure reactions or violent rage, depending upon the specific nuclei affected. Animals with all brain tissue above the hypothalamus removed can still exhibit complicated, highly organized patterns of emotional or motivated behavior, including autonomic effects.

In many of these cases, however, the behavior is directed at an inappropriate object. An extremely important function of the hypothalamus is its control of the pituitary gland and endocrine system. Feedback loops between this region and glands throughout the body control reproductive cycles, sexual receptivity, and autonomic responses to stressful stimuli. Homeostasis (a consistent internal environment) is maintained by hypothalamic systems regulating feeding, drinking, and internal temperature. Arguments for the existence of true brain "centers' were long supported by the critical role of the hypothalamus in homeostasis.

The hypothalamus is intimately related to a group of cerebral structures known as the limbic system. The system derived its name from the fact that it forms a border or rim (Latin: limbus) encircling the top of the brainstem, lying between that region and the cerebral cortex. The major limbic regions are the amygdala, septum, hippocampus, and limbic areas of the cortex. The behavioral functions of limbic nuclei are difficult to define. Lesion, stimulation, and recording studies indicate that they exert subtle modulatory effects on sensory and learning processes. Amygdala lesions in primates have been shown to affect social behavior and in human studies, hippocampal damage has been associated with memory deficits. It is possible that the true role of the limbic system does not conform to any presently defined behavioral function, but, at this point, its role in affective systems seems clear.

A full exposition of our anatomy and physiology is of course beyond the scope of this book as well as its author's expertise. The essential point to be made here, along with introducing some important terminology is that we cannot truly understand our emotional life and it relates to our will without a healthy respect and basic knowledge of anatomy and physiology, especially our brain and nervous system.

Brain Facts: a Primer On The Brain and Nervous System published by the Society of Neuroscience is a clearly written reference guide.

2) Individual Experience, Programming and Conditioning. Each of us, have a separate and independent existence. We all have a personal 'self,' put most basically as a body out of which we sense and experience reality. Our anatomy and physiology represent the structure and function of this self. Our experience is the inner workings of our anatomy and physiology and the sum of our growth and development over time, which involves our health, learning and interaction with external forces.

Our programming and conditioning are the patterns of our thinking and feelings which operate on an instinctual or subconscious level, or the process that creates such patterns. Our ability, as individuals, to make decisions and exercise will to affect our own experience is impacted by the strength of our individual programming and conditioning, which is the sum of our memories, knowledge, and habits, and the intensity of the emotions associated with each of them. A program is a self-contained script or pattern that works in whole, and automatically, once initiated, triggered or stimulated by something. Conditioning is the repetition of a thought, emotion, or act that may eventually become a regular and unconscious pattern of behavior or program of actions within us. Anything that we do in order to willfully affect our emotions and the intensity of our emotional states represents our control over our programming and conditioning.

3) Cultural Experience, Programming and Conditioning. While each of us has an individual reality, we also have a cultural reality – our interaction with external forces and their influence upon us – which shapes our reality and affects our anatomy and physiology, and influences our individual experience, which includes our health and learning, among other factors. These external forces can include persons, institutions, events, circumstances, and the natural environment. Our experiences with parents, neighbors, classmates, and the satisfaction of our basic needs and wants – like food, clothing and shelter – represents much of our cultural experience, programming and conditioning. Our individual experience inevitably leads to a cultural experience, beginning first, with our relationship with our mothers in the womb.

To speak of these three factors determining our emotional life separately is only helpful as an introduction.
They all affect one another and drive the creation of our value systems and beliefs.

Our anatomy and physiology relates to our individual experience which relates to our cultural experience in a never ending cycle which shapes and continues to evolve our value and belief systems. It is our values and our beliefs as a result of these three factors working in a never-ending cycle which most greatly affect our emotions and our emotional states which impact our minds.

It is all of these forces which affect our senses and how we perceive reality and vice-versa.

From the entrepreneurial perspective this of course means that all of these forces affect whether or not, and *what* opportunities we perceive (and to what degree) as well as how we decide to pursue them and how we create the organizations – businesses – to do so.

Of the three factors we have just introduced – anatomy and physiology; individual experience programming and conditioning; and cultural experience, programming and conditioning – we have a measure of individual control over all three.

We can affect our anatomy and physiology by diet, exercise, and movement, for example. We can affect our individual conditioning and programming by learning and determining how we will respond to any stimulus from the external environment, for example. We can affect our cultural conditioning and programming by deciding with whom we will associate and what we will expose ourselves to, for example.

Of the three, in a certain sense we have the least amount of control over anatomy and physiology and our cultural conditioning and programming. With anatomy and physiology, in one sense, the production of our bodies was an act that took place without our knowledge or involvement in a proactive sense, and there are a great many properties of our bodies that we do not appear to be able to change. And, with cultural conditioning and programming, we simply have very little control over others and how they think, feel and act. Now, in both cases we still exert a level of control, but the multitude of factors beyond our control or understanding far exceed those that we do control, when compared to our ability to condition and program ourselves.

But this might suggest that we should spend most of our focus on what we are more likely to control, our individual experience.

This is not necessarily the case because *what we control is not necessarily what is affecting us the most.* It may be better to focus on how we relate to what we can't control, in order to better understand and experience what we desire in relation to that part of reality. In that sense a greater knowledge of anatomy and physiology and our cultural experience might produce a greater impact on behalf of what we want.

Of all of the factors that affect us the most – our physical nature (physiology and anatomy) and environment (cultural experience, conditioning and programming) it is culture that probably affects our emotions and emotional states in more ways than any other.

This view is informed by the views of cultural psychologist Dr. Carl Ratner.

His insights imply how our minds and emotions can best serve the entrepreneurial self-community.

Dr. Ratner maintains that emotions are cultural phenomena because a) they are socially constructed artifacts b) their characteristics reflect (recapitulate) the social organization of activities and the cultural content of concepts; c) emotions are formed through socialization which ultimately reflects social activities and cultural concepts; and d) emotions support, or reproduce, cultural activities.

He acknowledges that emotions depend upon anatomy and physiology that make a wide range of emotional reactions possible, but he does not believe that anatomy and physiology strictly determine any said emotions. He writes that, "the socially organized ways in which people act, think, and are treated in their cultural activities – e.g., their responsibilities, rights, obligations, behavioral norms, opportunities, rewards — stimulate the development of emotions, are reflected in the characteristics of emotions, and are the ultimate function of emotions."

He describes his views as a revised activity theory of emotions.

He writes in articles published on his web page (http://www.humboldt1.com/~cr2/):

Emphasizing the activity basis of emotions produces the most vivid description and explanation of emotions because it ties them to the vibrant richness of real life. It relates emotions to the dynamic changes which are occurring in the world economy, to the kinds of governments and legal systems people live in, to the manner in which medical care is dispensed, to changes in family relations and the educational systems children grow up in, to the art that is produced and the media that people are exposed to, to spectacular technological innovations/artifacts, and to the changing physical infrastructure of towns and cities. Overlooking activity leads to overlooking many specific cultural features of emotions. It also leads to incomplete explanations of emotions' characteristics, formation, and function.

Dr. Ratner believes that his view places emotions within the realm of rational analysis and transformation. By acknowledging the cultural influence on emotions, Dr. Ratner believes "inappropriate, debilitating, and antisocial emotions can be overcome through altering their cultural characteristics. Since these characteristics rest upon cultural concepts and activities, substantive emotional change among large numbers of people requires changes in cultural activities and cultural concepts — as historical evidence on anger, fear, and love demonstrate."

That culture shapes human emotions and even sensory perception is hard to deny in the face of evidence that anthropology provides. Dr. Ratner points to the comparative studies of emotions in different societies, writing:

Rural Fiji Indians differentiate a whole class of social emotions from individual emotions. Social emotions, such as camaraderie, are positive, constructed only in social interaction (typically religious rituals), experienced by numerous individuals together, experienced only by men who are the sole participants of such interactions, are considered to be expressive acts not as internal states, and are regarded as the only true emotions. Emotions which are experienced by solitary individuals are transient and devalued as quasi-emotions which happen on occasion but which are not constructed according to people's will (Brenneis, 1990).

Cultures vary greatly in the number and kind of emotions they recognize. No one pattern is standard or normal (Russell, 1991). Some cultures have a few broad emotional concepts rather than finely differentiated Western emotional concepts. For example, people in Uganda have an emotional concept that combines elements of Western anger and sadness. Australian aborigines have one concept that combines elements of Western fear and shame. Samoans have one concept that spans Western hate and disgust and does not distinguish them. Conversely, certain societies make exceedingly fine distinctions among emotions. The Pintupi differentiate 15 kinds of fear.

And others compliment Dr. Ratner's point of view through their examination of different cultures and societies. From *Pain: The Gift Nobody Wants* we see:

Whether consciously or subconsciously, the mind largely determines how we perceive pain. Laboratory tests reveal that... people reared in different cultures environments experience pain differently. Jews and Italians react sooner and complain louder than their Northern European counterparts; the Irish have a high tolerance for pain, Eskimos the highest of all.

Some cultural responses to pain nearly defy belief. Societies in Micronesia and the Amazon Valley practice a childbirth custom called *couvade* (from the French word for "hatching"). The mother gives no indication of suffering during delivery. She may break from work a mere two or three hours to give birth, then return to the fields. By all appearances it is the husband who bears the pain: during the delivery and for days afterward he lies in bed, thrashing about and groaning. Indeed, if his travail seems unconvincing, other villagers will question his paternity.

Traditionally, the new mother waits on her husband and sits by his side to entertain the relatives who drop by to offer him congratulations.

Ronald Melzack tells of another cultural anomaly.

In East Africa, men and women undergo an operation – entirely without anesthetics or pain-relieving drugs – called "trepanation," in which the scalp and underlying muscles are cut in order to expose a large area of the skull. The skull is then scraped by the *doktari* as the man or woman sits calmly, without flinching or grimacing, holding a pan under the chin to catch the dripping blood. Films of this procedure are extraordinary to watch... There is no reason to believe that these people are physiologically different in any way. Rather, the operation is accepted by their culture as a procedure that brings relief of chronic pain.

Have East Africans truly mastered the art of surgery without anesthesia? Whose pain is more "real," that claimed by a typical childbearing mother in Europe or a *couvade*-practicing father in Micronesia? Both examples demonstrate the mysterious power of the human mind as it interprets and responds to pain.

Dr. Ratner does acknowledge what we have described as the individual experience, conditioning and programming and recognizes that people can change their emotions and emotional states without considering the broader influence of culture. However, these changes "are superficial in the sense that they do not challenge the basic content, or quality, of emotions," he maintains. Dr. Ratner argues that substantive changes in emotions require understanding and altering the cultural activities and concepts that organize them.

Our worldview agrees with Dr. Ratner's assessment of emotions as being more broadly influenced by culture, but we depart a bit from his conclusion that substantive changes "require understanding and altering the cultural activities and concepts which organize them." Research shows that through independent conditioning and programming, lasting changes to emotional states can be made, independent of altering cultural activities, for instance.

And this point of agreement and departure turns us in the direction of what undergirds emotions and emotional states. Essentially our emotions and emotional states rest on the dual foundation of our value and belief systems. By value we mean what one assigns significance to; and by belief we mean an expectation or conviction one has.

Obviously people assign significance to persons, places and things related to their basic necessities like food, clothing, and shelter, and they have expectations regarding persons, places and things. Thus, it is not hard to recognize that there is a good and sound basis to believe that our values and beliefs pertain more to our cultural experience than our individual experience. This is logical, especially if external factors overwhelmingly outnumber internal factors, in terms of what influences the thinking and behavior of most people.

However, the human being does have free will, and no matter how persuasive the process of cultural activity is, the person must still choose or select the meaning of their experience. Even if all of the options of behavior are presented culturally, the human being's will – their individual experience, conditioning, programming and decision-making – is what determines which behavior they select. And the human capacity to give new meaning to an experience – even outside of the culture with the most influence upon them – resides in the individual, and not the culture.

This is clearly a core element of our view, expressed last chapter. *Suffering is always both a cultural and individual activity, but the decision on how to handle it, and what decisions to make regarding it are always individual in nature.* It is the human being who has the final power to determine what meaning to give an event and how to respond to it.

This points to the tremendous power of the human will, when properly supported.

In his October 26, 1986 speech, "The Will Of God," Minister Louis Farrakhan presents that the human will must be nourished by desire; buttressed and supported by knowledge and faith; directed by love; and protected by attitude. The concepts of 'buttress,' 'support' and 'protect' are similar in very important ways.

The nexus point that we recognize in these three areas is that knowledge, faith and attitude represent the important elements of meaning, expectation, and reconceptualization that are critical to entrepreneurial success, which is always accompanied by pain, suffering and the overcoming of adversity.

What do we mean specifically?

When a shock, loss, or great emotional pain is suffered, the entrepreneur, if they are to turn tragedy into triumph; create a success equal to the temporary defeat they current experience; and rebound; will inevitably have to build will power and persevere through the turmoil. But this can only occur after they have found or given purpose to the experience, or minimized or given proper proportion to the power of that experience to define or limit.

When purpose, meaning, or a valuable lesson that can guide future effort are identified and accepted, an amazing form of energy is released in a person.

These concepts and process are seen clearly in the work of Viktor E. Frankyl, a psychiatrist, advocate of logotherapy and holocaust survivor, and they expose, again, a generally underserved area in the field of psychiatry and psychology.

From two separate writings of Mr. Frankyl we connect these three vital principles. How they relate to the entrepreneur, will hopefully be evident at this point. From his book *The Will To Meaning*, Mr. Frankyl writes (we place boldface on those points where we think agreement with our model most visibly exists):

What I term the existential vacuum constitutes a vacuum in psychiatry today. **Ever more patients complain of a feeling of emptiness and meaninglessness**, which seems to me to derive from two facts. Unlike an animal, man is not told by instincts what he must do. And unlike man in former times, he is no longer told by traditions what he should do. Often he does not even know what he basically wishes to do. Instead, either he wishes to do what other people do (conformism), or he does what other people wish him to do.

I hope that I shall be successful in conveying to the reader my conviction that, despite the crumbling traditions, life holds a meaning for each and every individual, and even more, it retains this meaning literally to his last breath. And the psychiatrist can show his patient that life never ceases to have a meaning. To be sure, he cannot show his patient *what* the meaning is, but he may well show him that there is a meaning, and that life retains it: that it remains meaningful, under any conditions. As logotherapy teaches, **even the tragic and negative aspects of life, such as unavoidable suffering, can be turned into a human achievement by the attitude which he adopts toward his predicament.** In contrast to most of the existential schools of thought, logotherapy is in no way pessimistic, but it is realistic in that it faces the tragic triad of human existence: pain, death, and guilt. Logotherapy may be justly called optimistic, because it **shows the patient how to transform despair into triumph.**

And then from Mr. Frankyl's, *Man's Search For Meaning* we read of the process of reconceptualization and the role of attitude in more detail – specifically in how it was a factor in the survival of holocaust prisoners:

As we said before, **any attempt to restore a man's inner strength in the camp had first to succeed in showing him some future goal.** Nietzsche's words, "He who has a why to live for can bear almost any how," could be the guiding motto for all psychotherapeutic and psychohygenic efforts regarding prisoners. **Whenever there was an opportunity for it, one had to give them a *why* – an aim – for their lives, in order to strengthen them to bear the terrible *how* of their existence.** Woe to him who saw no more sense in his life, no aim, no purpose, and therefore no point in carrying on. He was soon lost. The typical reply with such a man reacted to all encouraging arguments was, "I have nothing more to expect from life anymore." What sort of answer can one give to that?

What was really needed was a fundamental change in our attitude toward life. We had to learn ourselves and, furthermore, we had to teach the despairing men that it did not matter what we expected from life, but rather what life expected from us. We needed to stop asking about the meaning of life, and instead to think of ourselves as those who were being questioned by life – daily and hourly. Our answer must consist, not in talk and meditation, but in right action and right conduct. **Life ultimately means taking responsibility to find the right answer to its problems and to fulfill tasks which it constantly sets for each individual.**

Every entrepreneur – if they are to succeed – must accept that it is this attitude expressed above by Mr. Frankyl that is the only one that makes no excuses for failure, seeing life as a path to define one's self; solve problems; and find answers to difficult questions.

This is the attitude that embraces knowledge, attitude and faith, as the support and buttress for the will power necessary to persevere through life's difficulties.

So now, we are faced with the challenge of building our will in a manner that unites our heart, mind and soul – our volition, cognition, and conation. We can call this process the unification of our self-community.

In order to do so, we will need to work on both our conscious and subconscious minds, both of which affect emotions, thoughts and most importantly – our will power.

First, let's distinguish between both 'minds.'

According to many scientists, psychologists and psychiatrists, our subconscious minds have the greatest impact on creativity, memory, and emotional states. And our conscious minds excel at analysis, logic, math, and processing things in sequence.

We develop our conscious mind significantly by strengthening our ability to perform critical thinking. This aptitude is essential to analyzing opportunities once they are identified and weighing the possibilities, pros and cons, and factors affecting success or failure. It also aids us in planning.

We develop our subconscious mind primarily by three means – suggestion, visualization and prayer. One will find that in the lives of a great many successful entrepreneurs or businesspersons, these three activities were what built and sustained the will to persevere through difficulty, and remain confident in one's ability to obtain the objective.

Although we have tried to be as clear as possible in our arguments and advocacy of the human being's ability to manage and control their thinking and feeling, naturally, there are some reading this who may be thinking – *can one really learn how to think?* The question is far from inappropriate. A good answer to it can be found in *The Cambridge Handbook Of Thinking and Reasoning* edited by Keith J. Holyoak and Robert G. Morrison. In a chapter called, "Learning to Think: The Challenges of Teaching Thinking" by Ron Ritchhart and David N. Perkins we read of the Western perspective on this:

The idea that thinking can be taught, or at least productively nurtured along its way, is ancient. Beginning with the efforts of Plato and the introduction of Socratic dialog, we see attention to improving intelligence and promoting effective thinking as a recurring educational trend throughout the ages. Early in the twentieth century, Dewey (1933) again focused North American's attention on the importance of thinking as an educational aim. At the same time, Selz (1935) was advocating the idea of learning intelligence in Europe. In the 1970s and 1980s, specific programs designed to teach thinking took shape, many of which continue in schools today. Efforts to teach thinking have proliferated in the new millennium, often becoming less programmatic in nature and more integrated within the fabric of schools.

Despite this long history of concern with thinking, one reasonably might ask: Why do we need to "teach" thinking anyway? After all, given reasonable access to a rich cultural surround, individuals readily engage in situated problem solving, observing, classifying, organizing, informal theory building and testing, and so on, without much prompting or even support. Indeed, neurological findings suggest that the brain is hard-wired for just such activities as a basic mechanism for facilitating language development, socialization, and general environment survival. Furthermore, it might be assumed that these basic thinking skills are already enhanced through the regular process of schooling, as students encounter the work of past thinkers, engage in some debate, write essays, and so on. Why then, should we concern ourselves with the teaching and learning of thinking? Addressing these issues entails looking more closely at a fuller range of thinking, particularly what might be called high-end thinking, as well as examining the role education plays in promoting thinking.

Although it is true that the human mind comes readily equipped for a wide variety of thinking tasks, it is equally true that some kinds of thinking run against these natural tendencies. For example, probabilistic thinking is often counterintuitive in nature or doesn't fit well with our experience. We have a natural tendency toward favoring our own positions and interests – my-side bias – that can lead to poor conclusions in decision making and discernments of truth. We frequently draw conclusions and inferences based on limited evidence. The fundamental attribution error names the tendency, particularly in Westerners, to ascribe characterological traits to others based on limited but highly salient encounters.

Furthermore, sometimes our natural ways of making sense of the world actually stand in the way of more effective ways of thinking. For instance, our ability to focus attention can lead to narrowness of vision and insight. Our natural tendency to detect familiar patterns and classify the world can lock us into rigid patterns of action and trap us in the categories we invent. Relatedly, already developed understandings constitute systems of knowledge that are much more readily extended than displaced: We tend to dismiss or recast challenges rather than rethinking our understandings, which is a deep and general problem of learning. Our emotional responses to situations can easily override more deliberative thinking. The phenomenon of group-think, in which the dominant views of the group are readily adopted by group members, can lead to limited processing and discernment of information. These are just a few thinking shortfalls suggesting that truly good thinking does not automatically develop in the natural course of events.

Even when our native tendencies do not lead us astray, they can usually benefit from development. The curiosity of the child for discovering and making sense of the world does not automatically [lead] into an intelligent curiosity for ideas, knowledge, and problem solving, for example. Our ability to see patterns and relationships forms the basis for inductive reasoning, but the latter requires a level of precision and articulation that must be learned. Our natural ability to make inferences becomes much more sophisticated through systematized processes of reasoning with evidence, weighing evidentiary sources, and drawing justifiable conclusions. Indeed, for most thinking abilities that might be considered naturally occurring, one can usually identify a more sophisticated form that such thinking might take with some deliberative nurturing. This type of thinking is what is often referred to as high-end thinking or critical or creative thinking. Such thinking extends beyond a natural processing of the world into the realm of deliberative thinking acts aimed at solving problems, making decisions and forming conclusions.

In light of this commentary on thinking, which indicates its ability to be 'learned,' it might be useful, then, to think of critical and creative thinking, in particular, as acquired skills which work on our conscious minds, and which can have a great impact on how we perceive and interpret reality.

Let's consider a bit more on how thinking is learned, and the relationship between creative and critical thinking, to drive the point home. On the subject from *Becoming A Critical Thinker* by Vincent Ryan Ruggiero we read:

You are staring into space, imagining you are headed for the airport. You picture yourself ready for a month's cruise in the Caribbean, your pockets stuffed with cash. Would this mental process be thinking?

Now imagine you're discussing politics with friends. "It's always the same with politicians," you say. "They're full of promises until they're elected. Then they develop chronic amnesia. I can't see why people get excited over elections." Would you be thinking in this case?

Thinking…is purposeful mental activity. You control it, not vice versa. For the most part, thinking is a conscious activity. Yet the unconscious mind can continue working on a problem after conscious activity stops – for example, while you sleep.

Given this definition, your ruminations about a Caribbean cruise are not thinking but daydreaming, merely following the drift of your fantasies. On the other hand, your discussion of politics may or may not involve thinking. We can't be sure. You might not be thinking at all but just repeating something you'd said or heard before.

Thinking is sometimes regarded as two harmonious processes. One process is the production of ideas (creative thinking), accomplished by *widening* your focus and looking at many possibilities. The key to this process is to resist the temptation to settle for a few familiar ideas. The other process is the evaluation of ideas (critical thinking) accomplished by narrowing your focus, sorting out the ideas you've generated, and identifying the almost reasonable ones.

Both processes are natural activities for human beings, but we rarely perform them well without training and diligent practice.

In a work book available in association with this book and via consulting services at CM Cap (http://www.cmcap.com/) we provide introductory "training and diligent practice" material designed to strengthen our ability in these two crucial areas.

But for now, let's narrow our focus a bit on critical thinking, of which Vincent Ryan Ruggiero states: "Critical thinking entails reflecting on the meaning and significance of observations and the reasonableness of ideas."

Now, an area where critical thinking is most helpful in strengthening our will is in the area of building our value and belief systems so that they support us emotionally and enable us to have the power necessary to pursue an opportunity and overcome adversity.

Beliefs can be constructed through critical and rational thinking and logic.

Remember, beliefs are only expectations and convictions regarding a person, place, thing or event. All one has to do is construct a series of statements (also called propositions in logic) that justify any belief we want to hold as true.

So, for example, say I want to establish a belief that I could start a profitable business selling and repairing laptops in a certain town, I could first start by trying to identify five true statements which support that belief. They could be: 1) there is no other laptop repair or retail store in a twenty mile radius 2) I have spoken to over twenty people in the last 3 months who have expressed a desire for such a store 3) many people don't feel comfortable buying computers online and would like a local expert to guide them through the process 4) I worked at a major laptop retail and repair shop in a major city for five years and understand the business from the inside out 5) there is a major corporate center and shopping plaza within one mile of where I would like to open the store, and both could be a source of early and regular business for my new establishment.

With enough reasons, strong and true enough, I could form a belief that could launch me into business.

By the same token I could challenge the conclusion (another term from logic) – that I should go into this laptop retail and repair business by forming five true statements that support a belief that I should not go into such a business. By comparing the strengths and weaknesses of these two beliefs, I can perhaps make a more informed decision. But if the purpose is to get a belief off the ground, it is best to first construct it as strongly as possible. To make a belief as firm as possible, true and strong arguments should be combined with a lot of emotion (we will get into this in the section on suggestion in influencing the subconscious mind).

Similarly, we can use critical thinking and logic to unearth our value systems and modify them.

An easy exercise in this area would be to list five things that you value about being an entrepreneur, placing each value on a ladder as a rung or step, with the most important value at the top, and the least important at the bottom. For example you might list in order of importance 1) status 2) money 3) sense of accomplishment 4) independence 5) sense of adventure.

As you look at your value ladder you may feel that something is not right – that status, perhaps, is too important, and you want to change that. So you switch your first and third values and end up with a sense of accomplishment as most important. In addition on reflection, you come to think that a sense of adventure has caused you to take too many risks in business and that you want to de-emphasize that and find a more empowering value. So, you remove a sense of adventure from the bottom rung and replace it with "a contribution to my legacy," because you feel this value is very important and it will have the effect of moderating what risks you take out of concern that you might destroy a great reputation and good works for which you will be remembered.

Again, depending upon how accurate these values are in reflecting your personality, character and motives, and depending upon how strongly you identify with them emotionally, they have the power to strengthen and nurture your will.

The act of entrepreneurship is one of creativity, rationality, and persistence. The nexus point between these three factors is the relationship between the conscious and subconscious mind. Understanding this enables one to understand what they can and can't directly do to control their thoughts and emotions.

To put it simply, while knowledge is important, we must admit that we do not need to know every detail of how something works in order to utilize it and benefit from it.

The brain and mind is a classic example.

While no publicly recognized scientist has explained how or why to the masses, it is a fact that even though you may have consciously stopped doing so, your brain and mind continue to work on thoughts, ideas, and concepts you once contemplated. Even when we are pre-occupied with something else or sleeping, our brain continues activity in ways that produce thoughts, concepts, ideas, and answers to questions, seemingly out of nowhere.

Just exactly what is it that causes us to receive a sudden and powerful insight, or what people call an epiphany?

An epiphany is defined by the *Merriam-Webster Online Dictionary* as:

a usually sudden manifestation or perception of the essential nature or meaning of something (2): an intuitive grasp of reality through something (as an event) usually simple and striking (3): an illuminating discovery, realization, or disclosure b: a revealing scene or moment

All of us have experienced such moments – that mixture of new information and understanding combined with emotional stimulation, excitement and pleasure.

Yet, I have never met anyone who could explain what causes this to happen and all of the steps involved.

This comes as no surprise as the most respected scientists of this world are also at a loss.

A June 19, 2009 article in *The Wall Street Journal* "A Wandering Mind Heads Straight Toward Insight" by Robert Lee Hotz explained:

It happened to Archimedes in the bath. To Descartes it took place in bed while watching flies on his ceiling. And to Newton it occurred in an orchard, when he saw an apple fall. Each had a moment of insight. To Archimedes came a way to calculate density and volume; to Descartes, the idea of coordinate geometry; and to Newton, the law of universal gravity.

Five light-bulb moments of understanding that revolutionized science.

In our fables of science and discovery, the crucial role of insight is a cherished theme. To these epiphanies, we owe the concept of alternating electrical current, the discovery of penicillin, and on a less lofty note, the invention of Post-its, ice-cream cones, and Velcro. The burst of mental clarity can be so powerful that, as legend would have it, Archimedes jumped out of his tub and ran naked through the streets, shouting to his startled neighbors: "Eureka! I've got it."

In today's innovation economy, engineers, economists and policy makers are eager to foster creative thinking among knowledge workers. Until recently, these sorts of revelations were too elusive for serious scientific study. Scholars suspect the story of Archimedes isn't even entirely true. Lately, though, researchers have been able to document the brain's behavior during Eureka moments by recording brain-wave patterns and imaging the neural circuits that become active as volunteers struggle to solve anagrams, riddles and other brain teasers.

Following the brain as it rises to a mental challenge, scientists are seeking their own insights into these light-bulb flashes of understanding, but they are as hard to define clinically as they are to study in a lab.

Much of this difficulty in definition and study revolves around the subconscious mind, and the nexus point between it and our conscious mind.

The subconscious mind is much more complicated than the conscious mind, and the three means of reaching it that our model recommends –

suggestion, visualization and prayer – warrant some more elaboration. Here is a bit more on each:

Suggestion. As we have seen from our earlier look at advertising and psychological warfare – human beings are suggestible, to varying degrees, in different states of mind. But generally speaking, the more relaxed and more comfortable (on one extreme) or the more intense of an emotional state one experiences at the time a suggestion is made (on the other extreme) the more likely it is to take root.

The reason that both of these extremes are viable is because of how the brain works.

The relaxed state of mind works because of our susceptibility to suggestion when our brains are operating at certain brain waves.

We have four brain waves, measured in cycles per second: Beta is one, which is an alert state where the brain pulses at 13 to 30 cycles per second. As you relax, you go into another state – the Alpha cycle – which is 8 to 12 cycles per second. Next is Theta, 4 to 8 cycles per second and finally, Delta, which is less than 4 cycles per second. In the states of relaxation other than beta, the person is open to suggestion, and in the theta and delta cycles, the brain has more power to create and sustain images in response to detailed suggestions.

With a trusted companion, a tape recorder and even only yourself, your hearing of the repetition of certain statements, suggesting a desired outcome in detail, can strengthen your will, as your subconscious mind is less likely to reject suggestions while one is in this state.

To learn more about auto suggestion (words that come from ourselves, also known as 'self suggestion') and heterosuggestion (words which come from others) we consult *The Power Of Your Subconscious Mind* by Joseph Murphy and *Think And Grow Rich A Black Choice* by Dennis Kimbro:

First Dr. Murphy writes, in a section called "How Autosuggestion Banishes Fear":

The term *autosuggestion* means suggesting something definite and specific to oneself. Like any tool, wrongly used it can cause harm, but used properly it can be extremely helpful.

Janet R. was a talented young sister. She was invited to try out for an important role in an opera production. She desperately wanted to audition, but she was also terribly apprehensive.

Three times before, when she had sung for directors, she had failed miserably. The reason was fear of failure. She had a wonderful voice, but she had been saying to herself, "When the time comes for me to sing, I'll sound awful. I'll never get the role. They won't like me. They'll wonder how I have the nerve even to try out. I'll go, but I know it'll be a failure."

Her subconscious mind accepted these negative autosuggestions as a request. It proceeded to manifest them and bring them into her experience. The cause was an involuntary autosuggestion. Her fears had become emotionalized and subjectified thoughts that in turn became her reality.

This young sister was able to overcome the force of her negative autosuggestions. She accomplished this by countering them with positive autosuggestion. What she did was this. Three times a day, she went alone into a quiet room. She sat down comfortably in an armchair, relaxed her body, and closed her eyes. She stilled her mind and body as best she could. Physical inertia favors mental passivity and renders the mind more receptive to suggestion.

To counteract the fear suggestion, she repeated to herself, "I sing beautifully. I am poised, serene, confident, and calm." At each sitting she repeated this statement slowly, quietly, and with feeling from five to ten times. She had three such sittings during the day and one immediately before going to sleep.

After one week, she was completely poised and confident. When the fateful day came, she gave a wonderful audition and was cast in the part.

In another section called, "Some Comments On Heterosuggestion" Dr. Murphy writes:

The term *heterosuggestion* means suggestion from another person. In all ages and in every part of the world, the power of suggestion has played a dominant part in the life and thought of humankind. Political creeds, religious beliefs, and cultural customs all flourish and perpetuate themselves through the power of hetero-suggestion.

Suggestion can be used as a tool to discipline and control ourselves. However, it can also be used to take control and command over others who have not been taught to understand the laws of mind. In its constructive form it is wonderful and magnificent. In its negative aspects it is one of the most destructive of all the response patterns of the mind. Its results can be enduring patterns of misery, failure, suffering, sickness, and disaster.

Dr. Murphy continues in a section called, "Have You Accepted Any Of These?" with the following:

From the day we are born, we are bombarded with negative suggestions. Not knowing how to counter them, we unconsciously accept them and bring them into being as our experience.

Here are some examples of negative suggestions:

- You can't.
- You'll never amount to anything.
- You mustn't.
- You'll fail.
- You haven't got a chance.
- You're all wrong
- It's no use.
- It's not what you know but who you know.
- The world is going to the dogs.
- What's the use, nobody cares.
- There's no point to trying so hard.
- You're too old now.
- Things are getting worse and worse.
- Life is an endless grind.
- Love is for the birds.
- You just can't win.
- Watch out, you'll catch a terrible disease.
- You can't trust a soul.

By accepting heterosuggestions of this kind, you collaborate in bringing them to pass. As a child, you were helpless when faced with the suggestions of others who were important to you. You did not know any better. The mind, both conscious and unconscious, was a mystery you did not even wonder about.

As an adult, however, you are able to make choices. You can use constructive autosuggestion, which is a reconditioning therapy, to change the impressions made on you in the past. The first step is to make yourself aware of the heterosuggestions that are operating on you. Unexamined, they can create behavior patterns that cause failure in your personal and social life. Constructive autosuggestion can release you from the mass of negative verbal conditioning that might otherwise distort your life pattern, making the development of good habits difficult or even impossible.

In *Think and Grow Rich A Black Choice* we read:

Self-suggestion. How many times have you heard it said, "Just believe you can do it and you can!" Many stories have been told of the great reserves of the subconscious mind, how under its direction and by imparting its enormous strength, frail men and women have been able to perform feats far beyond their normal powers. It is the act of believing that is the starting force or generating action that leads great men and women to accomplishment. "Come on, men, we can beat them," shouts someone in command. Whether in a game, or on a battlefield, or in the strife of life, that sudden voicing of belief, challenging and electrifying, reverses the tide. "I can do it...I can do it...*I can do it!*"

Similarly, a man engaged in concentrated effort often talks to the man within. This "self-talk" or "self-suggestion," as it has been called, is completely self-contained. Self-talk is often the power that inspires the machinery of achievement into operation, and causes the subconscious mind to begin its creative work. It is the repetition of words or phrases that transforms faith into belief, and finally into accomplishment. Autosuggestion can take the form of thinking, seeing, hearing, feeling, tasting, and smelling through the power of your imagination.

...These are fundamentals of major importance that prepare the mind for the expression of faith. The man who has faith in himself brings under control and direction those powers of his subconscious. He also inspires a similar feeling in the minds and hearts of others with whom he comes in contact. A study of achievers will disclose the proof that those who "arrive" or "do things" are marked by a deep intuitive faith in themselves. These individuals overcome temporary defeat and use their failures as stepping-stones to ultimate victory.

Earlier we mentioned the two emotional states best suited for suggestion – that of deep relaxation and that of emotional intensity. The reason why the other extreme – an intense emotional state – is also fertile ground for a person to receive a suggestion is because of the way the brain and nerves make associations.

Whenever you are in an intense emotional state, your brain begins to look for the reason why. It looks to see whatever is happening at the same time this emotion is being experienced, and it begins to look for whatever appears unique – something not normal or usual according to one's memory and neural associations. The brain makes an association – right or wrong – and it files it into our memories so that it can be checked again quickly in the future. This process is happening all of the time.

So, therefore if a person is able to suggest something to themselves while they are in a pleasurable or positive state of mind they actually create a neural pathway which is actually a physical connection in the body. With suggestions repeated with emotional intensely, in a state of belief, a link between that feeling and that statement and attitude will be made even stronger.

In his book, *Awaken The Giant Within*, in describing the power of a neural pathway, Anthony Robbins writes, "When we do something for the first time, we create a physical connection, a thin strand that allows us to re-access that emotion or behavior again in the future. Think of it this way: each time we repeat the behavior, the connection strengthens. We add another strand to our neural connection. With enough repetitions and emotional intensity, we can add many strands simultaneously, increasing the tensile strength of this emotional or behavioral pattern until eventually we have a 'trunk line' to this behavior or feeling. This is when we find ourselves compelled to feel these feelings or behave in this way consistently."

Yes, thoughts and feelings that we have been made to believe are formless, are in actuality real physical and material realities.

Visualization. What is visualization? From *Visualization and Concentration* by Fenwicke L. Holmes writes:

One may be said to have a concrete idea of a thing if he can make a mental picture of it. A true mental picture has definiteness of detail, outline, and finish. Such a picture cannot be made in ignorance of the subject, and therefore the making of it means study, preparation, fitness. The inventor must understand something of principles in order in order to create the mechanism.

…The rules of visualization are simple. First, decide what you want. You cannot hope to create what is indistinct as a desire. My first question to all… is, "What do you want?" If you do not know, find out. Have a desire, an ambition, a purpose.

Second, see it as clearly with mental vision as you can.

Shakti Gawain – author of *Creative Visualization: Use the Power of Your Imagination to Create What You Want in Life*, writes: "In creative visualization you use your imagination to create a clear image of something you wish to manifest. Then you continue to focus on the idea or picture regularly, giving it positive energy until it becomes objective reality; in other words, until you actually achieve what you have been visualizing."

Visualization expert, Lee Pulos describes the process more bluntly when he says in *The Power Of Visualization*, "Visualization is a kind of pretending that becomes more real with practice." In an introduction and part of a session on his audio tape series he explains his evolution into the field, and the nature and power of the visualization process:

Like yourself I have been unconsciously using visualization all of my life. I day-dreamed excessively as a youngster, creating scenarios that sometimes went beyond imagination. For a number of reasons, valid at the time, I became a high-school drop-out at the age of 16, ran away from home, and joined the Navy. Fortunately I was assigned to a psychologist's office, assisting in the administering of paper and pencil tests. I loved what I was doing and the fire was lit. I wanted to become a psychologist. Day in and day out, I dreamed, imagined, and fantasized, every facet of my career before taking special tests that allowed me to enter college as a veteran on the G.I. Bill. The waking dreams continued and today imaging and visualizing, or programming my dreams is as much a part of my daily routine as eating or working out.

I have used visualization from everything ranging from accelerating the healing response following knee surgery, to achieving financial goals and achieving success as an author...

There's no end to modern day examples of achieving goals through visualization. In his classic self-help book, *Psycho-Cybernetics*, Dr. Maxwell Maltz described how Conrad Hilton created mental pictures of himself owning a hotel before he acquired his first one. James Hickman reported that when Bruce Jenner was preparing for his 1976 Olympic decathlon, for which he won the gold medal, he would train by doing a mental workout with a hurdle in his living room, each evening after dinner. These mental movies and rehearsals became so ingrained into his subconscious that the visualizations continued during sleep and his wife could always tell which event he was imaging by the way his body moved and angled while dreaming. Incidentally, Jenner claimed that most of his athletic successes were due to his strict regimen of mental practice since age 5, as he didn't feel he was a natural athlete.

...But where does the power of visualization come from? Is it a relatively new concept of the twentieth century or is it simply a New Age idea as practiced by persons in spiritual disciplines such as meditation and healing?

The earliest cultures dating from 60,000 B.C. to 10,000 B.C. believed in the power of the image to effect reality...

Philosophers and priests of every culture believed in the primacy of mind over material things and used visualization as a tool for personal growth and re-birth. The Hermetic philosophers of Egypt over 4,000 years ago, believed that mental images could transmute hate into love, fear into courage, illness into health. During the Middle Ages, powerful forms of focused visual concentration became the basic tool of alchemy – the idea of being able to transmute lead into gold or moving matter from one molecular structure or frequency domain into another.

Another powerful visualization practice described by ancient mystics and psychiatrist Carl Jung was to focus on ...a beautifully balanced circle of colors, images and symbols, as a technique for centering and unifying the different parts of the psyche and mind. This would probably be the ancient equivalent for training persons to use both hemispheres for full brain thinking.

There are countless modern day examples of mental rehearsal.

Roger Bannister claims he broke the four-minute mile because he visualized it many times before his historic race in 1954. The successful East German bobsled team at the 1980 Winter Olympics reported that for every actual run down the course, the team members visually and successfully ran the course 100 times – more time was spent mentally rehearsing than actually doing training runs on the course.

…What can I do to become a better visualizer? How can I create more vivid images? Are there exercises that will help me create clear mental pictures? 'It is so frustrating to be able to close my eyes and not be able to see anything.' The answer of course is that with relatively little training most people can become excellent visualizers. The ability to visualize like any other talent is distributed in the population within the range of the now familiar bell-shaped curve. Approximately 6 to 10% of the population are visualizing virtuosos. They have more recently been identified as 'fantasy-prone' individuals. Some of their characteristics are – a very active and imaginative fantasy life; a great capacity for self-absorption and losing themselves in their activities, creative activities come easily for them, they are usually quite suggestible and they make excellent hypnotic subjects. The rest of us have varying degrees of proficiency in creating mental movies. But with practice we can very quickly move ourselves up to within the virtuoso range. Of course, no one needs to be reminded that everyone in the world visualizes vividly, in color, every night during our two hours or so of dream time.

…the details of mental imagery are just as important or even more so, in some instances, than the vividness of an image. True. However, as you focus on the details of a specific outcome that you are programming for your life, you will find that the image will become increasingly more lucid, thereby making it more real for the subconscious. It would be analogous to listening to music through quadraphonic speakers, adding new dimensions to your experiencing rather than through the single channel limitations of one speaker. By increasing the realness of an image it becomes more likely that the mental picture will "take" with your deeper mind and increase the likelihood of that reality manifesting in your life.

As I reviewed the history of creative imagination and visualization I was struck by the number of disciplines over the ages that emphasize the importance of regular practice to enhance the vividness of closed eye visualization…

In the late 1800s geneticist and statistician Sir Francis Galton attended several sessions by a French educator who trained his students to visualize clearly in three dimensions. The students were urged to examine an object carefully so they could form a clear mental image. Next, they were directed to draw it in mid-air so they could develop muscular memories of the object. After practicing for several weeks, the students could summon images with ease and had developed the capacity for clear, vivid images. Conversely, some of the students neglected to continue their practice and their ability for visualizing atrophied. This is true of any system of the body that is not nurtured. In other words, *use it or lose it.*

The use of imagery in personal growth and psycho-therapy was pioneered by Sigmund Freud. He would evoke images by pressing on his patients' foreheads. Later, by having his patients recline on a couch with eyes closed, they would free-associate to whatever thoughts would enter their minds. With very little practice his patients began to report a flooding of images which in time became a waking dream.

Early in my career I trained in psycho-analytic therapy and was astonished at how easily I could evoke images by simply free-associating to my thoughts, and then, actively describing what appeared on my minds' eye screen. The more I described the detail in my images the more clearer they became.

Freud's colleague, Carl Jung regarded mental imagery to be a fundamental creative aspect of the psyche for personal growth. He developed the technique of active imagination that he considered superior to dreams in quickening psychological development. After World War II, psychiatrists Hans Carl Loiner and Robert Desoille developed a technique called guided-affective imagery which evoked rich, waking dreams and improved a person's capacity for directing clear mental images.

Again, I took special training in these traditions as I realized how simple and how powerful these techniques were for developing insights and accelerating personal growth.

The various imaging techniques have similar commonalities and they have all been brought together in a book entitled, *Psycho-Synthesis* by Roberto Assagioli.

In my personal experiences, I was directed to lie down, progressively relax each of my muscle groupings, and then was asked to begin describing every detail of what was on my mind's eye screen. Initially there was just the darkness of my closed eye lid. But as I began to actively describe, out loud, each small shadow, blob, germinal image, or phosphene (which looks like a comet going across your visual field), within minutes the imagery became clearer, richer and more vivid. I was elated, as I always thought of myself as a non-visualizer in those days. My patients began to report similar experiences improving their visualizations and I became convinced that everyone has the potential and the innate capacity for creating clear, mental movies.

The reason for providing you with this brief historical background on enhancing imagery is to introduce you to the process we will be using to help you learn clear easy-to-sense visual images. The technique has been labeled, 'image streaming.'

...Image streaming has been widely used for personal growth, corporate problem solving and think-tanking. An additional and unexpected benefit is that in at least one study with physics students at South West State University in Minnesota, the students experienced an average 20 point increase in their I.Q.'s after only 25 hours of practicing image streaming. Your left brains are probably wondering, 'hey how can that be?' How can a person increase their I.Q. when intelligence is considered – in most professional circles – to be inborn and determined by the laws of heredity?

I initially subscribed to that notion, even though many psychologists could not come up with an agreed upon definition of intelligence other than what I.Q. tests measured.

Today, one of the most recurring themes in defining intelligence is that *it is the art of paying attention.* Thus, image streaming relies on visualizing, paying attention to the minutest of details, free association, *some* intellectual analysis and speaking out loud. By doing all these functions simultaneously, one ends up stimulating different brain regions. This is referred to...as pole-bridging which links sub cortical or subconscious functions to the visual cortex, the speech area, sensory motor areas of the bridge, and the frontal lobes into single combined activities.

Thus, intelligence could be increased by building up communication channels from disparate parts of the brain.

There certainly is some support for this theory from several laboratories investigating brain function. As animals are hyper-stimulated in learning tasks, after as little as two weeks training, the wiring of their brains become denser and more complex. The neurons or brain cells become thicker in the axon or stem. And the synapses which are glove-like endings at the end of the axone develop additional fingers.

In PET scans and other imaging studies of more intelligent persons' brains the wiring is indeed more complex but it takes less energy or work to solve problems. Thus, image streaming could conceivably increase overall intelligence in problem-solving. Long term image streamers have reported an increase in their ability to sustain focus and concentrate; a much better attention span; an improvement in their powers of observation; a sharpening of one's awareness of the world in general *and* an increase of the vividness, frequency and recall of their dreams not to mention, of course, regaining the lucid visualizing abilities they once had as children.

Visualization, like suggestion best takes place when one is relaxed or in a peak emotional state. The reasons are essentially the same but the techniques are a little different. In his book, Lee Pulos recommends six different ways to visualize with five different forms of imagery in a deep state of relaxation. Anthony Robbins recommends imagining whatever it is you are trying to accomplish and rehearse it again, over and over again, with emotional intensity.

Both approaches instill belief, persistence and perseverance in the pursuit of an objective. In our workbook we offer an easy introductory visualization regimen.

Visualization and imagination affect the brain and mind in real physical ways, proving that such 'unseen' forces as intention, faith, motivation, belief, and conviction are associated with our anatomy and physiology and can be influenced through programming and conditioning.

Some may not understand why visualization and affirmation work in two extreme states of mind – deep relaxation or an intense peak emotional state. This confusion, and some may say apparent contradiction, points again to the reality that scientists don't yet fully understand how the brain and mind works and why some insights and ideas come to individuals in different states of mind and thinking processes.

For some, it is rational thought and reasoning that lead to insight, for others, it is intense relaxation, and still more it is random daydreaming and an apparent idle mind.

In the previously referred to article, "A Wandering Mind Heads Straight Toward Insight" we read:

To be sure, we've all had our "Aha" moments. They materialize without warning, often through an unconscious shift in mental perspective that can abruptly alter how we perceive a problem. "An 'aha' moment is any sudden comprehension that allows you to see something in a different light," says psychologist John Kounios at Drexel University in Philadelphia. "It could be the solution to a problem; it could be getting a joke; or suddenly recognizing a face. It could be realizing that a friend of yours is not really a friend."

These sudden insights, they found, are the culmination of an intense and complex series of brain states that require more neural resources than methodical reasoning. People who solve problems through insight generate different patterns of brain waves than those who solve problems analytically. "Your brain is really working quite hard before this moment of insight," says psychologist Mark Wheeler at the University of Pittsburgh. "There is a lot going on behind the scenes."

In fact, our brain may be most actively engaged when our mind is wandering and we've actually lost track of our thoughts, a new brain-scanning study suggests. "Solving a problem with insight is fundamentally different from solving a problem analytically," Dr. Kounios says. "There really are different brain mechanisms involved."

By most measures, we spend about a third of our time daydreaming, yet our brain is unusually active during these seemingly idle moments. Left to its own devices, our brain activates several areas associated with complex problem solving, which researchers had previously assumed were dormant during daydreams. Moreover, it appears to be the only time these areas work in unison.

"People assumed that when your mind wandered it was empty," says cognitive neuroscientist Kalina Christoff at the University of British Columbia in Vancouver, who reported the findings last month in the Proceedings of the National Academy of Sciences. As measured by brain activity, however, "mind wandering is a much more active state than we ever imagined, much more active than during reasoning with a complex problem."

She suspects that the flypaper of an unfocused mind may trap new ideas and unexpected associations more effectively than methodical reasoning. That may create the mental framework for new ideas. "You can see regions of these networks becoming active just prior to people arriving at an insight," she says.

In a series of experiments over the past five years, Dr. Kounios and his collaborator Mark Jung-Beeman at Northwestern University used brain scanners and EEG sensors to study insights taking form below the surface of self-awareness. They recorded the neural activity of volunteers wrestling with word puzzles and scanned their brains as they sought solutions.

Some volunteers found answers by methodically working through the possibilities. Some were stumped. For others, even though the solution seemed to come out of nowhere, they had no doubt it was correct.

In those cases, the EEG recordings revealed a distinctive flash of gamma waves emanating from the brain's right hemisphere, which is involved in handling associations and assembling elements of a problem. The brain broadcast that signal one-third of a second before a volunteer experienced their conscious moment of insight – an eternity at the speed of thought.

The scientists may have recorded the first snapshots of a Eureka moment. "It almost certainly reflects the popping into awareness of a solution," says Dr. Kounios.

In addition, they found that tell-tale burst of gamma waves was almost always preceded by a change in alpha brain-wave intensity in the visual cortex, which controls what we see. They took it as evidence that the brain was dampening the neurons there similar to the way we consciously close our eyes to concentrate.

"You want to quiet the noise in your head to solidify that fragile germ of an idea," says Dr. Jung-Beeman at Northwestern.

At the University of London's Goldsmith College, psychologist Joydeep Bhattacharya also has been probing for insight moments by peppering people with verbal puzzles.

By monitoring their brain waves, he saw a pattern of high frequency neural activity in the right frontal cortex that identified in advance who would solve a puzzle through insight and who would not. It appeared up to eight seconds before the answer to a problem dawned on the test subject, Dr. Bhattacharya reported in the current edition of the Journal of Cognitive Neuroscience.

"It's unsettling," says Dr. Bhattacharya. "The brain knows but we don't."

So far, no one knows why problems sometimes trigger an insight or what makes us more inclined to the Eureka experience at some moments but not at others. Insight does favor a prepared mind, researchers determined.

Even before we are presented with a problem, our state of mind can affect whether or not we will likely resort to insightful thinking. People in a positive mood were more likely to experience an insight, researchers at Drexel and Northwestern found. "How you are thinking beforehand is going to affect what you do with the problems you get," Dr. Jung-Beeman says.

By probing the anatomy of 'aha,' researchers hope for clues to how brain tissue can manufacture a new idea. "Insight is crucial to intellect," Dr. Bhattacharya says.

Taken together, these findings highlight a paradox of mental life. They remind us that much of our creative thought is the product of neurons and nerve chemistry outside our awareness and beyond our direct control.

"We often assume that if we don't notice our thoughts they don't exist," says Dr. Christoff in Vancouver, "When we don't notice them is when we may be thinking most creatively."

One aspect of this phenomenon should not be a mystery, especially if you have gotten this far in *The Entrepreneurial Secret* (or simply just read the last chapter) and that is, suffering can produce various states of mind and cause people to open themselves up to alternative ways of thinking and behavior.

We can predict that intense emotional suffering can force people to think more rationally and creatively. *But the route people choose in order to resolve such suffering or which kind of thinking is best suited to each individual* cannot be predicted by us.

Prayer. In writing this book I conducted quite a bit of research on prayer from a variety of perspectives, particularly theological, psychological, and anthropological. While each area of study seems to have constructed a worldview of prayer that is incompatible with the other, a common and unified theme does seem to emerge from a review and comparison of available literature on the subject. And that theme is prayer represents some form of communication – verbal expression, thought, emotion and movement – regarding the relationship between one's self and the unseen (or Unseen).

The question of to what, whom (or Whom) a prayer might be directed is important, but it starts the dialogue several stages beyond where it could begin and where it might be more likely to generate broad reasoned discussion – between the religious, agnostic and atheistic individual, for example, and the communities they may represent.

That it can be argued that prayer can be practiced and take place where there exists no organized belief in God or religion is not disputed.

Furthermore, not every prayer is a communication directed toward any object in particular. Prayers can be petitions, pleas, rhetoric, the expression of a desire, a confession, an invocation, praise, thanksgiving, venting, or simply thinking.

But of all of these possible actions that qualify as prayer, the debate over what constitutes a prayer essentially revolves around two questions and the difficulty in verifying the effect of prayer. Making this point clear is Anna Wierzbicka whose analysis, "What is Prayer? In Search of a Definition" is included in the book, *The Human Side Of Prayer*.

She writes:

The question whether prayer involves 'saying something' or 'saying something to someone' is as interesting as it is difficult. The intention is, no doubt, to say something *to someone*; it is less clear, however, whether or not the actual words are necessarily addressed to someone. One argument in favor of just 'saying something' (without 'to someone') could be based on the prayer of people who don't believe in God and who nonetheless try to reach him. This applies, for example, to Levin's prayer in Tolstoy's *Anna Karenina* (at his brother Nikolai's deathbed):

"During the sacrament Levin prayed too, and did what he had done a thousand times before, unbeliever as he was" (Tolstoy, 1982, p.522).

The same scene, however, could also be interpreted as yielding support to the opposite hypothesis, for Tolstoy continues as follows:

'Addressing himself to God, he said, 'If Thou does exist, heal this man (it would not be the first time such a thing has happened) and Thou wilt save him and me."

So, the proof that prayer is made to an object (Object) and that such an object (or Object) 'hears' the prayer and responds accordingly is hard to come by in a way that would satisfy individuals from a variety of backgrounds and enable agreement. Often, in discussions on prayer, a greater emphasis is placed upon the question of the existence and power of the object (or Object) of prayer as opposed to the process and other aspects of prayer that are more accessible and easier to consider and agree upon.

Even for Believers in a Supreme Being and External Reality to Whom much of prayer is directed, it is clear that in significant ways the prayer activity is meant to signify, educate, and demonstrate principles *more for the benefit of the person making the prayer* than *to Whom* they are directing it.

At other times, the relationship between the two parties (the prayer-maker and the Object of prayer) is what is being focused upon in the act of prayer. I discussed this with 96-year old Nation Of Islam Minister Lucius Bey, considered the 'dean' of all of the Honorable Elijah Muhammad's Ministers, as early as the time period when Malcolm X became a registered member of the Nation. In fact, Minister Lucius Bey – who joined the Nation in 1946 – was living in the home of the Honorable Elijah Muhammad when Malcolm X was in prison.

According to Minister Bey many of the letters Malcolm X wrote from jail to the Honorable Elijah Muhammad would be read by Mr. Muhammad to Minister Bey, right at the dinner table, before Malcolm X was released from prison in 1952.

In an interview published at BlackElectorate.com in October of 2004 (http://www.blackelectorate.com/) I discussed the principles of prayer with Minister Bey:

Cedric Muhammad: You have shared this with me before. Could you go through just some of what you learned from the Honorable Elijah Muhammad about the movements in prayer?

Minister Lucius Bey: Well, I learned that the different movements were an indication of an outward expression of something inwardly. Just as you would put your hands up to your ear and say Allah-u-Akbar four times turning, you are acknowledging outwardly that Allah is the God of the East, North, West, and South, and that your ears are open to hear him. Well, now if we don't mean that from the heart then we just went through a formality with no substance. The substance is carried out in our actual heart and practice. And all of the different bows are different forms of our condition and position of what Allah has brought us from. (The significance of the "ruku" position is that) He brought us from the earth (that is why) we look down. And (the sitting and prostrate positions – "jalsah" and "sajdah") we were once crawling like a baby – like an animal even. Now we stand up (in the qiyam position), and since we stand up, our prayers are to keep us reminded of what Allah has brought us from. That ought to keep us strong. But sometimes we just go through the (motions). And I just give a general statement sometimes that the different forms (of prayer) are an outward expression of an inward struggle.

Prayer is about more than the reality or existence of a Supreme Being, prophets, ancestor spirits, or supernatural forces. It is about one's internal conversation and thinking regarding themselves and the unseen – whether a Supreme Being or an unfulfilled desire or goal.

This is particularly relevant to our model of the entrepreneurial process – one's view of self and the ability for one to perceive an opportunity (that which was 'unseen' previously) and envision (visualizing the unseen) how to obtain it. The entrepreneurial act therefore has much in common with the process of prayer and perhaps can be aided by it.

Prayer, regardless to which of its most common definitions one accepts, invariably grows out of a form of self-consciousness, and the recognition of an inner self. In his 1916 book, *The Psychology Of Religion*, George Albert Coe, according to *The Human Side Of Prayer* "found the functions of prayer in its coherence and in our capacity to beget 'the confidence that tends toward victory over difficulties.'" In his book, Mr. Coe writes that prayer may be "the organization in to the self of the very things that threaten to disorganize it."

Clearly Mr. Coe's view of prayer is compatible with ours in that prayer is an act that apparently bolsters the Will and unites 'self.' And the act of prayer, in terms of its communication connects the self, where it currently is, with that which is outside of it – not only in terms of another being or a 'supernatural force,' but also the unseen reality that the prayerful one longs to see or desires. In that sense it is what Coe referred to as a "social form of personal self-realization."

But Coe's belief that prayer contributes to 'the confidence that tends toward victory over difficulties' is an important one to us, particularly as it relates to what we have already put forth regarding the necessity of suffering and the overcoming of adversity and difficulty in the entrepreneurial process.

The belief in prayer's ability to increase one's confidence is shared by millions, if not billions of people. That prayer has enabled a person to overcome difficulties is also a widely held position. But if prayer is an act that organizes the self, bringing it closer to what is currently unseen (in the common physical sense of that word), then it can be said to have the same effect as suggestion. In fact some have even considered prayer as a form of suggestion or auto-suggestion.

But if prayer is a 'form of internal conversation," capable of organizing the self and enabling it to obtain victory over difficulties, as Coe wrote, how is this done? Coe describes a process, the "evolution of prayer" that starts with a desire and "ends as the organization of one's own desires into a system of desires recognized as superior and then made one's own."

In *The Psychology Of Religion* he offers five propositions on the general study of human desires, which explain his view that desire evolves into an organized value system, in the self and society:

First, human desire is not extinguished when its immediate satisfaction is attained. This is plain enough in the case of our higher values. Knowledge, once attained, does not dampen but inflames the desire for knowledge. The acquisition of money rarely fails to restimulate and intensify the process of acquisition. Even in our directly instinctive desires a parallel overflow occurs. Our so-called "bestial" excesses are hardly bestial, for the way of a beast is to satisfy his appetite and then stop, whereas the way of a man is to extend his appetite. And appetite, as we have seen, does not always move upon a single level statically fixed, but rather grows refined, and sometimes becomes the servitor of ideal ends. Note, for example, how a single term, "love," is used for all grades of reaction, from merely instinctive sex attraction to the most deliberate self-devotion in which the original biological connotation has completely disappeared.

Secondly, human desires undergo a process of organization toward the unity of the individual. The way of human desiring is to take account of wants. Thereby we objectify our desires, compare them, and arrange them in scales, more or less refined...

Thirdly, human desires come thus to include a desire to have desires. The desires of the lower animals become organized after a fashion. Rats and mice learn not to touch the tempting morsel that the trap displays. A frog that is making for shore stops – "freezes" – if a bass approaches. Here is a kind of regulation of desire. Men as well as other species are molded in this stern manner. But men mold themselves. They form desires, not merely to have this or that object, but also to be this or that kind of man. Here lies the deeper meaning of education. It is socially organized desire that certain desires rather than others should control human life.

Fourthly, human desires undergo a process of organization toward social as well as individual unity. Education considered as socially organized desire is only one instance. That the individual is not a mere individual, but that individuality itself has a social reference, is now a commonplace of genetic psychology.

Fifthly, human desire, growing by what it feeds on, refining itself, judging itself, organizing itself, becomes also desire for the conservation of the human desire-and-satisfaction type of experience. Education, for example, has already come to involve enormous expenditure for ends that are to be realized only gradually after the death of those who pay the cost. National consciousness in general endows the future with present value. We shall not fully understand the passion of the patriot until we see within the economic causation of national conduct a desire that economic values shall be assured to future generations, and, within loyalty to a people's culture or institution, the identification of present interests with history yet to be made. The larger thought, too, of a world-destiny, or even of cosmic meaning, involves a present desire that desire-and-satisfaction as we know it may never end. Thus we desire to endow our values with the added value of time-defiance.

What name have we for this whole desire-within-desire, this whole revaluation of values that both makes us individuals and organize us into society? In each phase of life a part of the process appears. We revalue the seeing of the eye and the hearing of the ear, and aesthetic values emerge, art is born. We reflect upon what we want when man meets man, and moral values emerge as a control even of the instincts out of which they arise. So, also, out of relatively thoughtless thinking there springs a search for norms of thought and for a self-evidencing or rational standpoint. Here, then, are three points at which desire has organized itself by reference to ideal values – aesthetic values, ethical values, and noetic values [*author's note*: noetic means: of, relating to, or based on the intellect]. That this is a characteristic human process probably no one will deny.

The concept of a person in prayer moving from an initial desire to a multiple of desires, into a superior system of desires that is claimed by that person is relevant to the value of prayer to an entrepreneur. Prayer's ability to feed and organize desire(s) in a way that causes one to gain 'the confidence that tends toward victory over difficulties,' as Coe wrote, makes it a valuable weapon in the arsenal of a person facing difficulty after difficulty.

What George Albert Coe saw regarding the relationship between prayer and desire, from the perspective of psychology, others recognize, in different and very profound ways.

In his Study Guide # 6: Building The Will Part II, Minister Louis Farrakhan says, "…constant Prayer feeds, directs and elevates Desire…" In another section he writes, "This study course 'Self-Improvement: The Basis For Community Development' is centered around the action of Prayer as the root of our success or failure in fulfilling our purpose in life. Prayer is the most humble and the most exalted state of man at the same time."

In another section Minister Farrakhan states:

… We must overcome the force from within that would cause us to retreat and turn our backs on the difficulties we must overcome; we must resist the internal force that cause us to hoard and withhold; we are created impatient, that is, we are fretful when under stress and niggardly when we receive the benefits of life (from the Beneficent). The Holy Qur'an tells us plainly, that we possess these traits, whether we admit them or not, and we will continue to walk under the weight of them, EXCEPT THOSE WHO PRAY…WHO ARE CONSTANT AT THEIR PRAYER…

One can see a powerful relationship between prayer, desire and will-power in what Minister Farrakhan is articulating when his previous statement "…constant Prayer feeds, directs and elevates Desire…" is connected with this excerpt of the study guide:

Before He said "Be!", Allah (God) had the DESIRE to BE. DESIRE is the food that builds the Will. Desire causes us to achieve whatever the object of our desire is. You will recall that Desire was defined in the GLOSSARY in Study Guide 3, "Overcoming Difficulty" [*author's note*: that definition was, 'An earnest wishing for something; longing; yearning. A request or prayer']. Remember Minister Farrakhan's words from analysis of Question # 3 of that study guide:

"The *desire* to attain a goal brings us face-to-face with difficulty. When we undergo the trial of difficulty, the trial may be so intense that it <u>extinguishes the light of the desire to attain the goal</u>."

As we embark upon the course of building the Will, we see the importance of keeping alive the light of Desire. For the Will is exercised only as long as there is a Desire. Continuing, perpetual Desire generates continuing, perpetual exercise of the Will.

Without Desire, we have lost the nourishment to strengthen our Will, which weakens and is ultimately starved to death...

In years of practicing prayer and in studying it I have come to realize that prayer is not conducted or ordered for the benefit of the One to Whom I am praying. It is for *my* benefit on two levels: 1) that I may access blessings, favors, power, wisdom and insights from the One to Whom I am praying and 2) that it internally organizes my *self* – values, desires, and will.

Now from what forces should we protect the will?

The answer is as long as the list of those things which can keep a human being from following through on what they have determined to do, as well as those things which corrupt the will, perverting it and leading it into a direction other than what was originally intended.

One can easily think of those external forces coming from the outside like criticism, discouragement, slander, libel, competition, political and economic developments etc...But what about those forces *inside* of the human being that run counter to what they have determined to do?

In "The Will Of God," Minister Farrakhan lays bare seven such forces and what they are capable of doing:

Fear

Did you know that Fear is what the enemy of Allah (God) at hand, uses to restrict the Power of your own Will? What are you afraid of? Once someone can make you afraid, they restrict the Power of your own being to express itself.

Look at how many people today live in fear. I'm on a job and I am afraid that I am going to be fired (by a cantankerous boss or foreman). Think of it. So the foreman is threatening your security. You are afraid, so it restricts your Will. And, in a sense, it helps to make the individual not just a worker on the job, but a slave to the job.

Anytime you are afraid to think, to move, to express ourselves, for fear of being censured, for fear of losing a job; then you need to get away from that type of job, for you have lost the most precious thing that you could have and that is a Free Will. That is what Allah (God) has given you. But if your choices are made out of Fear, then you have made yourself a slave.

Fear is a distressing emotion; aroused by impending pain and danger. Of course, the Scriptures teach us that the Fear of Allah (God) is the beginning of Knowledge and that, of course, is true.

The Fear of Allah (God) is restricting, but it does not restrict us in a way that damages our development. The Fear Of Allah (God) frees us to act in accordance with His Will.

Vanity

The next thing that hurts the Will, redirects the Will, and redirects the Power of our being in a negative direction, is something called Vanity.

Vanity is excessive pride in one's appearance, one's qualities, one's abilities, and/or one's achievements. It is Conceit. Vanity can lead to arrogance. And, of course, anything that is done with the spirit of Conceit lacks real value. In fact, it is hollow and worthless. And those of us who are self-conceited; who are overly concerned with ourselves and who see too much importance in ourselves in our relationships to others; our acts are shallow. Our words are hollow; they have no real value. Consequently, we are considered, in the Eyes of Allah (God), worthless.

Pride

The next horrible distortion, or that which distorts the Will, is Pride. Pride is a high or inordinate opinion of one's own dignity, importance, merit, or superiority. Whether this is cherished in the mind or expressed openly by our bearing or conduct, makes no difference.

Once the mind is beset with Pride and we swell up with Pride, this directs the Power of our being. So we do things to enhance our merit, our superiority, our sense of importance. And we come blinded, by Pride, to the Will of Allah (God) and even feign humility, while in reality, the heart is a boiling cauldron of False Pride which has now corrupted the Will and redirected it toward an end that makes Man a slave of his own self-conceit, importance and, really, Delusion...

Envy

This is another emotion that can absolutely corrupt and redirect the Will. Envy is a feeling of discontent, usually with ill-will, at seeing someone else's superiority, advantages, or success. How many of you – how many of us – are plagued with this disease of the heart, right now? You are angry with someone whom you feel has an advantage or success that you believe should be yours. This is a terrible corruption of the Will of Allah (God); of the Will of Man.

Lust

Lust is a voracious appetite; a sexual appetite that is inordinate. It is out of the Divine Law. It is out of the way of the Order of Allah (God). It is something that we feel we have to do. It is a compulsion. And we allow that drive, that sexual drive, that Lust, to actually corrupt our Will and direct our Will towards ends that are nonproductive of good.

Anger

To those of us who are angered much, Anger can direct the Will. Anger directs the power of our being toward the object of our Anger. And oftimes, in our Anger, we can do very destructive things to Self and others. Anger is something that must be controlled.

Greed

And of course, lastly, there is Greed. Greed is the accepted inordinate or rapacious desire for wealth, power, food, or drink. Allah (God) wants us to be satisfied. But when we are overcome by Greed, this lust for wealth or power or food or drink, it manifests itself in our conspicuous consumption. It manifests itself in our directing our Will to destroy those who stand in the way of our assumption of Power. It leads to obesity, where one destroys one's health because of one's Greed; or destroys one's health because of uncontrolled urges.

All of the forces that Minister Farrakhan describes as redirecting the will have been the motivation for entrepreneurs in the past. And this should not be surprising. As we know not all motivations are pure, and not every act that ends up good, starts that way. And of course, human beings have the free will to choose options available to them.

Just as food for thought on this point we offer this interesting comment from the *Encyclopedia of Creativity Volume I, Mark* – A. Runco and Steven R. Pritzker, Editors In Chief – on the relationship between creativity (which is what entrepreneurship is in our model) and a force that can re-direct the will:

In our proclivity for linking creativity with inspiration and divine principles, we ignore its close affinity with hubris, the sin of pride. One of history's earliest legends has to do with creation of the Tower of Babel, where every artifice was employed to devise a tower so magnificent that it could reach the very portals of Heaven. Humankind would thereby be able to climb to the gates of Paradise and claim its blessings without moral deserving. According to the story, their punishment was to have their language confused and "to be scattered abroad across the face of the earth." Pride and conceit underlay their misuse of the gift of creativity, and this ultimately led to humankind's mutual estrangement. From that point on, all human inventions, from the chariot wheel to atomic fission, seem to bear the stigma of the Babel experience. Hence the lament in Ecclesiastes, "God made men upright, but they have sought out many inventions," and the Psalmist's echo, "They became unclean in their acts, and played the harlot with their inventions."

The view presented in this book is not that suffering always produces a morally purifying effect or a righteous endeavor or 'invention.' Our position is that it encourages deeper thinking, innovation, and that tends to produce an *entrepreneurial* act.

It is very possible that many who are suffering, will begin to identify with one of these forces, mentioned by Minister Farrakhan and use the energy of those forces to propel them into business. While that might be enough to fuel the will to get a business off the ground, it is not enough to maintain and grow a business.

If consistent progress is to be made in any endeavor motion must always be disciplined by order and obedience to scientific process, immutable laws and universal principles – many of which are referred to throughout the chapters of this book.

What also deserves further mentioning on these forces is that they reflect values and belief systems about one's self and others. And all value and belief systems affect perception.

Values, beliefs and perception – this is an important dynamic. Their relationship can determine what we believe is possible in life.

Values are the *what*, and *why* for which you do something, beliefs are what enable or hinder you, in the pursuit them. How?

Through our five senses (sight, smell, hearing, tasting, feeling) our brain identifies or receives over 2 billion pieces of data coming into it every second. A network of cells called the Reticular Activating System (RAS) handles the job of acting like an antennae, notifying your brain about certain stimuli, and generally filtering these pieces of data so that only a small portion of this 2 billion comes through. Otherwise our brains would be overloaded.

The RAS allows data in that meets any one or combination of three criteria: 1) The stimuli is important to our survival 2) it is new or unusual and 3) it has high emotional content associated with it. Ordinary routines and familiar stimuli do not get the RAS' attention. They don't reach its three-criteria threshold. It is looking for that which is critical to survival, unique and emotional.

If data and stimuli don't meet that threshold then they don't get noticed. Therefore the RAS can be a vital ally or enemy in your pursuit of what you are trying to obtain because, it helps you notice things that are critical to the accomplishing of your goals. On this point, in the book, *Neuro-Linguistic Programming For Dummies*, Romilla Ready and Kate Burton write:

Your beliefs will affect the threshold level of the RAS. Someone who believes that he is a poor speller may not 'see' an advertisement for a reporter's job, even though this shortcoming can be helped with spelling technology and he may be much better at investigating stories than someone who may not have a hang-up over their spelling ability and who applies for the job.

By being aware of your beliefs, you can identify how these beliefs may be stopping you from achieving your goals. Think of a time when you really wanted to do something but, for whatever reason, couldn't find the opportunity to achieve your goal. Now examine your beliefs. You may discover that these beliefs were stopping you from noticing openings that could have enabled you to achieve your goal.

Therefore we should remember that our values and beliefs affect our perception, which affects our will, level of faith, and emotions, against or in the service of our goals and quality of life.

And this is another concern that Minister Farrakhan has placed upon the forces that can redirect the will. In a letter introducing his Study Guide # 12, "Four Great Impediments To Self-Development" he writes in part, "…How we perceive reality is based upon the condition of our heart and mind and the quality of our faith…Anger does not permit us to see properly. Greed. Lust. Pride. Vanity. Envy. Hypocrisy. These are impediments to proper perception….how we perceive any set of facts reveals us, because based upon our perception and faith, we react accordingly."

What we value and believe is possible, affects what we notice and how we perceive, thereby determining our level of faith and the strength of our will to accomplish what we desire and obtain what we pursue. For the entrepreneur, *nothing should concern us more than these dynamics.*

<<<<>>>>

Now. Let's put it all together. It all boils down to a four-step process from a variety of angles. First, due to some stimuli – external or internal – we arrive at an idea or image we anticipate obtaining. Next we make that image more powerful through visualizing it more clearly and in more detail. Then we begin an internal process of reasoning, examination of our values and beliefs in support of and against our pursuing the idea or making the image we visualize a reality. Lastly, we make a decision. If in the positive, we determine to accomplish what we desire and envision and we feed, nurture, buttress, support and protect the will to achieve it.

Remember creative thinking produces ideas. Critical thinking evaluates ideas.

Similarly we can see essentially the same four steps laid out by Dr. Frank Channing Haddock who in *Power of Will* outlined:

We thus perceive four steps connected with the act of willing:

1) Presentation in mind of something that may be done;
2) Presentation in mind of motives or reasons relating to what may be done;
3) The rise in mind of Sufficient Reason;
4) Putting forth in mind of Volition corresponding to Sufficient Reason.

From the perspective of religion and scripture we see this same foundational four-step process. From the Holy Qur'an we read in the Yusuf Ali translation, the following on Surah 87 and its footnote:

In the name of Allah, the Beneficent, the Merciful.

1. Glorify the name of thy Lord, the Most High.
2. Who creates, then makes complete,
3. And Who measures, then guides,

Footnote: V.V. 2 and 3 speak of four Divine acts, *khalq* or creation, *taswiyah* or completion, *taqdir* or measuring, and *hidayah* or guiding. Everything in this universe is subject to these four laws, and so is man. He is created from a very humble and low beginning, his first condition being that of a life-germ which cannot be seen. Then it develops gradually to complete human form. This is the subject-matter of v.2. The third verse then lays down that everything in creation is held under control: it is made according to a measure and its progress lies along a certain line; and that is God Who guides it or makes it walk along that line. The whole is in special reference to the spiritual advancement of man through Divine glorification.

In the book, *Religion of Islam* by Maulana Muhammad Ali we read, "Four things are mentioned regarding every object of creation, including man: its creation (*khalq*), its completion (*taswiya*), its measure (*taqdir*), and its guidance to its goal (*hidaya*)

In lining our model up with what is written in the Qur'an we would consider the step one which is the idea stage as the creative act or *khalq*; the process of visualization as 'completing' the image and idea or *taswiyah*; the reasoning process as representing the measuring or third stage of *taqdir;* and lastly the building of the will which is the self-directing force we can liken to the power of guiding or *hidayah*.

We can see these four steps again from the perspective of Minister Louis Farrakhan's Study Guide, "The God Within," wherein he describes:

Who are the angels? Why did Allah (God) inform them of His intentions beforehand?

There is but one force: the Life Force. Each of the 99 attributes of Allah (God) is a force. Beneficence is guided by a force; Mercy is guided by a force. Retribution is guided by a force. In sharing Himself with man, God has placed these same forces or powers in the human being.

These forces may be used for negative ends or positive ends. In order to serve positive ends the forces must be controlled. Allah (God) is the uniting principle bringing these forces into submission to His singular Will, to accomplish a certain objective. The dialogue taking place in Holy Qur'an 2:30 is actually the God, the Ruler, reasoning with the forces within Himself. He says, "I", for He is the uniting principle, "am going to place a ruler in the earth." Then He allows the contrariness of the various forces (angels) to come up. Through reasoning with them, He unites them behind His Will; He Unites His own Self-Community that He may go on With His Plan.

The same process occurs within us, as He has placed some of Himself within us. When we think to do a thing, other thoughts come up within us, questioning the move, or objecting to the move. We must then reason with ourselves to reach a conclusion, for confusion within Self has a chilling effect on movement. When we are confused, unsure, we cannot take action. So here, Allah (God), says to the questioning forces within Himself, "I know what you know not."

In these three sentences of what the Minister has written we can see the four stages (numbering in boldface places emphasis on the order): **(1)** **and (2)** He says, "I", for He is the uniting principle, "am going to place a ruler in the earth." **(3)** Then He allows the contrariness of the various forces (angels) to come up. Through reasoning with them, He unites them behind His Will; **(4)** He Unites His own Self-Community that He may go on With His Plan.

Here we can see that first the idea and image are created and described (visualized), then a reasoning process takes place, then the decision is supported by the will to move forward to the objective.

Directly in terms of our entrepreneurial model another way to see this process is again, from the perspective of four factors or elements:

The Creative Thinking Process (Steps 1 and 2) involves the process of receiving an external stimuli or producing a thought or idea which represents the perception of an opportunity, which is followed by an accompanying image and the visualization process, which gives that thought or idea greater structure and form.

The Critical Thinking Process (Step 3) involves the process of comparing and contrasting values and beliefs in relation to the perceived opportunity that has been visualized. Logic is used to make arguments pro and con. This represents consensus-building through an internal dialogue and debate, characterized by rational thinking and reasoning.

The Execution Process (Step 4) involves –in the event of a positive decision – determining to accomplish the goal; supporting, protecting, nourishing, buttressing the will to do so; and planning, creating an organization to pursue the opportunity to doing so (successfully launching business).

Even Napoleon Hill's most powerfully concise statement seems to embody this four-step process. He wrote, "Every human being who reaches the age of understanding of the purpose of money wishes for it. *Wishing* will not bring riches. But (1) *desiring* riches with a (2) state of mind that becomes an obsession, then (3) planning definite ways and means to acquire riches, and (4) backing those plans with persistence which *does not recognize failure*, will bring riches."

This four-step process takes place in a larger context and that is the reality of how we view our selves. So, let's consider the impact of self-image, self-actualization and self-perception, which support or hinder our ability to think, visualize, reason, and make and sustain determined decisions toward a goal.

In other words, we should look deeper at the importance of not just the Self, and the Uniting of The Self-Community, but also *one's own view of Self.* It is important for us to realize that how we *view* ourselves – our self-concept – is just as important as what we *do* with ourselves. In fact, many argue that the power of one's self is determined, unleashed, or limited, by how we think and feel about ourselves. This is an important aspect to the teachings of Psycho-Cybernetics which exploded in popularity in the 1960s and 1970s with the publication of *Psycho-Cybernetics* by Maxwell Maltz. In a new updated version of that work, Maxwell Martz describes the evolution of the study of 'self', the impact his contribution has had, and why the way one views one's self – one's self-image – is critical to everything else:

A revolution in psychology began in the late 1960s and exploded in the 1970s. When I wrote the first edition of Psycho-Cybernetics in 1960 I was at the forefront of a sweeping change in the fields of psychology, psychiatry, and medicine. New theories and concepts concerning "self" began emerging from the work and findings of clinical psychologists, practicing psychiatrists, and even cosmetic or so-called "plastic surgeons" like myself. New methods growing out of these findings resulted in dramatic changes in personality, in health, and even in basic abilities and talents. Chronic failures became successful. Shy, retiring, inhibited personalities became happy and outgoing. At the time, I was quoted in the January 1959 issue of Cosmopolitan Magazine, in which T. F. James summarized these results obtained by various psychologists and MDs as follows:

Understanding the psychology of the self can mean the difference between success and failure, love and hate, bitterness and happiness. The discovery of the real self can rescue a crumbling marriage, recreate a faltering career, transform victims of "personality failure." On another plane, discovering your real self means the difference between freedom and the compulsions of conformity.

This was barely predictive of everything that has occurred in the four decades that followed.

When Psycho-Cybernetics was first published, if you visited a bookstore to obtain a copy, you might have found it nestled on an obscure shelf with only a dozen or so other so-called "self-help" books. Today, of course, "self-help" is one of the largest sections in the entire bookstore. Psychologists, psychiatrists, and therapists have proliferated, new specialists have emerged, such as sports psychologists and corporate performance coaches, and the stigma of seeking such help has disappeared to such an extent that in some circles doing so is trendy. Self-help psychology has become so popular it even has found a place in television infomercials!

...I would argue that the most important psychological discovery of modern times is the discovery of the self-image. By understanding your self-image and by learning to modify it and manage it to suit your purposes, you gain incredible confidence and power.

Whether we realize it or not, each of us carries within us a mental blueprint or picture of ourselves. It may be vague and ill-defined to our conscious gaze. In fact, it may not be consciously recognizable at all. But it is there, complete down to the last detail. This self-image is our own conception of the "sort of person I am." It has been built up from our own beliefs about ourselves. Most of these beliefs about ourselves have unconsciously been formed from our past experiences, our success and failures. Our humiliations, our triumphs, and the way other people have reacted to us, especially in early childhood. From all these we mentally construct a *self* (or a picture of a self). Once an idea or a belief about ourselves goes into this picture it becomes "truth," as far as we... are concerned. We do not question its validity, but proceed to act upon it *just as if it were true.*

Specifically, all your actions, feelings, behavior, even your abilities, are always consistent with this self-image. Note the word: always. In short, you will "act like" the sort of person you conceive yourself to be. More important, you literally cannot act otherwise, in spite of all your conscious efforts or willpower. (This is why trying to achieve something difficult with teeth gritted is a losing battle. Willpower is *not* the answer. Self-image management is.)

The person who has a "fat" self-image – whose self-image claims to have a "sweet tooth," to be able to resist "junk food," who cannot find the time to exercise – will be unable to lose weight and keep it off no matter what he tries to do consciously in opposition to that self-image. You cannot long outperform or escape your self-image. If you do escape briefly, you'll be "snapped back," like a rubber band, extended between two fingers, coming loose from one.

The person who perceives himself to be a "failure type person" will find some way to fail, in spite of all his good intentions or his willpower, even if opportunity is literally dumped in his lap. The person who conceives himself to be a victim of injustice, one "who was meant to suffer," will invariably find circumstances to verify his opinions.

You can insert any specific into this: your golf game, sales career, public speaking, weight loss, relationships. The control of your self-image is absolute and pervasive. The snapback effect is universal.

The self-image is a "premise," a base, or a foundation upon which your entire personality, your behavior, and even your circumstances are built. As a result, our experiences, seem to verify and thereby strengthen our self-images, and either a vicious or a beneficent cycle, as the case may be, is set up.

For example, a student who sees himself as an "F"-type student, or one who is "dumb in mathematics," will invariably find that his report card bears him out. He then has "proof." In the same manner, a sales professional or an entrepreneur will also find that her actual experiences tend to "prove" that her self-image is correct. Whatever is difficult for you, whatever frustrations you have in your life, they are likely "proving" and reinforcing something ingrained in your self-image like a groove in a record.

Because of this objective "proof," it very seldom occurs to us that our trouble lies in our self-image or our own evaluation of ourselves. Tell the student that he only "thinks" he cannot master algebra, and he will doubt your sanity. He has tried and tried, and still his report card tells the story. Tell the sales agent that it is only an idea that she cannot earn more than a certain figure, and she can prove you wrong by her order book. She knows only too well how hard she has tried and failed. Yet, as we shall see, almost miraculous changes have occurred both in grades of students and the earning capacity of salespeople – once they were prevailed upon to change their self-images.

Obviously, it's not enough to say "it's all in your head." In fact, that's insulting. It is more productive to explain that "it" is based on certain ingrained, possibly hidden patterns of thought that, if altered, will free you to tap more of your potential and experience vastly different results. This brings me to the most important truth about the self-image: It *can* be changed.

Numerous case histories have shown that you are never too young or too old to change your self-image and start to live a new, amazingly different life.

…One of the reasons it seems so difficult for a person to change habits, personality, or a way of life has been that nearly all efforts at change have been directed to the circumference of the self, so to speak, rather than to the center.

Numerous patients have said to me something like the following: "If you are talking about 'positive thinking,' I've tried that before, and it just doesn't work for me." However, a little questioning invariably brings out that these individuals employed positive thinking, or attempted to employ it, either on particular external circumstances or on some particular habit or character defect ("I will get that job." "I will be more calm and relaxed in the future." This business venture will turn out right for me." And so on.) But they never thought to change thinking of the self that was to accomplish these things.

Jesus warned us about the folly of putting a patch of new material on an old garment or of putting new wine into old bottles. "Positive thinking" cannot be used effectively as a patch to the same old self-image. In fact, it is literally impossible to really think positively about a particular situation, as long as you hold a negative concept of self. Numerous experiments have shown that, once the concept of self is changed, other things consistent with the new concept of self are accomplished easily and without strain.

One of the earliest and most convincing experiments along this line was conducted by the late Prescott Lecky, one of the pioneers in self-image psychology. Lecky conceived of the personality as a system of ideas, all of which must be consistent with each other. Ideas that are inconsistent with the system are rejected, "not believed," and not acted on. Ideas that seem to be consistent with the system are accepted. At the very center of this system of ideas – the keystone, or the base on which all else is built – is the individuals' self-image, or his conception of himself.

Lecky was a school teacher and had an opportunity to test his theory on thousands of students. He theorized that if a student had trouble learning a certain subject, it could be because (from the student's point of view) it would be inconsistent for him to learn it. Lecky believed, however, that if the student could be induced to change his self-definition, his learning ability should also change.

This proved to be the case. One student, who misspelled 55 words out of 100 and flunked so many subjects that he lost credit for a year, made a general average of 91 the next year and became one of the best spellers in school. A girl who dropped from one college because of poor grades, entered Columbia and became a straight 'A' student. A boy who was told by a testing bureau that he had no aptitude for English won honorable mention the next year for a literary prize.

The trouble with these students was not that they were dumb or lacking in basic aptitudes. The trouble was an inadequate self-image ("I don't have a mathematical mind"; I'm just naturally a poor speller"). They "identified" with their mistakes and failures. Instead of saying "I failed that test" (factual and descriptive), they concluded "I am a failure." Instead of saying "I flunked that subject," they said "I am a flunk-out." (For those who are interested in learning more of Lecky's work, try to find a copy of his book: Self-Consistency, A Theory of Personality.)

Lecky also used the same method to cure students of such habits as nail biting and stuttering.

My own files contain case histories just as convincing: the woman who was so afraid of strangers that she seldom ventured out of the house and who now makes her living as a public speaker. The salesman who had already prepared a letter of resignation because he 'just wasn't cut out for selling" and six months later was number one man on a force of one hundred salespeople. The minister who has considering retirement because "nerves" and the pressure of preparing a sermon every week were getting him down, and who now delivers an average of three "outside talks" a week in addition to his weekly sermons and doesn't know he has a nerve in his body.

Following Dr. Lecky's breakthrough thinking on this subject, born from observation, as well as my own observations and thoughts chronicled in the earlier editions of this book, a mountain of more sophisticated scientific research and anecdotal evidence has led to the acceptance of the controlling self-image by most of the academic psychological community.

The crux of what Maxwell Martz presents is compatible with our model. As we have earlier noted about value and belief systems, a person must support the will with reason, suggestion, and emotional intensity. That is why critical thinking, prayer, visualization and affirmation are recommended.

But in all of these processes, the person must remember the importance of their view of their own value, potential, and ability. Without the awareness of the power of one's self image and its impact on our Will, we will not adequately unite our self-community in the service of our entrepreneurial endeavor. Who we think we are is just as important as what we are trying to accomplish. **Our self-concept is intertwined with our entrepreneurial vision.**

All of what we have just considered brings us to an important but sticky concept – that called faith. Faith is a concept every single entrepreneur is involved with and should seek to understand. The word is widely used, and has come to take on an enormously broad application that touches will power, belief, knowledge, and hope. A surprisingly (for some) good place to begin looking at this term and concept is theology and religion.

There we are able to look at faith from perhaps the fields that have been the most influential in determining the popular views of the concept.

From the *Encyclopedia of Christian Theology* edited by Jean-Yves Lacoste we read from the entry on faith:

Faith is the inner attitude of one who believes. The words of the Bible that we translate as "faith" or "fidelity" (*'emunah*, *'emet*), and as "believe" (*he' emin*), come from the same Hebrew root (*'mn*); Greek shows the same relationship in *pistis*, "faith" and *pisteuein*, "believe." The underlying idea in Hebrew is that of firmness; in Greek, that of persuasion.

In English, "believe" can denote either an uncertain opinion or a strong conviction, based on an interpersonal relationship. The latter meaning is the one that is found in the Bible; hence the frequency of the vocabulary of faith in the Psalms (84 times); see also Deuteronomy (23 times). Isaiah (34 times), and Jeremiah (21 times).

Of the usage of the word faith in the New Testament, the *Encyclopedia of Christian Theology*, states:

...Jesus proclaimed the imminent coming of the Kingdom of God (Mt. 3:17 and parallel passages). Mark summarizes his message in the terms of the first Christian preaching: "Believe in the gospel" (1:15). But Jesus had already brought to the fore the fundamental significance of faith. He says to the person whom he has cured: "Your faith has made you well" (Mt 9:22 and parallel passages' Mk 10:52 and parallel passages; Luke 7:50). "All things are possible for one who believes" (Mk 9:23; see Mt 7:20 and parallel passages; 21:21 and parallel passages)...He does not specify in whom one should have faith. He does not say, "Believe in me," but the circumstances reveal that the faith in God that he wants to encourage is linked to a faith in his own person. "He was teaching them as one who had authority" (Mt 7:29 and parallel passages), as a fully accredited envoy. The expression "Amen, I say to you" is peculiar to Jesus (the Hebrew *'amen* affirms certainty)...

An element of personal confidence or certainty, as we can see from the above, is wrapped up in the word 'faith.' In the scriptures, the relationship between faith and certainty is made clear in a variety of passages and words. From the Bible we read of "evidence of things unseen..."; and "know of a surety"...And from the perspective of Islam we get acquainted with a view of how personal experience determines levels of certainty. There are four levels of certainty according to some Islamic scholars. One, Yusuf Ali, in his translation of the Holy Qur'an writes of Surah 69:51 which he renders in part as: "...verily it is Truth of assured certainty:"

"All Truth is in itself certain. But as received by men, and understood with reference to men's psychology, certainty may have certain degrees. There is the probability or certainty resulting from the application of man's power of judgment and his appraisement of evidence. This 'lim-ul-yaqin, certainty by reasoning or inference. Then there is the certainty of seeing something with our own eyes. 'Seeing is believing.' This is 'ani-ul-yaqin, certainty by personal inspection...Then as here, there is the absolute Truth, with no possibility of error or judgment of the eye (which stands for any instrument of sense-perception and any ancillary aids, such as microscopes, etc.) This absolute Truth is the haqq-ul-yaqin spoken of here."

The connection between these concepts and the entrepreneurial act is that the entrepreneur has to have a high level of two qualities – desire and faith – in order to successfully pursue an opportunity. If the entrepreneur can properly reach the level of certainty appropriate to them, the power is explosive.

One will remember that in our model, desire feeds the will and faith supports it, driving an individual to fulfill the image and vision they have in their mind and heart regarding a business venture. The successful entrepreneur is one who confidently expects to obtain a goal and faithfully strives in that pursuit. Faith is more than hope in that it represents the full confidence in the actualization of an image and vision adhered to by the entrepreneur, as well as the evidence that substantiates – or the reason(s) that justifies – the hope for success.

We know faith when they see it, *even those of us who do not accept the belief system or the object of the faithful one.* People frequently reject a cause and accept the effect when considering faith. That is just how powerful a firm confidence in the future and belief and perseverance in the face of adversity is. It compels respect, admiration and awe. Its ability to animate, motivate, and strengthen the resolve of the human being is evident to many, even if the Source of such power – as identified by the person embodying it – is rejected.

A fine example of this can be found in the book, *Life Of Mahomet*, by Sir William Muir, which speaks of the great faith of Muhammad of 1,400 years ago and what it allowed him to overcome and accomplish. Keep in mind, as you read what follows, that Sir William Muir was a disbeliever in Islam and a formidable opponent of its scholars and theologians.

His criticisms have been considered mean-spirited, vicious, and even 'attacks' on him, by some. Yet and still, Mr. Muir, in his book, published in 1861, in a chapter called, "The Person and Character of Mahomet" (keep in mind spellings of names, places and events, vary from source to source on Muhammad of 1,400 years ago, in both historical and contemporary literature) is still compelled to acknowledge the irresistible power of the faith, confidence, and belief of the Prophet of Islam:

The growth in the mind of Mahomet of the conviction that he was appointed to be a Prophet and a Reformer, was intimately connected with his belief in a special providence, embracing as well as the spiritual, the material world: and simultaneously with that conviction there arose an implicit confidence that the Almighty would crown his mission with success. The questionings and aspirations of his inner soul were regarded by him as proceeding directly from God; the light which gradually illuminated his mind with a knowledge of the divine unity and perfections, and of the duties and destiny of man, – light amidst gross darkness, – must have emanated from the same source; and he who in his own good pleasure had thus begun the work would surely carry it to an end. What was Mahomet himself but a simple instrument in the hand of the great Worker? It was this belief which strengthened him, alone and unsupported, to brave for many weary years the taunts and persecutions of a whole people. In estimating the signal moral courage thus displayed by him, it must not be overlooked that for what is ordinarily termed *physical courage* Mahomet was not remarkable. It may be doubted whether he ever engaged personally in active conflict on the battle field: though he accompanied his forces, he never himself led them into action, or exposed his person to unavoidable danger. And there were occasions on which (as when challenged by Abdallah to spare the Bani Cainucaa, alarmed by the altercation at the wells of Moaisi, or pressed by the mob at Jierrana,) he showed symptoms of a faint heart. Yet even if this be admitted, it only brings out in higher relief the singular display of moral daring.

Let us for a moment look back to the period when a ban was proclaimed at Mecca against all the citizens, whether professed converts or not, who espoused his cause; when they were shut up in *Sheb* or quarter of Abu Talib, and there, for three years without prospect of relief, endured want and hardship. Those must have been steadfast and mighty motives which enabled him, amidst all this opposition and apparent hopelessness of success, to maintain his principles unshaken. No sooner was he released from confinement, than, despairing of his native city, he went forth to Tayif and summoned its rulers and inhabitants to repentance; he was solitary and unaided, but he had a message, he said, from his Lord. On the third day he was driven out of the town with ignominy, blood trickling from the wounds inflicted on him by the populace. He retired to a little distance, and there poured forth his complaint to God: then he returned to Mecca, there to carry on the same outwardly hopeless cause, with the same high confidence in its ultimate success.

We search in vain through the pages of profane history for a parallel to the struggle in which for thirteen years the Prophet of Arabia, in the face of discouragement and threats, rejection and persecution, retained his faith unwavering, preached repentance, and denounced God's wrath against his godless fellow citizens. Surrounded by a little band of faithful men and women, he met insults, menace, danger, with a high and patient trust in the future. And when at last the promise of safety came from a distant quarter, he calmly waited until his followers had all departed, and then disappeared from amongst his ungrateful and rebellious people.

Not less marked was the firm front and unchanging faith in eventual victory, which at Medina bore him through seven years of mortal conflict with his native city; and enabled him while his influence and authority were yet very limited and precarious even in the city of his adoption, to speak and to act in the constant and undoubted expectation of entire success.

It is the result of this 'unchanging faith in eventual victory,' leading to success in religion and the secular world which compelled Dr. Michael H. Hart to identify Muhammad as the most influential person in human history, in his book, *The 100: A Ranking Of The Most Influential Persons In History.*

And now a final point on perception. Earlier in this chapter we touched upon sensory perception and its relationship to our belief and value systems. In our model the entrepreneurial process is marked by an individual perceiving an opportunity. Their perception is what causes them to 'see' something that perhaps others haven't. This act of perception is the catalyst to the desire that causes the individual to decide to create an organization in order to pursue that.

We have looked at the Reticular Activating System (RAS) in the human being, and how this relates to perception, but that is not the entire story.

We don't perceive only by our physical senses.

We also perceive through reasoning, discernment and patience. Critical thinking helps us with discernment and patience. But patience is largely developed as a result of attitude, faith and will power.

There are some things that we can learn immediately. In other instances *time is required* – in both the unfolding of events, and for comprehension and understanding to arrive. By judging circumstances hastily, we can hurt and endanger ourselves and others. In business by judging circumstances prematurely or without guidance and the insight of others, we misperceive opportunity and make critical mistakes and errors that hurt our chances for success.

Two stories which are striking in this regard, and which have served as an instructive example of the importance of perception and patience, for me, are written of in the scriptures. One appears in both Bible and Holy Qur'an, while the other is only written of in the Holy Qur'an. The first is the story of Joseph and his Brothers and the other is commonly referred to by many as the story of "Moses and The Wise Man."

Let's first look at the latter story mentioned.

Although the man who Moses follows in this story is not given, he is referred to by Islamic scholars, commentators and translators as Khadir or Khidr. Below is that section, from Surah 18 verses 60 to 82 followed by the footnote commentary on those verses by the Holy Qur'an translator, Yusuf Ali (the relevant footnote numbers are in parenthesis):

60. Behold, Moses said to his attendant, "I will not give up until I reach the junction of the two seas or (until) I spend years and years in travel."

61. But when they reached the Junction, they forgot (about) their Fish, which took its course through the sea (straight) as in a tunnel.

62. When they had passed on (some distance), Moses said to his attendant: "Bring us our early meal; truly we have suffered much fatigue at this (stage of) our journey."

63. He replied: "Sawest thou (what happened) when we betook ourselves to the rock? I did indeed forget (about) the Fish: none but Satan made me forget to tell (you) about it: it took its course through the sea in a marvelous way!"

64. Moses said: "That was what we were seeking after:" So they went back on their footsteps, following (the path they had come).

65. So they found one of Our servants, on whom We had bestowed Mercy from Ourselves and whom We had taught knowledge from Our own Presence.

66. Moses said to him: "May I follow thee, on the footing that thou teach me something of the (Higher) Truth which thou hast been taught?"

67. (The other) said: "Verily thou wilt not be able to have patience with me!"

68. "And how canst thou have patience about things about which thy understanding is not complete?"

69. Moses said: "Thou wilt find me, if Allah so will, (truly) patient: nor shall I disobey thee in aught."

70. The other said: "If then thou wouldst follow me, ask me no questions about anything until I myself speak to thee concerning it."

71. So they both proceeded: until, when they were in the boat, he scuttled it. Said Moses: "Hast thou scuttled it in order to drown those in it? Truly a strange thing hast thou done!"

72. He answered: "Did I not tell thee that thou canst have no patience with me?"

73. Moses said: "Rebuke me not for forgetting, nor grieve me by raising difficulties in my case."

74. Then they proceeded: until, when they met a young man, he slew him. Moses said: "Hast thou slain an innocent person who had slain none? Truly a foul (unheard of) thing hast thou done!"

75. He answered: "Did I not tell thee that thou canst have no patience with me?"

76. (Moses) said: "If ever I ask thee about anything after this, keep me not in thy company: then wouldst thou have received (full) excuse from my side."

77. Then they proceeded: until, when they came to the inhabitants of a town, they asked them for food, but they refused them hospitality. They found there a wall on the point of falling down, but he set it up straight. (Moses) said: "If thou hadst wished, surely thou couldst have exacted some recompense for it!"

78. He answered: "This is the parting between me and thee: now will I tell thee the interpretation of (those things) over which thou wast unable to hold patience. (2421)

79. "As for the boat, it belonged to certain men in dire want: they plied on the water: I but wished to render it unserviceable, for there was after them a certain king who seized on every boat by force. (2422)

80. "As for the youth, his parents were people of Faith, and we feared that he would grieve them by obstinate rebellion and ingratitude (to Allah and man). (2423)

81. "So we desired that their Lord would give them in exchange (a son) better in purity (of conduct) and closer in affection. (2424)

82. "As for the wall, it belonged to two youths, orphans, in the Town; there was, beneath it, a buried treasure, to which they were entitled: their father had been a righteous man (2425): So thy Lord desired that they should attain their age of full strength and get out their treasure – a mercy (and favour) from thy Lord. I did it not of my own (2427) accord. Such is the interpretation of (those things) over which thou wast unable to hold patience."

Footnotes:

2421: The story and the interpretation are given with the greatest economy of words. It would repay us to search for the meaning in terms of our own inner and outer experience.

2422: They went on the boat, which was plying for hire. Its owners were not even ordinary men who plied for trade. They had been reduced to great poverty, perhaps from affluent circumstances, and deserved great commiseration, the more so as they preferred an honest calling to begging for charity. They did not know, but Khidr did, that the boat, perhaps a new one, had been marked down to be commandeered by an unjust king who seized on every boat he could get – it may have been, for warlike purposes. If this boat had been taken away from these self-respecting men, they would have been reduced to beggary, with no resources left them. By a simple act of making it unseaworthy, the boat was saved from seizure. The owners could repair it as soon as the danger was past. Khidr probably paid liberally in fares, and what seemed an unaccountably cruel act was the greatest act of kindness he could in the circumstances.

2423. This seemed at first sight even a more cruel act than scuttling the boat. But the danger was also greater Khidr knew that the youth was a potential parricide. His parents were worthy, pious people, who had brought him up with love. He had apparently gone wrong. Perhaps he had already been guilty of murders and robberies and had escaped the law by subtleties and fraud. See next note.

2424. The son was practically an outlaw – a danger to the public and a particular source of grief to his righteous parents. Even so, his summary capital punishment would have been unjustified if Khidr had been acting on his own. But Khidr was not acting on his own: see the latter part of the next verse. The plural "we" also implies that he was not acting on his own. He was acting on higher authority and removing a public scourge, who was also a source of extreme sorrow and humiliation to his parents. His parents are promised a better-behaved son who would love them and be a credit to them.

2425. The wall was in a ruinous state. If it had fallen, the treasure buried beneath it would have been exposed and would certainly have been looted, among so churlish and selfish a people....The treasure had been collected and buried by a righteous man. It was not, in any sense of the word, ill-gotten gains: it was buried expressly in the interests of the orphans by their father before his death. It was intended that the orphans should grow up and safely take possession of their heritage. It was also expected that they would be righteous men like their father, and use the treasure in good works and in advancing righteousness among an otherwise wicked community. There was thus both public and private interests involved in all the three incidents. In the second incident Khidr uses the word "we" showing that he was associating in his act the public authorities of the place, who had been eluded by the outlaw.

2427. Those who act, not from a whim or a private impulse of their own, but from higher authority, have to bear the blame, with the vulgar crowd, for acts of the greater wisdom and utility. In human affairs many things are inexplicable, which are things of the highest wisdom in the Universal Plan.

If ever there was a lesson in how patience is a virtue, and comes to the aid of our perception, it is evident in this story.

As for Joseph, and the power of perception, the most powerful commentary I have read regarding this scriptural story is that written of by Jabril Muhammad in the third edition of his book *This Is The One.*

He explains:

The book of Genesis is often called the book of beginnings. That book ends with Joseph's establishment of a family for God's use. He did this under the direct guidance of the Lord of the Worlds. This family, according to theologians, was to be the basis, for that, out of which would grow or develop a nation for God's glory. According to theologians the Messiah would eventually be born, from among the descendants of some of the members of this divinely produced nation.

...Out of the ugliest of motives, Joseph's brothers sold him into bondage. They were envious of him. He suffered through various ups and downs and finally landed in a dungeon. Even then there were those who were ungrateful to him for the favors God granted them through the insights of Joseph.

The ruler of the land and his people were in deep trouble. Joseph, who was already elevated in the sight of God, became elevated in the sight of those in power who previously did not properly recognize him. The king was in deep trouble: God blessed the ruler through Joseph. Joseph became powerful in the land. Famine arose. His brothers, among others, had to get in sort of a bread line. His brothers did not recognize him but he recognized them.

How did he handle those who were now under his sway or power? How did he handle those who once mistreated him? Joseph had the heart of God. This was evident in the way that he – with God's help – worked the circumstances in which he found his brothers and aided them to come to repentance. He did it in a manner that preserved their dignity. It was a magnificent plan which, of course, required the help of Almighty God for its perfect outcome. In fact the plan originated with God and was an aspect of His larger purpose. In the Holy Qur'an 12:76, we read: "Thus, We planned for the sake of Joseph."

His brothers came to know who he was. He was more than gracious in victory. He was more than gracious because God was using his heart to educate and elevate his family, which made it a victory for the entire family. Joseph was a magnificent instrument in the hands of God in the fulfilling of His grand design (which included His directive and His permissive will for the ultimate perfection of man.) In the Holy Qur'an 12: 90-93, and in Genesis 45: 4-15 we can read some of the most elevated and beautiful expressions of the heart of an elevated human being to be found anywhere. (I hope each reader will ponder the text for him/herself.)

The main point I wish to make, in briefly commenting on his words, was that Joseph did not focus on what others did *to* him. His prime focus was on what God was doing for him in what He allowed them to do *to* him. Thus, even though they did not know it, their evil served him.

Joseph saw *in* their selling him into bondage, God's sending him ahead of them to prepare that which was good *for* them, including the saving of their lives.

In both the story of Joseph and that of Moses and the Wise Man patience is clearly depicted as a virtue, as are other qualities, enabling clearer perception, over time. But the kind of patience the Holy Qur'an demonstrates as necessary to success is not the concept of that word that most people have in mind. That idea of patience, for many, amounts to little more than 'hanging in there,' almost helplessly, with a less than positive attitude. That is a far cry from the Arabic word *sabr* or *sabir,* which is translated in English as 'patience.' For a most accurate meaning of this rich word we consult footnote 61 in the Yusuf Ali translation of the Muslim holy book. It reads:

The Arabic word Sabr implies many shades of meaning, which it is impossible to comprehend in one English word. It implies (1) patience in the sense of being thorough, not hasty; (2) patient perseverance, constancy, steadfastness, firmness of purpose; (3) systematic as opposed to spasmodic or chance action; (4) a cheerful attitude of resignation and understanding in sorrow, defeat, or suffering, as opposed to murmuring or rebellion, but saved from mere passivity or listlessness, by the element of constancy or steadfastness.

So what is the secret of Willpower, you ask?

Unless you are able to marry creative and critical thinking, persevere and endure obstacles and challenges over time, without losing faith or confidence in your objective, you will not succeed in business, or in life.

We have just provided a deeply spiritual view of the entrepreneurial process, combining emphasis on the first half of that process, *the perceiving of an* opportunity with more science regarding the force of willpower that enables success in the second part of the entrepreneurial process – *creating an organization* to pursue that opportunity.

Now, to close *The Entrepreneurial Secret* we look at how both suffering and willpower – the innermost aspects of the entrepreneurial struggle relate to your most intimate relationships with others.

The Secret Of Will Power

- *Unseen does not mean unreal or invisible. There is nothing irrational in believing that there are realms, or mental levels, beyond the experience most of us live on.*
- *There are five primary means by which humans sense or engage reality: 1) taste (gustatory) 2) touch (kinesthetic) 3) hearing (auditory) 4) sight (visual) and 5) smell (olfactory).*
- *There are five primary means by which human beings learn: reading, observation, conversation, experience and revelation/intuition*
- *Advertising, and commercials to sell products and psychological warfare and propaganda used in warfare are two areas where the ability to persuade, manipulate and control human minds are essential. How much control over your own mind do you have?*
- *The heart, mind, and soul - or feelings and emotions; ideas and thinking; and purposeful determination - are all essential factors or the means by which the entrepreneur perceives an opportunity and then creates an organization to pursue it.*
- *Not a single great entrepreneur achieved and sustained success without developing and supporting the power of their will through suffering and adversity. Every great entrepreneur has practiced one, two, or all three of the following methods: prayer, affirmation, or visualization. They did so whether or not they claimed a religious or spiritual faith, or belief system.*
- *There are three factors that determine our emotions and our emotional states. They are: our anatomy and physiology; our individual experience, programming and conditioning; and our culture experience, programming and conditioning.*
- *Through our five senses (sight, smell, hearing, tasting, feeling) our brains have over 2 billion pieces of data coming into it every second. A network of cells called the Reticular Activating System (RAS) handles the job of acting like an antennae, notifying your brain about certain stimuli, and generally filtering these pieces of data so that only a small portion of this 2 billion comes through*
- *Creative thinking produces ideas. Critical thinking evaluates ideas. There is a four-step process that brings them both together.*
- *How we view ourselves - our self-concept - is just as important as what we do with ourselves. Who we think we are is just as important as what we are trying to accomplish. Our self-concept is intertwined with our entrepreneurial vision*
- *In business by judging circumstances prematurely or without guidance and the insight of others, we misperceive opportunity and make critical mistakes and errors that hurt our chances for success. Patience improves the clarity of our perception.*

Chapter 15: The Secret Of Personal Relationships – The Entrepreneur and Those Around Them

"...they say: Why has not a treasure been sent down for him...?"
—portion of Holy Qur'an, Surah 11:12

"She was proud to support her husband's dream of building a business. But five years is a long time to watch someone focus on his company at the expense of everything – everything – else."
—**Confessions of an Entrepreneur's Wife,** *Inc.* **magazine (March 2006)**

"The men who have accumulated great fortunes and achieved outstanding recognition in literature, art, industry, architecture, and the professions, were motivated by the influence of a woman."
—***Think & Grow Rich* by Napoleon Hill**

"I have stood by the Law Of Success lecture and my 15 points for more than seven years. At times they only seemed to mock me, when I was talking of success to others while my own family suffered for necessities. I have not known just why I did this. At times I wondered, as you have done, if I would not have been better off to have forgotten it all and have gone back to some little job as a bookkeeper, where I could have earned at least a modest living. BUT there was something that would not let me do it... I have stood my ground, suffered, been disappointed, and given disappointment to others all because I could not do otherwise. I was simply helpless in the matter...I would have changed my course a dozen times in the past six or seven years IF I COULD HAVE DONE SO."
—***Napoleon Hill, in a June 13, 1925 letter to his wife (as detailed in A Lifetime of Riches)***

"In the new book "Renegade," about Obama's barrier-breaking run for the presidency, author Richard Wolffe recounts a stretch in 2000 when the Obama's marriage was a lot frostier than it appears today. There was little conversation and even less romance," Wolffe, who covered Obama's campaign for Newsweek magazine, wrote of that period. "She was angry at his selfishness and careerism; he thought she was cold and ungrateful."
—**"President Obama and Michelle's picture perfect marriage wasn't always so, says new book 'Renegade' by Michael Saul and David Saltonstall"; June 2, 2009;** *New York Daily News*

"I pointed to the stars and all you saw was my finger-tip."
—**Sukuma Proverb: Tanzania**

If there is one word and question that I hope this book will help you to respect the power of, it would be "why?" It is a question you – as an entrepreneur or business person – will ask of *yourself*, but more importantly, for the purposes of this chapter, it is the question that those closest around and dearest to you will ask both you <u>and</u> themselves, often <u>without telling you</u>.

Why couldn't she have just taken a job? Why did he have to risk so much? Why is it taking so long for her to get this off of the ground? Why is he placing me second to his work? Why does she have so little time for me? Why won't he accept that this isn't going to work? Why won't she spend money on me and herself rather than putting everything back into the business? Why won't he try a different approach? Why won't she ask for help?

Whether 'they' tell you or not these (and others) are the kind of thoughts that go through the mind of your best friends, sisters, parents, brothers, husbands, wives, boyfriends, girlfriends, and children.

If you are an entrepreneur or business owner be prepared because everyone who learns about what you are doing is evaluating or judging you according to their own value system.

Unfortunately (or fortunately) you have very little or no control over the worldview of others, and are not able to read their most secret thoughts.

The entrepreneurial paradox is that while you believe you have performed a supreme act of *un*selfishness by starting a business, giving it your all, sacrificing your comfort and risking your own wealth, others close to you simultaneously may view your decision and hard work, as a supreme act of *selfish*ness. To them, and in their minds, you have put them second to your pursuit.

Of course this is compounded and becomes even worse of a situation, when you maintain in your own mind that you are doing what you are doing *for them*.

It can be a mess.

But I am here to tell you that it is normal.

My only goal in this chapter is to help you become more aware of this challenge, and to think of ways, most appropriate to your circumstances, value system, and belief, to manage the stress it brings into your relationships, and the energy it saps from your entrepreneurial drive.

It all starts with a good look at yourself, and acknowledging there is probably something very special about your personality and make-up.

In a May 6, 2009 article entitled, "Poor Children of the Rich and Successful," in *The Financial Times*, Luke Johnson writes, "I spend most of my time working with entrepreneurs, and I really believe that they are not the same as other people. They have an ambition, a competitive urge and a lust to take risks that is way beyond the norm."

This certainly sounds good, right? Sounds like we are members of an elite secret society or something, no? All good.

Well, maybe not *all* good.

Mr. Johnson later adds, "Driven characters tend to work long hours and, as a consequence, are at home with their families less. Such absence can mean strained relationships and endless guilt."

Oh, right, forgot about that part.

In sum, the problem boils down to this: entrepreneurship is a deeply personal act, and even spiritual in the sense that it represents an intensely motivational, creative and painful act. It is usually an individual decision – not always made in consultation with those closest to you. As a result, a divide can immediately develop between the <u>thing</u> you may care about the most, and which needs great care – a business – and the <u>people</u> you care about the most: family and friends.

Every truly great entrepreneur, scientist or artist understands what this dilemma feels like – and in a different way so do their loved ones and inner circle.

When you combine the elements of:

1) the need for privacy
2) different communication styles
3) levels of ignorance
4) different value systems
5) possibly radically different concepts and expectations regarding love (and how it is demonstrated), loyalty, commitment, suffering, sacrifice, risk, and reward
6) financial constraints and responsibilities
7) different thresholds for patience and pain
8) respect for time

9) milestones for success
10) fear

It is not hard to see how explosive entrepreneurship can be in your personal life and the prospects of success for your business.

Take the element of fear for instance, in a two person relationship.

Even though one person in the relationship may genuinely support and be loyal to another person, it does not mean that they will be able to handle the amount of risk and anxiety involved in starting or running a small business.

Any decision the entrepreneur makes, or any act they perform can trigger a host of fears in another person, who is relating to them – possibly even judging them – according to their own value system.

In the book, *Feel the Fear and Do It Anyway*, Susan Jeffers, Ph.D. writes:

Fear can be broken down into three levels. The first level is the surface story, such as the ones described above. This level of fear can be divided into two types: those that "happen" and those that require action. Here is a partial list of Level 1 fears divided into these types:

LEVEL 1 FEARS

Those that "Happen"	*Those Requiring Action*
Aging	Going back to school
Becoming disabled	Making decisions
Retirement	Changing a career
Being alone	Making friends
Children leaving home	Ending or beginning a relationship
Natural disasters	Using the telephone
Change	Asserting oneself
Dying	Losing weight
War	Being interviewed
Illness	Driving
Losing a loved one	Public speaking

Accidents	Making a mistake
Rape	Intimacy

...One of the insidious qualities of fear is that it tends to permeate many areas of our lives. For example, if you fear going to parties, having intimate relationships, applying for jobs, and so on.

This is made clearer by a look at the second layer of fear, which has a very different feel from that of Level 1. Level 2 fears are not situation-oriented; they involve the ego.

LEVEL 2 FEARS

Rejection	Being conned
Success	Helplessness
Failure	Disapproval
Being vulnerable	Loss of image

Level 2 fears have to do with inner states of mind rather than exterior situations. They reflect your sense of self and your ability to handle this world. This explains why generalized fear takes place. If you are afraid of being rejected, this fear will affect almost every area of your life – friends, intimate relationships, job interviews, and so on. Rejection is rejection – wherever it is found. So you begin to protect yourself, and, as a result, greatly limit yourself. You begin to shut down and close out the world around you. Look over the Level 2 list once again, and you will see how any one of these fears can greatly impact many areas of your life.

Level 3 gets down to the nitty-gritty of the issue: the biggest fear of all – the one that really keeps you stuck. Are you ready?

LEVEL 3 FEARS

I CAN'T HANDLE IT!

"That's it? That's the big deal?" you may ask. I know you're disappointed and wanted something much more than that But the truth is this:

AT THE BOTTOM OF EVERY ONE OF YOUR FEARS IS SIMPLY THE FEAR THAT YOU CAN'T HANDLE WHATEVER LIFE MAY BRING YOU.

Let's test this. The Level 1 fears translate to:

I can't handle illness.
I can't handle making a mistake.
I can't handle losing my job.
I can't handle being alone.
I can't handle making a fool out of myself.
I can't handle not getting the job.
I can't handle losing him/her.
I can't handle losing my money…etc.

The Level 2 fears translate to:

I can't handle the responsibilities of success.
I can't handle failure.
I can't handle being rejected…Etc.

Thus Level 3 – simply, "I can't handle it!"

Each day, in a very complicated and unpredictable way, human beings move in and out of these levels of fear in response to individuals, circumstances, events, and institutions.

It is difficult enough managing *our own* emotional states, much less that of others.

Entrepreneurship and business ownership is a recipe for misunderstanding, hurt feelings, confusion, and disappointment between people.

In addition to accepting that the closest and most intimate relationships can bring together two persons with different value systems and concepts of fear, further consideration should be devoted to the reality that different people may react differently to your idea or vision due to their character and how they relate to external forces.

This relates to the levels of fear previously referred to.

This becomes especially important when dealing with persons who have given you their word – whether support as a loved one or friend, or even as a trusted business partner.

You may be surprised, and even feel betrayed when that person begins to fall away from you and the idea that they claimed to believe in as much as you.

It is hard to know where the most fertile soil is for your business concepts and ideas. That is because it is difficult to read minds and to know the heart of others, much less what they will do when confronted with difficult and unexpected situations.

Perhaps one of the clearest pictures of this phenomenon – how people may respond to the same idea inn dramatically different ways – is contained in the Bible. It is known as the Parable of The Sower and is found in the 13th chapter of the book of Matthew:

[1] Later that same day Jesus left the house and sat beside the lake. [2] A large crowd soon gathered around him, so he got into a boat. Then he sat there and taught as the people stood on the shore. [3] He told many stories in the form of parables, such as this one:

"Listen! A farmer went out to plant some seeds. [4] As he scattered them across his field, some seeds fell on a footpath, and the birds came and ate them. [5] Other seeds fell on shallow soil with underlying rock. The seeds sprouted quickly because the soil was shallow. [6] But the plants soon wilted under the hot sun, and since they didn't have deep roots, they died. [7] Other seeds fell among thorns that grew up and choked out the tender plants. [8] Still other seeds fell on fertile soil, and they produced a crop that was thirty, sixty, and even a hundred times as much as had been planted! [9] Anyone with ears to hear should listen and understand."

[10] His disciples came and asked him, "Why do you use parables when you talk to the people?"
[11] He replied, "You are permitted to understand the secrets of the Kingdom of Heaven, but others are not. [12] To those who listen to my teaching, more understanding will be given, and they will have an abundance of knowledge. But for those who are not listening, even what little understanding they have will be taken away from them. [13] That is why I use these parables,

For they look, but they don't really see.

They hear, but they don't really listen or understand.

[14] This fulfills the prophecy of Isaiah that says:

'When you hear what I say, you will not understand. When you see what I do, you will not comprehend. [15] For the hearts of these people are hardened, and their ears cannot hear, and they have closed their eyes— so their eyes cannot see, and their ears cannot hear, and their hearts cannot understand, and they cannot turn to me and let me heal them.'

[16] "But blessed are your eyes, because they see; and your ears, because they hear. [17] I tell you the truth, many prophets and righteous people longed to see what you see, but they didn't see it. And they longed to hear what you hear, but they didn't hear it.

[18] "Now listen to the explanation of the parable about the farmer planting seeds: [19] The seed that fell on the footpath represents those who hear the message about the Kingdom and don't understand it. Then the evil one comes and snatches away the seed that was planted in their hearts. [20] The seed on the rocky soil represents those who hear the message and immediately receive it with joy. [21] But since they don't have deep roots, they don't last long. They fall away as soon as they have problems or are persecuted for believing God's word. [22] The seed that fell among the thorns represents those who hear God's word, but all too quickly the message is crowded out by the worries of this life and the lure of wealth, so no fruit is produced. [23] The seed that fell on good soil represents those who truly hear and understand God's word and produce a harvest of thirty, sixty, or even a hundred times as much as had been planted!"

One could compare the seed to an idea, vision or concept. Look at the reasons why the 'seed' did not take root:

- people don't understand the idea
- people don't last long
- people fall away as soon as they have problems or are persecuted for believing
- the idea is crowded out by the worries of this life and the lure of wealth

The idea or seed only takes root among those who truly hear and understand.

And there is always a relationship between what we perceive (hear and understand) and the condition of our mind, heart, and soul.

<<<<>>>>

Let's look at the inter-personal dynamics of this from another story outside of the business world (although wealth is definitely a dominant factor in the storyline) many of us have heard some aspect of.

We referred to it in a previous chapter.

One of the most widely available examples of how what is happening to a person is understood differently by that person, and those closest to them, because of their different perspectives, value systems and beliefs, is the story of Job, in the Bible.

According to Wikipedia (as of the date of this writing):

The **Book of Job** (Hebrew: בוֹיא) is one of the books of the Hebrew Bible. It relates the story of Job, his trials at the hands of Satan, his theological discussions with friends on the origins and nature of his suffering, and finally a response from God. The Book itself comprises a didactic poem set in a prose framing device and has been called "the most profound and literary work of the entire Old Testament". The Book itself, along with its numerous exegeses, are attempts to address the problem of evil, i.e. the problem of reconciling the existence of evil or suffering in the world with the existence of God. Scholars are divided as to the origin, intent, and meaning of the book.

As we previously looked at this story from the perspective of suffering, review again how radically different Job's experience is being interpreted by his inner circle. Remember, the view represented in the Bible is that of a Supreme Being, which ultimately Job, as a Believer, is striving to access, and come into harmony with.

From the previously referenced material by Christian theologian Dr. Thomas 1. Constable in his "Notes on Job" 2006 Edition, we learn in response to the question of 'Why do the godly suffer?' the following:

Person(s)	Answer	Evaluation
Job's wife	God is unfair.	Never
Job's three friends	God is disciplining (punishing) them because of sin.	Sometimes
Job	God wants to destroy them because of sin.	Sometimes
Elihu	God wants to direct (educate) them because of ignorance.	Sometimes
God	God wants to develop them and to demonstrate His glory.	Always

We saw previously from Dr. Constable's writing that "the different characters in the book based their understanding and their convictions on different sources of knowledge," as follows (author's note: epistemology is the branch of philosophy that studies the nature of knowledge and how valid it is; rationalism is the reliance on reason as the best guide for belief and action; empiricism is the view that experience, especially of the senses, is the only source of knowledge):

Person(s)	Epistemological base
Job's wife	Empiricism
Job's three friends	Rationalism
Job	Rationalism
Elihu	Human inspiration
God	Revelation

Dr. Constable notes that "Job's three friends each had a different basis of authority."

Person	Authoritative base
Eliphaz	Experience
Bildad	Tradition
Zophar	Intuition

In their various views of Job's circumstance, Job's friends placed greater weight or gave greater authority to different aspects of their learning.

They judged him according to their own worldview.

Now apply the lessons of Job to *your life* and scenario as an entrepreneur-business owner:

How do you view the difficulty of what you are going through? Why is it so painful and challenging?

Now, ask – how do you think those closest to you are dealing with it, mentally and emotionally?

What is the base of your knowledge – is it rational thought, empirical evidence, or religious and spiritual teachings? Something else?

What is the base of the knowledge of those dearest to you?

On what authority do you rely for evaluating individuals, circumstances, institutions, and events?

Is it the same as those closest to you?

And there is another dynamic that should be weighed.

How do those persons *closest to those, who are closest to you,* view you, and what you are going through and attempting to do?

You may be surprised to learn that the source of the value system, conclusions, opinions and judgments regarding you and your business endeavor are coming *from* other people *through* your family and friends.

"Cedric, don't ever do that again! You had me scared. We didn't know what happened to you."

I was absolutely shocked by these words. They came not from one of my very closest childhood friends, but from *his* fiancée who became my friend through him, in college.

I felt bad, and was touched at the same time.

In pursuit of an entrepreneurial goal I had suddenly disappeared from the lives of people with whom I had previously been in regular contact. I think I had been 'gone' for around 4 months.

I had been in my zone – in my own little world – caught up in the entrepreneurial passion and I had not stayed in regular communication.

I did enough to let some people know I wasn't dead, I think (smile).

But, maybe not.

I certainly was not in the same rhythm I had been, in terms of phone calls and pages (yes this was the era of the beeper.)

Here I was having not seen a person who was practically my best friend and his soon-to-be wife, and when I physically re-surfaced in their lives, I returned with one thing primarily, and almost exclusively in mind – the good news of my adventures and progress in the music business.

I had no inkling of what I had done to others whom I related to not as super entrepreneur, but just as friend. I had even less of an idea that my friend's fiancé was probably also reflecting *his* unspoken feeling (although like any good friend, he showed more interest in my Hip-Hop escapades).

To this day, she remembers what happened, and so do I. I still feel a bit bad, and touched by her expressed concern.

Yes, we entrepreneurs are something else. Re-read the chapter on Suffering if you want to understand more of why we act the way we do.

Our greatest strength in pursuit of building an organization out of nothing can be our greatest shortcoming or imperfection in our personal relationships – in either a real sense or through the perception of others.

What can account for these diametrically opposed aspects of our entrepreneurial and personal lives?

In a sense it is our split personality.

Let me explain.

You will remember that in this book we define an entrepreneur as one who conceives of or perceives an opportunity and creates a business organization in pursuit of it.

That act requires both the freedom of creativity and boundless optimism and the discipline of form and healthy skepticism.

The entrepreneurial act reflects the first two laws of the universe: motion and order. But motion always comes first.

In a sense Donald Trump summed it up when he wrote in his 1987 best-seller, *Art Of The Deal*, "You can't be imaginative or entrepreneurial if you've got too much structure."

The duties, obligations, and responsibilities of familial ties and friendships represent structure. Whether too much or not, each entrepreneur (and their inner circle) will have to determine.

As we have hopefully made clear from a previous chapter, entrepreneurship is a deeply intense spiritual, psychological and emotional undertaking. We looked at this a bit from the perspective of psychology, sociology, and psychiatry and considered that entrepreneurs are experiencing a *passion* of sorts, and could technically even be considered to be going through a traumatic experience by definitions from the worlds of science and medicine.

This is why this book does not shy away from terminology in those fields. In fact we embrace them.

Nothing wrong with recognizing something is off a bit, even possibly wrong with you – at least until the money starts rolling in, right? [Is it not interesting that so many who complain about the strange ways of entrepreneurs have no problem in concept or reality with spending the money they would or already do receive from them?]

Some of the most successful figures in business understand that entrepreneurs go through 'something' pretty heavy, that may border on insanity.

In *Art Of The Deal* Trump writes:

One of the keys to thinking big is total focus. I think of it almost as a controlled neurosis, which is a quality I've noticed in many highly successful entrepreneurs. They're obsessive, they're driven, they're single-minded and sometimes they're almost maniacal, but it's all channeled into their work. Where other people are paralyzed by neurosis, the people I'm talking about are actually helped by it.

I don't say this trait leads to a happier life, or a better life, but it's great when it comes to getting what you want.

What is going on here – are entrepreneurs saviors of societies, or weapons of mass destruction destroying personal relationships?

Both – depending upon who you talk to.

<<<<>>>>

What makes for all of this tension inside of us, entrepreneurs?

Over many years and in various settings, I have been blessed to work with, manage or advise entrepreneurs, entertainers, politicians, businesspersons, religious leaders and spiritual teachers. It has been an educational, spiritually rewarding, and illuminating experience.

Among the insights that I have been blessed to receive through such relationships and interactions—with said individuals, and those that work closely with them—is an understanding, to a degree, of the complimentary and sometimes tense relationship between creative thinking **and** critical thinking.

One of the areas where this dynamic plays out is in the arena of *planning*.

I've learned not just what planning is and its importance, but also what it (and other such 'grind' and 'grunt' work) *does* to certain types of entrepreneurs and creative people.

'Balanced' and 'happy' are two descriptive words that you may not find coming out of the mouths of those around you, regarding what they observe of your earliest struggle to plan and get a business off of the ground.

Much of that grueling tension that disallows peace of mind, can come from aspects of the creative nature and personality, and the fact that at times, elements of the planning effort involve areas of critical thought— like research, reasoning, debate, and even *the proper use of doubt*— that can appear to be the total opposite or even the *enemy* of the creative process which initiated the business effort.

In other words, many of us feel that such attributes, qualities and processes of creative thought like desire, intuition, spontaneity, affirmation, and "brain storming" are hindered by certain more deliberative aspects of critical thought. We can feel that somehow the freedom, joy, and comfort that we find in the rise or expression of an intense desire or new idea is *hurt* by the discipline of critical thought.

By the same token, many of us (often subconsciously) who are well-studied and comfortable relying upon analysis and critical thought often believe that planning is incompatible with spontaneity, intuition, and even *revelation*. Some of the more creative aspects of entrepreneurship can be very uncomfortable to those of us with that disposition.

But both worlds – creative and critical – are essential to success, and there is no way to get around having to incorporate them into your effort.

This civil war of sorts that goes on inside of the entrepreneur, also can take place on the outside, with those in the inner circle (again people who are also struggling to find a creative-critical balance) who love them.

Your most intimate companions may have different leanings in their own personality which may make them misperceive or prematurely judge what is happening to you. And to make matters worse – neither they nor you can be sure what costs the journey will require everyone to pay.

Nowhere is this more poignant and painful than in the relationship between life partners – a husband and a wife, even when the supportive spouse is rational in thought and has expertise and a background in business. Sometimes the personal sacrifice of a companion or family member is the greatest investment of all that an entrepreneur receives (sometimes without even asking for or expecting it).

From a March 2006 *Inc.* magazine article, 'Confessions of an Entrepreneur's Wife," by Phaedra Hise we read:

Some of the names in this story have been changed.

We were on vacation at the lake when my husband decided to start a company. Our five-year-old, Lily, was napping, so we had some rare adult time to talk about the opportunity Bill was considering. He wanted to leave his job as general manager for an industrial laundry plant to partner with a guy who had invented a drink that was carbonated but also 100 percent juice. It seemed to Bill like the chance of a lifetime, given that he had worked for a number of entrepreneurial companies before, most notably a few beer businesses. And I agreed. As we aged it would only become harder for him to take a big risk like that. We had some money saved and had recently relocated from Boston to Richmond, Virginia – a pretty affordable town. Why not go for it?

I knew what we were in for. I had been a business journalist for a dozen years (five of them on staff at *Inc.*) and had written countless articles and a couple of books about managing start-ups. My husband was a smart M.B.A. with entrepreneurial drive, I told myself, and I would be the supportive wife with exceptional business sense. In five years, he would sell the company to Coke or Pepsi and cash out.

Of course you've already guessed it: I was dead wrong on nearly every count. Neither of us could have predicted the company's surprising trajectory. Watching Bill navigate the entrepreneurial life, I see now just how little I really knew about starting and building a business. In the five years since Bill embarked on his great adventure, I've come to realize the only thing I was right about originally is that my husband is, indeed, a smart M.B.A. – and he has more entrepreneurial drive, much more, than either of us knew.

…By this point I was raising Lily alone, going solo to her concerts and swim meets. I was making the decisions about her education, health, and social life with little input from her father. One night she and I were sitting at the dinner table and the meal was over before I realized that I had forgotten to tell her that Daddy was out of town. She had quit asking where he was.

In the spring of 2003 Lily's school decided to send a few teachers to Spain for a month of language immersion at summer school. Lily loved Spanish, and at one point I had been fluent. I found myself wishing we could do something similar. I brought it up casually with Bill, figuring he would say I was crazy. Secretly I was hoping he would say, "Great, let's all go!" Instead, he looked relieved. "I'm going to be really busy this summer," he said. "It's probably best if you guys are out of here." So Lily and I spent July in Mexico, taking classes in the morning and swimming each afternoon. Bill was home three days that month.

I worried about his health. He was gaining weight and had started smoking. I also worried about his moodiness. The man I married 15 years earlier had been a social powerhouse, cracking jokes and cooking gourmet meals for large dinner parties. This new Bill was a short-tempered monosyllabic hermit. When I did occasionally drag him to a party full of my friends, I was shocked at how many he had never even met.

I had originally thought of this as *his* company, *his* work, *his* life. But now Lily and I were also paying a price. With Bill rarely home, I soon lost the time and energy to focus on my work. Left with no profession, and essentially no husband, I became frustrated and resentful. I found myself thinking that it might be easier if Lily and I lived alone, with no illusions about being able to depend on Bill. Fortunately we found a good therapist and held our marriage together, but it became clear that Bill just didn't have the mental or physical energy to maintain much of a personal relationship. I knew he wanted me to be happy, but I couldn't stop picking fights about his lack of time at home. I wanted him to succeed, but I hadn't expected the company to so deeply invade our personal lives.

If you are an entrepreneur, or the spouse or child of one – any resemblance between persons and circumstances from the previous story are *not* coincidental.

So what is the secret of personal relationships you ask?

Previously, emphasis was placed on ten elements that impact an entrepreneur's personal or domestic life: 1) the need for privacy 2) different communication styles 3) levels of ignorance 4) different value systems 5) possibly radically different concepts and expectations regarding love (and how it is demonstrated), loyalty, commitment, suffering, sacrifice, risk, and reward and 6) financial constraints and responsibilities 7) different thresholds for patience and pain and 8) respect for time 9) definitions of progress or milestones for success and 10) fear.

These elements are always in play and intersecting in your entrepreneurial and private life.

The problem is however, that we have a personal life already developed *before* we enter into or fully mature into the entrepreneurial mindset. In other words, we don't decide when we are born and to whom. We have selected our childhood friends, and have fallen in love before we identify an entrepreneurial idea. And we enjoy company and companionship for reasons that have nothing to do with our future or current business interests.

So, the drive, time, energy and sacrifice required – on its own merit – to build something from nothing, is always going to be in conflict with the obligations, duties, and expectations that were established before the great idea and exciting new venture manifested, or emerged.

As a result, there are times where the entrepreneur and those closest to them will realize that temporary or permanent separation is natural, logical, and desirable – especially when 1) efforts to tone down the high octane of entrepreneurship or 2) efforts or promises of an entrepreneur's companion to reach a higher level of understanding, or assistance, never materialize.

In his book *Objective Hate*, the enormously popular and successful multi-media personality, Troi "Star" Torain of Star and Buc Wild writes humorously but sharply of a relationship in the earlier days of his development as an entrepreneur:

So I'm in Queens with this poor man's version of Halle Berry, and I'm frustrated and trying to avoid robbing a grocery store. All of a sudden we start fighting. The cute witch wanted to get married, but I told her I wasn't ready for that game. So to ease the tension I concentrated on the role I had been playing as Mister Mom. I'd get the kids up in the morning and take them to school, then pick Kia up from work in the evening. This went on for a little under four months. The relationship didn't even last a year, because our perceptions on life were just different.

The straw that broke the camel's back came one night as I was sitting at the kitchen table, looking at some designs I'd done on the computer back at Round The Globe. It was the outline for a magazine idea I'd had: Around The Way Connections. It was based on the dating ads I had seen in the Village Voice. Kia came into the kitchen and I said, "Hey, sit down. I want to show you something." I started explaining my idea for the magazine to her, showing her the layout ideas and the outlines. The…looked at me and said, "Sounds like a good scam, but my kids need school uniforms. What are you gonna do about that?" I could see that she wasn't even trying to hear me out; it was as if she'd spit in my face. But I couldn't blame her – some people are just shortsighted. That second I knew that I had to get the…away from her; she was a vampire…

Star saw something in Kia that every entrepreneur hates – disrespect for their vision and demonstrated progress. She did not see, or care to see what he did in the humble and early stages of his progression. Kia's concern was an immediate need for clothing for her children, which she evidently did not see being met through this particular entrepreneurial endeavor.

Their concepts of time, vision, and responsibility were radically different.

Star determined them to be irreconcilable and moved on.

There are millions of entrepreneurs in relationships right now with persons with whom such views are similarly irreconcilable.

In a sense this is not the fault of any party involved.

When duty and responsibility to mutually agreed upon (or implied in the case of children or individuals unable to take care of themselves) commitments and obligations are challenged or interfered with by the demands of the entrepreneurial process, something has to give – either the pursuit of business or a modification or elimination in the expectations associated with duty and responsibility.

This latter option – a process of reconciliation between current demands and expectations with the reality of the business development process – of course, has to involve both parties in the relationship.

Again, each entrepreneur will have to think through these dynamics from their own perspective and hopefully with an enlightened self-interest.

When all is said and done, although entrepreneurs may need or crave opposition in order to refine their idea, or business organization, *no entrepreneur* wants the people closest to them – especially those whom they have voluntarily brought into their life – to be the opposition *leaders*.

At least I haven't met any, yet.

I've never heard any business owner tell me, "I want the *worst* enemy of my vision, work and efforts to be my spouse, parent, children, or best friend."

Yet and still, this is often the case. If that is the case, any individual who still succeeds in business is truly blessed through and by the painful experience.

On a more pleasant note we will close.

If having your own family and friends opposing your dream is the worst thing an entrepreneur can imagine, the opposite must be the most glorious – the unity between two life partners in business.

I have found one of the most inspiring stories of any entrepreneurial couple to be that of Mr. Junius G. Groves – an ex-slave – and his wife, and I would like to share it with you.

From Booker T. Washington's *The Negro In Business* we read:

Perhaps our most successful Negro farmer is Junius G. Groves, of Edwardsville, Kansas, who is often referred to as "The Potato King." Mr. Groves is a full-blooded Negro, and was born a slave in Green County, Kentucky, in 1859. He and his parents were made free a few years later by the proclamation of Abraham Lincoln. As soon as he was old enough he began attending the public schools of his neighborhood, but as he could be in school only during two or three months in the year, he did not secure a great deal of book knowledge. What he learned was enough, however, to give him a desire for education; for we find him, after he left school, continuing to study as best he could. By the time he reached manhood he was able to read and write and had some knowledge of figures.

In 1879 occurred what was known as the "Kansas Exodus," and Mr. Groves, with a large number of other colored people from the South, caught the emigration fever. When he reached Kansas he had just ninety cents in his pocket. The sudden influx of so many colored people in the state caused it to be somewhat overrun with cheap labor, and employment was hard to find. After an earnest search of some days Mr. Groves succeeded in finding employment at a farm at forty cents a day. He has told me that he agreed to begin to work for this wage because he knew that within a few days he could convince his employer that he was worth more. So faithfully did he work that by the end of the three months his wages had been increased to seventy-five cents a day. This was the pay which the very best farm hands were receiving in that neighborhood. Out of this small sum he had to pay for his board and laundering.

By the end of the year he had saved enough to go in search of what he hoped would be a better job. His travels through different parts of the state availed him nothing, and he finally decided to return to the place where he had first found employment. He had made such favorable impression upon his old employer that the latter offered to let him have a portion of his farm to cultivate on "shares." The conditions of the contract were that the employer should furnish nine acres of land, a team, seed and tools, and Groves should plant, cultivate and harvest the crop for one-third of what was made. This offer was gladly accepted, and Mr. Groves planted three acres in white potatoes, and three in water-melons.

Soon, after getting the crop planted Mr. Groves decided to marry. When he reached this decision, he had but seventy-five cents in cash, and had to borrow enough to satisfy the demands of the law. But he knew well the worth and common sense of the woman he was to marry. She was as poor in worldly goods as himself, but their poverty did not discourage them in their plans. Mr. and Mrs. Groves have told me with a great deal of satisfaction how they managed with much difficulty, the day after their marriage, to get a few yards of calico to make a change of clothes for Mrs. Groves so that she might begin work at once in the field by his side, where she has ever since been his steady companion. During the whole season they worked with never-tiring energy, early and late; with the result that when the crop had been harvested and all debts paid they had cleared $125. Notwithstanding their lack of many necessaries of life, to say nothing of comforts, they decided to invest $50 of their earnings in a lot in Kansas City, Kansas. They paid $25 for a milk cow, and kept the remaining $50 to be used in the making of another crop.

The success of the first year's work had convinced the landlord that he would be taking no risk in renting Groves and his wife a larger acreage; so their holding the second year was increased to twenty acres. From his year's earnings they purchased a team. They now began to feel that they could take an even more independent step. I say *they* advisedly, because all through these laborious years Mrs. Groves worked on the farm constantly at the side of her husband, and even now, when occasion demands it, she does active work in the field.

The third year they rented sixty-six acres of good farm land near the town of Edwardsville, Kansas, at an annual rate of $336. Of this amount they were able to pay one-third in cash in advance. As this was more land than they could personally cultivate, a small portion was sub-rented. Seldom have two people worked harder or sacrificed more than did Mr. and Mrs. Groves that year. They not only worked the farm, but raised pigs and fowls and sold milk and butter. In the winter, when other farmers were idle, they cut wood and sold it in town. They were determined to succeed.

Space will not permit me to mention all the devices Mr. and Mrs. Groves employed or relate all the adventures he met in accumulating his first capital. Suffice it to say that at the end of the year, in 1884, after they had paid all debts, and their bank-book was balanced, they found that they had to their credit in the local bank, as the result of their labor for the three previous years, $2,200. During the greater portion of the time they were earning this money, this young man and his wife were living in an old shanty, with one broken-down room. They decided now that they would buy a farm for themselves, and agreed to pay $3,600 for eighty acres of land near Edwardsville, in the Great Kaw Valley – a section comprising about 3,400 acres of the most fertile land in the state. Mr. and Mrs. Groves paid on the land the $2,200 which they had saved, and closed a contract to pay the remaining $1,400 at the end of the year. Letting the hired man live in the house on the place, they built a shanty for themselves on the place until the crop was grown. After Mr. Groves had taken possession of the farm, nearly all of the neighbors began to tell him that he had made a bad bargain, and to prophesy that he would not only be unable to pay the $1,400 at the end of the year, but would lose his $2,200 besides. Mr. Groves told me that this was the first and only occasion in his life when he became discouraged; and that he would not take heart again until he began to inquire who they were who were seeking to discourage him, and found that they were poor, shiftless people who owned no land themselves. Mr. Groves then determined to succeed, not only for his own sake, but to disappoint those who had predicted his failure. Enough was realized from the one year's crop to pay for the whole farm, with a neat little surplus, which they used in improving their house and stocking their farm.

Mr. and Mrs. Groves continued to work hard and with success on this farm until they were able, in 1887, to pay cash for two small adjoining farms. In 1889, they bought a fourth farm, and in 1896 the fifth one. They now own 500 acres of the finest land in the Kaw Valley – land that is easily worth from $125 to $250 an acre. They no longer occupy the little one-room shanty, but have advanced to a large, beautiful, well-appointed dwelling, built at a cost of $5,000. It has fourteen rooms and modern improvements, including a private gas-plant which furnishes twenty-seven lights, a private water system, and a local telephone. The house is supplied with bath-rooms and everything necessary to make it comfortable and convenient.

...But why is Mr. Groves called "The Negro Potato King?" Let me answer. In one year alone he produced upon his farm 721,500 bushels of white potatoes, averaging 245 bushels to the acre. So far as reports show, this was 121,500 bushels more than any other individual grower in the world had, at that time, produced. And besides the potatoes raised on his farm, Mr. Groves buys and ships potatoes on a large scale. In 1905 he bought from white growers in the Kaw Valley and shipped away twenty-two cars of white potatoes. He also bought fourteen cars of fancy seed potatoes in North and South Dakota, which he sold to growers in the Kaw Valley, and in Oklahoma and the Indian Territory. Mr. Groves says that he ships potatoes and other farm products to nearly every portion of the United States, and to Mexico and Canada.

He says that he has never found his color to be a hindrance to him in business. During his busy season as many as fifty laborers, white and black, are employed on his farm. It is maintained at its highest productivity by persistent effort and constant energy on the part of Mr. Groves. As I have said, he received little education when a boy, but he has persevered until he has now reached the point where he can analyze and classify the soils upon his farm, and apply just the proper fertilizer to the various plots. He uses nothing but the latest improved cultivators, potato-planters, potato weeders, and diggers, and in fact, all work that can be done with machinery is done in that way.

Besides his farming interests, Mr. and Mrs. Groves have large holding in mining stocks in the Indian Territory and Mexico, as well as banking stock in their own state. They own four-fifths interest in Kansas City Casket and Embalming Company, of Kansas City, Kansas, and take the deepest interest in their own state and throughout the country. Mr. Groves, in speaking of his larger interests, always says "we," meaning Mrs. Groves and himself. In the most beautiful manner, and with the greatest tenderness, he never fails to give Mrs. Groves due credit for all that she has helped him to accomplish.

...In speaking of what they have been able to accomplish, Mr. Groves said in a very modest way (both he and his wife are among the most simple and modest people I have ever met): "I think that our success shows that a Negro can and will make his way if given a chance. If we could start with but seventy-five cents and succeed as we have, other people of our race can do the same thing."

I have never heard a more beautiful and inspiring story about love in entrepreneurship than this one.

In closing, it is possibly most important to be more sober about *this* particular secret than any other. Your personal relationships are powerfully impacted by your suffering as an entrepreneur, and the entrepreneurial process is profoundly impacted by the people that mean the most to you – for better or worse.

Be fully aware and sensitive to this fact.

Choose your personal companions carefully with the prospects of success in mind, but also realize that others have chosen you too, with still more, like small children, having no say in the matter at all.

If you want your loved ones to support your business ventures, seek and work for it, but just don't be naïve enough to think it will always come.

Just like with the success of your business – there is no guarantee.

The Secret of Personal Relationships

- *If you are an entrepreneur or business owner be prepared, because everyone who learns about what you are doing is evaluating or judging you according to their own value system.*
- *The entrepreneurial paradox is that while you believe you have performed a supreme act of unselfishness by starting a business, giving it your all, sacrificing your comfort and risking your own wealth, others simultaneously may view your decision and hard work, as a supreme act of selfishness.*
- *Entrepreneurship and business ownership is a recipe for misunderstanding, hurt feelings, confusion, and disappointment between people.*
- *You may be surprised to learn that the source of the value system, conclusions, opinions and judgments regarding you and your business endeavor are coming from other people through your family and friends.*
- *Some of the most successful figures in business understand that entrepreneurs go through 'something' pretty heavy, that may border on insanity.*
- *Balance and happiness are two words that you may not find coming out of the mouths (or more importantly) the hearts of those around you, regarding what they observe of your earliest struggle to plan and get a business off of the ground.*
- *The problem is that we have a personal life already developed before we enter into or fully mature into the entrepreneurial mindset. So, the drive, time, energy and sacrifice required – on its own merit - to build something from nothing, is always going to be in conflict with the obligations, duties, and expectations that were established before the great idea and exciting new venture manifested, or emerged simultaneously with these other priorities.*
- *There are times where the entrepreneur and those closest to them will realize that temporary or permanent separation is natural, logical, and desirable.*
- *If having your own family and friends opposing your dream is the worst thing an entrepreneur can imagine, the opposite must be the most glorious – the unity between two life partners in business. One of the most inspiring stories of any entrepreneurial couple to be that of Mr. Junius G. Groves – an ex-slave – and his wife.*

Epilogue – The Greatest Secret of All

The current economic environment of today demands that first-time entrepreneurs, start-up businesses, and small businesses with less than a handful of employees immerse themselves in three areas – information, instruction, and inspiration.

To me, there are three books or reference works that separately embody these vital categories. The most informative book I have ever reviewed on the subject of business is the over 2,000 page 'encyclopedia,' *Business: The Ultimate Resource.* The book filled with the most instruction, to me, is *E Myth Mastery: The Seven Essential Disciplines for Building a World Class Company* by Michael E. Gerber. And the work with the most inspiration for business, is *Think And Grow Rich* by Napoleon Hill.

It is these three books that I recommend to all of my clients and which I believe come closest to embodying the three elements of business knowledge: the technical, the practical, and the spiritual.

I have attempted to write a book that will contribute to the unification of these three areas of knowledge.

The best Book to do so has yet to be revealed to us, but is certainly on the way.

The successful entrepreneurs of the next decade will be continuous learners in these three areas. They will gain insights from newspapers, magazines, books, blogs, social networks, mentors, broadcast programming, professional societies, and consultations, in combination with the best teacher of all – personal experience in business. The application of such 'book knowledge,' 'street knowledge,' motivation and persistence, to the daily process of conceiving ideas, developing plans and coordinating people and systems in an organization in this increasingly competitive environment, is what will determine success.

I believe that in the post-crisis environment it will be an eclectic group of those with the fewest options who will emerge, survive and thrive as entrepreneurs. Their creative and skillful application of the 'secrets' of this book will surprise and intrigue many, writing the success stories of this generation – many of which will be turned into movies.

Who will they be?

It will be the members of strongly-knit kinship and family like systems – whether West Indian communities, members of fraternities and sororities, religious groups, even former teammates on sports teams or members of street organizations like gangs – who are best positioned to tap into the power of trust and unity to find alternative ways to finance new businesses. They are more likely to accept the harsh realities that come with the knowing the Secrets of Commercial Banking, Securitization, Group Economics, and Capital described in this book.

It will be the independent-minded, small business owner, perhaps a female sole proprietor running a beauty salon or virtual administrative assistant business who understands that there is nothing wrong with being a member of a single political party, but that only voting with members of one party on every issue is not in the best interest of the bottom line of their business. This young female entrepreneur is more likely to understand the Secret Of Policy and that pursuing an enlightened self interest in business requires one to speak the language of *power* (money, votes, physical presence, and media influence) and not just party loyalty.

It will be the recently laid off middle manager and supervisor of a multinational corporation with twenty years of experience in office politics who will understand the real consequences of not learning the Secrets of a Personal Power Base, Etiquette and Networking, and Negotiating. This experienced professional is most likely to do what it takes to apply the techniques and best practices of interpersonal relationships and such skills as subordination and socialization which lead to new contacts, new leads, and new sales.

It will be the family, located in a small community, that has struggled to keep a 'Mom and Pop' business open for the last 10 to 15 years who will learn the Secret of Substitutes. The combined effects of shopping malls, technology, and demographic change have cut into their profits year-by-year. Their commitment to doing things the same way, was once an asset. Now it has blinded them to threats and competition well beyond the store on the other side of town, selling the same product or service.

The four childhood friends, inspired to start a business together are best acquainted with the Secret of Team and the reality of the 9 Personality Types. After hours of conversation, planning, small investments made, and even written commitments, they begin to realize that that each of them has different levels of motivation, temperaments, and expectations for success over time. The different strengths and weakness of the group have become sources of division rather than a means to compliment one another.

The former musician, signed to a record label deal, who for years had a manager, accountant, and legal team handle all of their paperwork will be shocked by the Secret of Planning and Presentation, which reveals that there is far less writing and talking than they believed, involved in the initial business plan and presentation that they will need to put together to start their new multi-media company.

The previously incarcerated and homeless individuals are the apparently unlikely group prepared to accept the Secrets of Suffering and Will-Power. It is they that know that intense personal pain and the ability to endure and make it through extremely difficult circumstances is what strengthens character, inspires ideas, and allows one to learn powerful lessons from their own mistakes and errors.

It is the one-time executive who has voluntarily left his job and risked it all: status, personal savings, and their home who grasps the Secret of Personal Relationships and the devastating impact that entrepreneurship can have on their most intimate companions, and friends. It is they who experience the sense of betrayal when a wife shows that they don't believe in them or their idea. It is they who experience the intense sense of guilt when they know that their personal sacrifice has created an even greater one in their children. Yet, it is also this executive who will experience the joy of their entire inner circle supporting them, expecting nothing but success!

Although there may be likely candidates and people best suited to learn this or that particular Secret, there is no telling when or what Secret will matter the most in the personal, professional, or spiritual life of any particular entrepreneur.

And it is that unpredictability that may be the biggest Secret of all – the point of intersection between necessity, chance, and faith. I do not know the idea, insight, and the decision (nor its timing) that an entrepreneur will make, that will be most critical to their success in life and in their business.

It is still a mystery to me.

Therefore, I simply could not write that chapter.

Therefore this book will forever remain incomplete, without *you.*

So, I leave that for you to do, and would be so honored if you would share it with me.

You can write me, personally at:
theentrepreneurialsecret@cedricmuhammad.com

August 17, 2009